Library
Publishing
Toolkit

Edited by Allison P. Brown

IDS Project Press
2013

Published by IDS Project Press
Milne Library, SUNY Geneseo
1 College Circle
Geneseo, NY 14454

ISBN-13: 978-0-9897226-0-5 (Print)

ISBN-13: 978-0-9897226-1-2 (e-Book)

ISBN-13: 978-0-9897226-2-9 (EPUB)

Book design by Allison P. Brown

About
the Library Publishing Toolkit

An RRLC Incubator Project

A joint effort between Milne Library, SUNY Geneseo

& the Monroe County Library System

The Library Publishing Toolkit is a project funded by the Rochester Regional Library Council. The Toolkit is a united effort between Milne Library at SUNY Geneseo and the Monroe County Library System to identify trends in library publishing, seek out best practices to implement and support such programs, and share the best tools and resources.

Principal Investigators:

Cyril Oberlander
SUNY Geneseo, Milne Library, Library Director

Patricia Uttaro
Monroe County Library System Director

Project Supervisor:

Katherine Pitcher
SUNY Geneseo, Milne Library, Head of Technical Services

Project Sponsor:

Kathleen M. Miller
Executive Director, Rochester Regional Library Council

Contents

vii

Foreword

Makerspaces for the Mind

Walt Crawford

Libraries have always been places for creation, at least indirectly—the research required for nonfiction, the inspiration required for fiction, and, not infrequently, the atmosphere that helps the creative juices flow.

Recently, "makerspaces" have been touted as great new service ideas for public and academic libraries. Definitions of makerspaces can be as cloudy as those of Library 2.0, but for now I'll use "a place where people have an opportunity to explore their own interests, learn to use tools and materials, and develop creative projects." Most definitions also involve *gathering*—that is, that makerspaces involve teamwork—but that's not always either necessary nor desirable: some creative projects should be solitary.

This essay isn't the place to explore the general desirability of makerspaces. I'd say that makerspaces—especially those involving things like 3D printers—are great ideas for *some* larger libraries and absolutely out of the question for thousands of smaller libraries, which have neither the space, the funds, or the staffing to oversee use of 3D printers and their raw materials. But that's a different essay.

Every library, no matter how small or how large, including public, academic, and others, can and I believe should be a special kind of makerspace: a makerspace for the mind.

That is what library publishing and library support for patron publishing is all about: providing the tools to develop books, articles, and other publications—creations where the mind is the primary resource. It's a role that's suitable for public libraries as small as Brownell Public Library in Kansas or Cliff Island Library in Maine; it's a role that's suitable for the Little Priest Tribal College in Nebraska and the John Wesley College in North Carolina.

Baseline Publishing Makerspaces

What does it take to start a makerspace for the mind? The baseline is straightforward: three square inches of space in the stacks (that is, 0.4 linear inches at least 6.2 inches deep) and $50 for

a copy of my book *The Librarian's Guide to Micropublishing* (2011: Information Today, Inc.). Oh, and access to a computer with an Internet connection and Microsoft Word, LibreOffice, or OpenOffice.

That's not enough to build a library publishing program, but it is—with a little publicity added—enough to get your library into publishing. It means your library can help community members with niche publications they want to develop. That includes *millions* (maybe tens of millions) of family researchers who want to publish family histories for themselves and a few relatives, even though they know there's no commercial market. It includes people with stories to tell who'd like to see the stories handed down in durable form. It includes hobbyists who believe they have something worthwhile to say.

These people have been around ever since publishing's been around, but they've usually been discouraged by the substantial costs and special expertise needed to produce high-quality books. Now, with print-on-demand services that don't charge upfront fees (specifically Lulu, but also, for paperbacks, the CreateSpace division of Amazon), it's possible to produce a handful of books for very little money. With the templates we created and the methodology offered in *The Librarian's Guide to Micropublishing*, it's feasible for almost anyone to generate a *quality* book. (This isn't a pitch for my book—but the book does lower the barriers to high-quality/low-cost publishing.)

Expanded Library Involvement

Libraries can move from baseline makerspaces to full-fledged library publishing one step at a time, as people and other resources permit and to meet local needs—especially in academic libraries, where the need for library publishing seems likely to grow over time.

For public libraries, that can mean encouraging writing, editing, and maybe even proofreading circles to make better use of micropublishing resources. It can mean directly publishing local histories, the results of teen poetry clubs, and all sorts of other publications generated in or by the library. For *very* large public and academic libraries, it might mean installing an Espresso Book Machine or equivalent so the PDFs generated using micropublishing techniques can be turned into professional-quality trade paperbacks right on the spot.

I can imagine public libraries creating their own imprints for community-generated publications. I don't have to *imagine* academic libraries creating their own imprints: that's already happened and it's likely to happen more often in the future, for at least three reasons:

- Smaller academic institutions that don't have university or college presses, and larger ones where the university press has shut down or is in trouble, *still* have faculty and researchers—and students, for that matter—with important things to say. With micropublishing techniques, enhanced by more advanced software and deliberate provision of editing and publicity resources, libraries can found and maintain virtual university presses with minimal physical investment. You don't need to determine whether you can sell the 500 to 1,000 copies you might need to make a press run feasible: If a scholarly monograph turns out to have a natural audience of 15, a virtual university press will yield 15 copies, with no waste and very little overhead. (At today's prices, the production *and fulfillment* costs for 15 copies of a 200-page trade paperback would be about $130 or $8.50 a copy; make that $280 or $18.50 a copy for hardbound versions.)

- In institutions that *do* have stable university presses, there may be departments or areas that the university press doesn't handle well—or monographs and specialized publications that are worthy but can't meet the press's minimum saleability requirements. The library can help, again using micropublishing techniques.

- Some libraries already support open access journals, either on their own behalf or in association with other departments and societies. Open access journals require additional tools—e.g., systems for managing peer review and editing, ways to assure consistent layout for articles, and tools to maintain the website for each journal. Such tools are readily available in open source form. This seems likely to be a growth area for libraries as they protect their own budgets and improve access to the scholarly literature. There's even a possible role for micropublishing here, especially for smaller journals (say those publishing less than 750 pages per volume): It would be a truly trivial task to turn a set of articles in PDF form into an annual print volume, made available to those who desire it for the cost of printing—again, with no up-front capital expenses for the library. (A 700-page 8.5x11 hardback annual would cost less than $30 at today's prices, assuming color isn't required.)

The Rest of the Toolkit

I've focused on print publishing because I believe there's a real role for libraries in continued print publishing. That doesn't rule out e-first or e-only publishing. For open access journals, my assumption is that articles and issues would appear on the Web. For other publications, most of the techniques needed to produce high-quality books work equally well to create high-quality e-books.

At this point, going from a formatted Word document (done the right way, using styles and a template) to a Kindle e-book is trivial and requires no additional software. You may need additional software and a couple of additional steps to get from Word to EPUB, but those tools will become more available over time—and eventually, I suspect, will be incorporated into Word, just as Word and LibreOffice now generate PDFs directly.

The librarians who contributed to this publication offer a range of real-world examples and perspectives. I look forward to reading the results. If you haven't already done so, you should look forward to how your library can encourage appropriate publishing and even become a publisher: how you can provide a makerspace for the mind.

Acknowledgments

We'd like to thank all our contributors, supporters, and collaborators, especially: the project team at SUNY Geneseo and the Monroe County Library system: Greg Benoit, Joe Easterly, Adrienne Furness, Corey Ha, Bill Jones, Jay Osborne, Kate Pitcher, Leah Root, Betty Spring, and Bonnie Swoger; Sheryl Kron Rhodes for her editing; all who participated in interviews and so generously shared their experiences: Rivkah Sass, Gerald Ward, Krissie McMakin, Gina Bingham, Mark Coker, Henry Bankhead, Jamie LaRue, Cindy Gregory, Amber Hughey, Donna Feddern, Matt Clark, Cheryl Napsha, Monica Harris, Janie Hermann, and Richard Reyes-Gavilan; Mark Tullos at Bowker.

Introduction

Cyril Oberlander

Library Director, Milne Library, SUNY Geneseo

A t a time when some may question the future of libraries, it is clear libraries are an unparalleled and invaluable resource to local authors and readers. For public libraries, the 2010 Institute of Museum and Library Service[1] Public Library study indicates that U.S. public libraries serve over 297.6 million people, and had some 1.57 billion visits.[2] For academic libraries, the 2010 National Center for Education Statistics[3] shows that among the 3,689 U.S. academic libraries, over 22.5 million visited during one week in the fall of 2010, and during that same week, the total information services that required staff assistance exceeded 34.5 million.[4] In libraries, we see and assist countless readers busy researching and writing, some producing scholarly articles and books, others writing research papers, and yet others authoring a novel or posting to Web blogs. Libraries provide a resourceful, inspiring, and sustaining place for both the author and the reader. Libraries are looking to library publishing services because it serves author and reader in a holistic manner. Authors often acknowledge the libraries that provide crucial services, resources, and space to create their works. The tradition of supporting authors and creators of digital content is expanding to include new resources and publishing services.

Library publishing is well defined by the Library Publishing Coalition in this volume on page 370 as a "set of activities led by... libraries to support the creation, dissemination, and curation of scholarly, creative, and/or educational works." The mission of library publishing services is based on a core value of libraries: knowledge sharing and literacy are an essential public good. Libraries have been challenged in this mission as publishers develop content delivery platforms that focus on direct sales to customers. By developing library publishing services, libraries curate options for authors and readers that are missing from today's publishing market. Between commercial and self-publishing, there is a niche for authors and readers that can provide a winning solution to each. This solution can preserve public access to knowledge, and compensate authors who provide open or affordable access to their works.

Library publishing service models closely parallel a long library tradition: connecting author and reader. We do this, not simply by selecting and housing books, but by providing services to authors to publish their work to reach readers across the globe. Libraries provide

---

[1]   http://www.imls.gov/

[2]   Public Libraries in the United States Survey Fiscal year 2010, IMLS Jan. 2013. http://www.imls.gov/assets/1/AssetManager/PLS2010.pdf

[3]   http://nces.ed.gov/

[4]   Academic Libraries: 2010, First Look. http://nces.ed.gov/pubs2012/2012365.pdf

this service, regardless of whether the author is a famous writer, family genealogist, or student writing a paper. This seemingly significant role shift is primarily one of new workflow. We often assist authors with research, citation management, or copyediting services. Increasingly, academic librarians are assisting faculty with the production of alternative textbooks or digital scholarship, and public librarians are assisting writing groups, or helping writers produce their first manuscripts. In addition, because we are keenly aware of the market for new books and reader services, we are well-positioned to market the books we help authors create. We are experts at metadata and cataloging, and those skills are integral to facilitating the creation, marketing, and access of new works. Our digital libraries are moving beyond digital copies of content in public domain, and swiftly moving towards content our community creates and cares about.

Academic and public libraries are increasingly providing publishing services ranging from author workshops to publishing journals and books. Library publishing strategies and workflow design vary widely. Many academic library programs started as reprint, institutional repository, or digitization projects, and have been expanding to include scholarly communication programs such as hosting journals, publishing new manuscripts, and supporting digital scholarship. On the other hand, public library programs often started with reading and writers' groups, and have expanded to include developing community creativity centers or makers-spaces and workshop programming to develop writing or digital media.

The variety of publishing services among libraries often reflects local needs and interests, which is a positive sign that libraries are evolving to the needs of their users. However, without sharing knowledge of service designs and outcomes, libraries duplicate the challenging work of development, or worse, risk efficiency and minimize impact. We want the authors that utilize library publishing services to be successful and we know many are. However, publishing pilots can be problematic to authors, and that is one story libraries can ill afford. Similarly, if we neglect to share templates, we forget to address a library core value: the needs of the community. By sharing our stories, our templates, and the outcomes of our publishing services, we significantly strengthen the community of libraries. Sharing useful publishing practices improves efficiency and collaboration, thereby enriching and expanding publishing outcomes and providing value across authors and readers.

The Library Publishing Toolkit seeks to identify library publishing practices, share best practices, and expand services because trends among authors, libraries, publishers, and readers highlight the need to develop strong networks of library publishing services. Chief among the trends is the disruption of the pricing, distribution, and format of the traditional publisher and library markets. Issues of particular interest to libraries are as follows:

- Many publishers push to sell directly to consumers and appear no longer as interested in the library as a consumer.

- Libraries' lending and resource sharing traditions are often seen by publishers as revenue reducing practices.

- E-books and e-reader platforms with licensing terms and digital rights management negatively affect the library's ability to serve their readers.

- Emergent authoring systems and services are disrupting publishing by empowering anyone to publish anything at any time and of any quality.

- Self-publishing industries and open access are adding new players and new competition to publishing markets.

The Library Publishing Toolkit has been developed to identify and confront some of these trends in library publishing, seek out best practices, and share the tools and resources. It was funded by the Rochester Regional Library Council[5] and is a collaborative effort between Milne Library at SUNY Geneseo[6] and the Monroe County Library System[7]. Our goals include to:

- Develop strategies libraries can use to identify types of publishing services and content that can be created and curated by libraries.

- Evaluate and recommend regional and Web services, and software used for digital content creation and publishing.

- Assess trends in digital content creation and publishing that can be useful in libraries, and suggest potential future projects.

- Identify efficient workflows for distributing content for free online and with potential for some cost-recovery in print-on-demand markets.

- Develop a Library Publishing Toolkit to contribute to best practices strategies for libraries of all types, addressing the need for content creation and distribution.

In this first edition of the Library Publishing Toolkit, you will find a variety of useful resources and strategies that you can readily apply or adapt. The key to reading this Toolkit is to react to it; we hope that it inspires and expands library services to better meet the needs of authors and readers. We also hope you will share your thoughts, strategies, and workflows by adding your comments and suggestions to http://www.publishingtoolkit.org/.

With many thanks to the authors who contributed 37 articles, participants of 13 interviews and tours, and the hard work of our researcher and editor, Allison Brown, this Library Publishing Toolkit represents the first of many shared resources dedicated to library publishing services. The organization of the Library Publishing Toolkit includes essential information on a wide variety of programs and services that are intended to help frame, support, and/or inspire the development of library publishing services:

1. Publishing in Public Libraries
   ◦ E-book, self-publishing, and printing services

---

[5] http://rrlc.org/

[6] http://geneseo.edu/library

[7] http://www3.libraryweb.org/home2.aspx

- ◦ Author services ranging from writers' groups and celebrations to author incubator programs
- ◦ Inspirational spaces, creativity centers, and publishing digital media

2. Publishing in Academic Libraries
   - ◦ Trends and essentials in scholarly publishing: Assessment, e-journals, outreach, service models, XML, etc.
   - ◦ Books and e-books: Library and university press partnership, service models, and workflows
   - ◦ Journal publishers: Organizational aspects, outreach and sustainability, and workflows
   - ◦ Publishing original works and archives: Storytelling, student works, and archival projects
   - ◦ Organizational development: Collaboration with faculty, communication, consortia, and cooperative approaches

Although the Toolkit segments public and academic libraries, both library types are moving away from merely selecting and purchasing content, each independently heading toward similar futures in publishing and the business of creating, curating, and distributing digital content. That future is related to the phenomenal growth in self-publishing books and digital media, and the Internet services and software that provide easy-to-use platforms for creativity and social networking. The market growth and environment that enables authors and creators to share their work also enables library publishing opportunities. At SUNY Geneseo Milne Library, for example, we have used Amazon's CreateSpace to provide print-on-demand reprints of rare books in the public domain, and we have published an original new memoir, *Tagging Along,* by Stuart Symington, Jr.

Libraries are also re-examining the self-publishing business as a community service opportunity. In 2012, Bowker announced that the number self-published books created in the U.S. grew 287% since 2006, with a total number of titles exceeding 235,000.[8] Libraries are determining their role in collecting and providing access to self-published titles. Dilevko and Dali adeptly pointed this out in 2006:

"In public and academic libraries, there has been, for the most part, an awkward silence about how to deal with books from self-publishers, mainly because of the lack of reviews of self-published books in mainstream reviewing outlets."[9]

Important for libraries is recognizing the growth in self-publishing as a community of authors that use libraries and need library services, while at the same time, enables new opportunities for libraries. The work of scholarly communications or author services can inspire creativity; it can also serve as a strategy that promotes an alternative publishing model. Open access is

---

[8] http://www.bowker.com/en-US/aboutus/press_room/2012/pr_10242012.shtml

[9] (Dilevko, 2006, p. 211).

one of the library publishing models taking shape, along with affordable print-on-demand titles. Cumulatively, these alternatives have the potential to develop a more community- and academic-friendly publishing model that is sustainable and disseminates works to a wider audience.

In academic environments, unique digital content is produced extensively; papers, projects, theses, monographs, and data sets are produced every day. In response, SUNY Geneseo's Milne Library is piloting a number of publishing initiatives that are helping us establish publishing services, including:

- Digital Scholarship: Research, development, and production work for a collaborative digital humanities and scholarship initiative called Digital Thoreau.[10] This project involved Text Encoding Initiative[11] (TEI) training for the Technical Services staff, who in about six months completed the monumental work of encoding *Walden* and works by scholars Walter Harding and Ronald Clapper. Thanks to their TEI work, and using the Versioning Machine,[12] readers of *Walden* can see the variation in the seven published editions and annotations by Walter Harding, Ronald Clapper, and others.

- Publishing Books: Publishing of reprints and new works on Amazon's CreateSpace and e-books on Open Monograph Press, open source software developed by the Public Knowledge Project, and hosted online by Milne Library.[13] The reprints expand the access to public domain works that have not been digitized and holdings of which are very rare. We utilized GIST GDM[14] batch analysis, an open source tool, to automate identifying works that qualify. Providing both an open access version and a print-on-demand helps protect access to the content, as well as expand use. The sales of print help fund growing special collections and this program.

- Publishing Journals: Hosting journals using Open Journal Systems and hosting conferences using Open Conference Systems. Both open source software packages were developed by the Public Knowledge Project and are hosted by Milne Library.[15]

- Open Access Digital Projects: Hosting a variety of digital projects, including WalterHarding.org with Omeka, a digital exhibition tool developed by Roy Rosenzweig Center for History and New Media, and Gandy Dancer, SUNY's Online Literary Magazine using WordPress and Open Journal Systems.[16]

Each project provides an opportunity for the library to develop skills and understand the important connections between author, librarian, and reader. Milne Library sees these

[10]   http://digitalthoreau.org/
[11]   http://www.tei-c.org/index.xml
[12]   http://digitalthoreau.org/walden/solitude/text/05_solitude.xml
[13]   http://opensuny.org/omp/index.php/minerva
[14]   http://www.gistlibrary.org/gdm/
[15]   https://ojs.geneseo.edu/; http://eres.geneseo.edu:8080/ocs/
[16]   http://www.gandydancer.org/

publishing and related digital scholarship initiatives as vital to transforming scholarly communications. These initiatives enrich the learning environment and expand open access and affordable publishing models that strengthen education and lifelong learning. Milne's recently formed publishing team is looking at establishing best practices and workflows using a suite of publishing services and systems. The team's goals are to develop expertise and knowledge about publishing services, provide infrastructure, and create a streamlined workflow for the variety of publishing services.

At the Rochester Public Library, a member of the Monroe County Library System, digital content is created daily through the Digitizing Department at the Central Library. Thousands of pages of unique, rare, or out-of-print materials, significant to local history or genealogy research, have been digitized and made available as PDF files on the http://www.libraryweb.org website. This includes books, newspapers, letters, yearbooks, images, and more. In addition, finding aids unique to the digitized materials are also being created by staff. The Monroe County Library System is looking strategically at publishing digital content as an opportunity to serve their users. The Rochester Public Library is developing a new teen space focused on digital content production, leveraging the ideas and interest in makerspace and digital productions.

Among libraries, collaboration and sharing insights about publishing services has become critical at a time when libraries, publishers, and others are seeking opportunities and taking risks to adapt and rethink their position with the readers' market. For libraries, the mission of advancing, sharing, and preserving knowledge, inspiring lifelong learning, and strengthening our communities is seen as a vital role and responsibility. We see our role as serving both the author and the reader. Central to bringing libraries and publishers to a converging point is the focus on providing knowledge access to readers. There are several possible strategies to address the challenge of providing access to publishing services, and many with competing conclusions. The picture for library publishing needs focus and clarity to define effective library roles and services. With a clear vision and a collaborative framework, authors, readers, and libraries are building a sustainable and mutually beneficial future.

Bibliography

Dilevko, J., & Dali, K. (2006). The self-publishing phenomenon and libraries. *Library & Information Science Research*, 28(2), 208–234. doi:10.1016/j.lisr.2006.03.003

Part 1

Publishing in Public Libraries

Allison P. Brown

SUNY Geneseo

IN THIS SECTION

Introduction

Patricia Uttaro

Director, Monroe County Library System

An image imprinted indelibly in my mind is that of a line of people forming a human chain, hands clasped firmly together, protecting the Library of Alexandria from protestors and looters during the unrest in Egypt in 2011. Those people fully recognized and believed that the library and its contents were too important, too valuable to jeopardize and were willing to risk their own lives to protect it.

Libraries scare dictators, tyrants, zealots, terrorists—anyone who wields power based in fear and oppression—because the library represents knowledge which celebrates and records human achievement. For centuries, libraries have borne the responsibility of collection, management, and preservation of information; in 2013, however, libraries have the opportunity to broaden that responsibility to include the facilitation, creation, and interpretation of information or content.

Libraries are uniquely positioned to become facilitators of content creation as well as content creators in their own right. Libraries are connectors in their communities, whether located in a small town, city, suburb, or college campus. People seek us out for information, for access to equipment, for expert advice, for space to create. Why not broaden our focus from collection and preservation of information to facilitation and creation? Let's strengthen the connection between writers and libraries by helping independent authors navigate the Wild West of self-publishing and help create a vibrant author colony in our own communities. Many larger libraries have the tools necessary and are capable of acquiring and developing the staff expertise needed to jumpstart and maintain such an operation.

Additionally, many libraries are sitting on storehouses of content treasure, just waiting to be repurposed and reintroduced to readers and information consumers. Almanacs, poetry, letters, diaries, maps, images, scrapbooks, and so much more have been diligently collected and preserved by libraries all over the world; the opportunity exists now to bring those items to light and share them widely through such avenues as the Digital Public Library of America, HathiTrust, and regional projects such as the New York Heritage digital collection.

Content Creation Facilitation

Students

New York, along with 44 other states, has adopted the Common Core Standards for grade-level instruction, which requires students to "use technology, including the Internet, to produce and publish writing as well as to interact and collaborate with others".[1] Many students learning under these standards will become adults with highly developed collaborative skills and will expect access to the networks, equipment, and materials necessary to continue to participate in collaborative projects and content creation. At the same time, adults who embrace lifelong learning already turn to the library as a source for materials that satisfy their craving for knowledge, which often results in the creation of content. The students who use public and school libraries every day will soon, if not already, be asking librarians for assistance with content creation and publishing options.

In 2012, the Rochester (NY) Public Library joined 12 other communities nationwide in planning new digital learning centers inspired by YOUmedia, a teen space at the Chicago Public Library. This project is part of the Learning Labs in Libraries and Museums project begun in 2010 to develop collaboration among a variety of community institutions to increase student participation and performance in science, technology, engineering, and mathematics. Since then, the MacArthur Foundation and IMLS have committed to investing $4 million to support Learning Lab projects in museums and libraries nationwide.

Each Learning Lab uses a research-based education model known as connected learning, which facilitates and encourages discovery, creativity, critical thinking, and real-world learning through interesting activities and experiences that combine academic and social experiences through the use of digital and traditional media. The labs provide teens with a network of mentors and peers, often brought together via online social networks. Activities in Learning Labs enhance the education experience by merging it with the social, potentially leading to a richer and more satisfying life experience based on deeper communication and civic engagement.

"Digital media are revolutionizing the way young people learn, socialize, and engage in civic life," said Julia Stasch, Vice President of U.S. Programs for the MacArthur Foundation. "These innovative labs are designed to provide today's youth with the space, relationships, and resources to connect their social worlds and interests with academics and to better prepare them for success in the 21st century."

Teen Central at the Central Library of Rochester & Monroe County (NY) is the main site for YOUmedia within the Rochester Public Library, with the project dubbed HO-MA-GO (Hanging Out-Messing Around-Geeking Out). City branch libraries participate through backpack sets that include a variety of media equipment for youth to explore in the branch. At Teen Central, the first project is being developed in conjunction with the Rochester Teen Film Festival. Working

---

[1] http://www.corestandards.org/ELA-Literacy/CCRA/W, http://www.corestandards.org/ELA-Literacy/CCRA/W/6

with our main partner, Dr. Brian Bailey from Nazareth College, teens will learn about creating films and be encouraged to submit them to the annual film festival. The library will host a special red-carpet showcase event for all content created.

The Rochester Public Library is currently entering the second phase of development and recruiting youth to serve on a youth design council. The youth chosen will help design the layout of the physical space, the programs offered, and the types of media equipment purchased. The youth will also be trained on using the equipment and serve as peer mentors once the program is up and running. The variety and scope of content that could be created through the YOUmedia project is infinite, and the library will play multiple roles, including facilitator, content creator, and content collector. The library will become a creation space as well as a collection source, and youth will learn to use the library in a completely different way.

Adults

The swift growth of digital publishing has made it extremely easy for people to share their knowledge through both traditional print and digital publications. The market is being flooded with independent, personal publishing of content that bypasses the traditional publishing process, with ordinary people publishing all sorts of content, including memoirs, novels, cookbooks, and family histories. There has never been a time in history when so many people have access to the tools necessary to publish their work for the masses. However, these grassroots, independent writers do not have access to all the tools, expertise, and advice provided by publishers during the traditional publishing process. As a result, we see many independently published works that are full of bad grammar, typos, dense and awkward composition, and poorly constructed plots.

Libraries can step in and provide or facilitate pre-publishing services to our communities by providing staff trained to assist with such services or by establishing collaborative agreements with area writing groups or literary societies. Librarians are by nature a literary group. Investing in development of staff who have an interest in and a talent for language and writing can provide a valuable service to community members. Many libraries and librarians, in fact, already serve as trusted resources to researchers and writers. Taking that research assistance further and expanding it to include proofreading, critical reviewing, and even formatting and publishing is certainly feasible.

Imagine a collaborative writing and publishing space in a library. It has plenty of room for writing groups to meet for sharing and critiquing of works in progress but also plenty of quiet, private space where writers can work uninterrupted for varying lengths of time. Perhaps the library offers small study rooms that can be rented on a long-term basis, allowing a writer to create a personal workspace that includes access to the library computer network, including high-speed Internet and research databases. When the writer is ready to share his or her work with readers, the library provides a connection to a writing group, a local publisher, or to a staff member or other community member who can provide proofreading, copy editing, a critical review, or even graphic design and formatting assistance. Perhaps the library offers access to high-speed printing and binding equipment, as well as secure digital storage space, allowing the writer to write, edit, and publish all in one place.

Imagine the writers who use this space are part of a community of writers who meet regularly for support, discussion, technical assistance, and camaraderie. Their creativity and imagination is constantly challenged by the rich, stimulating environment created by the library, potentially resulting in significant contributions to the written record. These writers interact with the library staff, exchanging and debating ideas, writing and rewriting, performing, reading aloud and otherwise creating a dynamic atmosphere. Those writers who prefer solitude might also find that, and still have access to the research, materials, and equipment they need to create.

Once the writing is done and the piece is ready for publishing, what role does the library play? Technological advances have made it possible for a 300-page book to be printed and bound in a few minutes using equipment such as the Espresso Book Machine. Libraries can provide access to such machines, as they provided access in the past to emerging technologies such as photocopy machines and computers. Several libraries and bookstores in North America have experimented with such machines with varying results. What kinds of books might be printed on these machines? Think family histories, scrapbooks, cookbooks, yearbooks for homeschooling groups, poetry, and more. The possibilities are endless. Additionally, libraries can provide staff expertise to help writers learn to publish digitally. There are any number of sites available in 2013 that allow a writer to upload and publish an e-book; none of them are simple to use. Libraries can, and do, offer tutorials on how to use sites such as Blurb, Lulu, and even Amazon. In fact, none of the activities mentioned above are new to libraries, as the millions of people who attend programs and use library resources each year can attest.

Library as Content Creator

While the library as content facilitator is not such a stretch, the library as content creator is a distinctly different concept, especially for public libraries. Large public libraries have created content and published material for years, but most libraries have not had the resources to engage in wholesale digitizing or publishing of original content. Digitizing is becoming easier and more affordable, which provides a tantalizing opportunity for libraries to mine their collections for unique, non-copyrighted materials that would generate interest among the buying public. For example, the Central Library of Rochester and Monroe County owns the only copy (in the area) of a building code handbook from the 1960s that includes critical information for architects addressing renovations in pre-1960 structures. Staff have been asked repeatedly by architects who have driven many miles whether the library would ever digitize the book and make it available via the Web. This kind of material is exactly what should be identified in library collections and made available as digital content through partnerships with copyright owners. Libraries need to provide information where and when the user needs it, which is not necessarily within four walls.

The New York Public Library has taken a noteworthy approach to identifying unique content and presenting it in an attractive, appealing manner. Their Biblion project has created access to collections of World's Fair images and materials as well as Mary Shelley's *Frankenstein*. These fascinating collections can now be browsed by anyone at any time. On the other side of the pond, the British Library has produced a number of apps that provide access to varied collections as "High Seas Adventures," "History of Britain and Ireland," and "Novels of the 18th & 19th Century." Also available via an app are digitized "Treasures of the British Library," which offers access to unique manuscripts such as *Beowulf*, William Blake's notebooks, and illuminated manuscripts. While not in possession of such treasures as these, the Rochester Public Library is currently developing a project, "Rochester Voices," which provides app-based access to such unique items in their collection as letters, diaries, and music. All of this material is relevant to Rochester history and is unique to the library's collection. Once the "Rochester Voices" app is launched, access to this primary source material will be widespread.

There are exciting things happening at the state and national levels revolving around the creation of content, and libraries of all sizes have content to offer. The Digital Public Library of America, HathiTrust, the American Memory Project at the Library of Congress, and New York Heritage are just a few of the projects currently underway that will provide unprecedented access to primary source material. Imagine the scholarship that can be achieved through this improved access. Women's studies students will no longer have to read *about* Susan B. Anthony's letters; instead they can read the actual letters. Libraries all over the world have been the epicenters of preservation and collection of knowledge for centuries. We are now at a stage in history where access to all that material can be broadened in ways not imagined even 50 years ago.

Conclusion

The roles of the library as content facilitator and creator all come back to the consumer. As long as there is a desire and market for knowledge and an equal desire to share knowledge, imagination, and achievement, libraries will continue to serve as a linchpin in our culture. Whether providing services to help writers write and publish or mining our collections for unique material to share digitally, libraries and librarians will continue to fulfill the roles of information collectors, brokers, and creators.

About Publishing in Public Libraries

Allison P. Brown

Milne Library, SUNY Geneseo

Perhaps not surprisingly, libraries offering publishing services have a strong connection to independent local publishers and self-publishing authors. The works produced by this community are often stigmatized in discussions of validity or quality but continue to gain the support of both readers and authors. From a librarian's perspective, the focus on self-published titles is often on the hubris of publishing without the sanctioning of an established publishing company and a dislike of the details and standards that are missed when authors go it alone. There is distrust of content that does not fit into the standards we rely on publishers to provide.

Among the plethora of definitions and roles of the self-publisher, this one sticks out: "A self-publisher is a publisher: one who is undertaking the financial risk to bring a book to market and coordinating everything involved: advertising, marketing, printing, order fulfillment, etc."[2] The element of risk and the isolation of the writer are highlighted in this definition. The element of risk is tied to the image of the self-publisher as prideful and the isolation the root of what keeps the published works from conforming to the standards libraries love so dearly—and ironically both of these stigmas can be addressed by libraries themselves.

The other side of the issue is unsustainability within the current publishing model, especially in terms of e-content. In light of this climate, more libraries are turning to smaller and independent publishers to work together and create a counterpart model. Much like in the selection of content, most libraries rely on a combination of popular titles and more specific content to fulfill the needs of a unique community. Both models can thrive.

With other strong examples of how regulated media can coexist and benefit from crowdsourced material this juxtaposition has potential. So armed with knowledge of information and literature, keen discernment, and a prime position in the community, librarians are creating and assisting with the creation of a vast array of content. This section of the toolkit addresses these roles and asks how can libraries be more proactive in the creation, production, and access to content.

---

[2] "APPLICATION FOR AN ISBN PUBLISHER—ISBN.org." http://www.isbn.org/standards/home/isbn/us/printable/isbn.asp

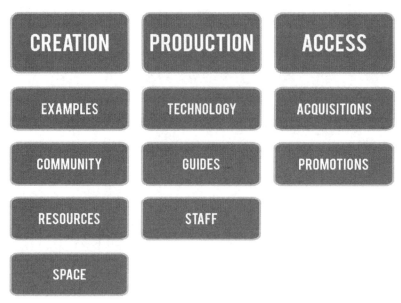

Common ways libraries support publishing.

Creation

When it comes to the creation of content, libraries already play an incredibly important role. Libraries house and promote the literature and content that inspire patrons to then go out and write their own stories. These functions are ever expanding; more and more libraries provide examples through what they do as much as the material they house. We can look at Idea Box, Oak Park's interactive exhibit area that invites patrons to interact, participate, and create. Buffalo & Erie County Public Library, as well as many other libraries, write and create local material to educate and entertain.

Community is similarly an ingrained part of what libraries do, and this function is evolving. We can see that through makerspaces and digital media labs the library is already bringing in and catering to a different type of patron than the traditional avid reader or casual Internet user. This is an opportunity to connect with already established organizations to offer space and mutual branding, and in doing so reach a new audience. Provincetown Public Library, in establishing their press, recruited community members to serve on their editorial board. Douglas County Libraries is similarly involving volunteers and local writers in writing and publishing support services. Resources—distinct from examples as specific craft, creation, and publishing information—also include locally created guides, instructions, and bibliographies. Specific and local resources for publishing are a frequent request both from patrons and librarians. Good examples of this can be seen at Sacramento Public Library's I Street Press and their informational and educational materials. Lastly, space is simple but very powerful. Offered to writing groups, hosting classes, promoting local authors, or simply designed to be open and flexible, this is one of the most simple ways libraries can open their doors to the creative community. A great example of this is Princeton Public Library: in opening their space to writers participating in National Novel Writing Month, they spurred the creation of a thriving writing group.

Production

Providing the technology needed for content creation and mindfully supporting that technology with accessible instructions and trained staff is becoming exceedingly important for libraries. Brooklyn's InfoCommons[3] houses such resources as well as hosts digital creation-centered programming. If libraries continue to embrace this role of providing technology and software that is not available freely elsewhere, there is potential to forge strong community relationships, increase the skill set and function of our own profession, and most importantly foster digital literacy that will only become more and more important to function successfully in our educational and professional lives. There are also examples of libraries providing production services using the Espresso Book Machine or e-book creation software to create works written by patrons or mined from the library's collection, and these services have proved fruitful for the library and the community.

Access

Providing or gaining access—especially to digital content—is a complicated discussion, but specifically looking at locally created content and self-published works, there are many opportunities for libraries. Local collections that include independently and self-published works, displays of local authors, and events that highlight these collections and people are already common in public libraries. However, there are generally only unwritten policies that reflect the acquisitions of these types of works. Developing these policies and practices could provide guidance for both writers marketing their books to libraries and librarians screening the titles. Two case studies in this section show libraries playing a role in this area in very different ways. Douglas County Libraries represents a very hands-on approach to both general issues of access in terms of e-content and the acquisition of independently published material, as well as a hands-on approach to communicating the policies and standards to local writers. Los Gatos Public Library provides an alternate example of providing support for self-publishers at the same time as making a commitment to access the published work but within the more common framework of acquisitions. While there are many intricacies in this area of publishing, libraries can be thinking about how they can assist in distributing locally created materials, how these materials can be integrated into existing collections, and how to represent the work in order to connect content with readers.

Case Studies

The case studies here represent libraries working in many combinations of these areas of publishing. I had the privilege of speaking or corresponding with 14 people at 12 libraries to hear the inspiration, planning, implementation, and upkeep of their services and programs that support writing and publishing. By sharing these stories and linking them to the larger climate of content creation, makers, and the uncertainty in the publishing world, we hope they will serve

---

[3]   "Shelby White and Leon Levy Information Commons " http://www.bklynpubliclibrary.org/locations/central/infocommons

13

as valuable examples and the starting point for brainstorming and inspiration as libraries find more ways to support not just the consumption, but the production of information, literature, and art.

Serving a Writing Community, Building a Writing Community

1 ## IN THIS CHAPTER

I noticed two common denominators when I spoke to libraries about their thriving writing communities: clever use of space and enthusiastic participants. Before talking about publishing print-on-demand titles, acquiring an Espresso Book Machine, or offering e-book publishing courses, libraries should be playing a role in supporting the writing process. If we have complaints about the standard of writing these days or the unpredictability of self-published titles, this is the place to start. Especially amidst the chaotic world of e-book distribution, licensing, and platforms, cultivating the direct author-library relationship can only help with awareness and support. Both

Jamie LaRue[4] and Mark Coker[5] in recent articles have addressed their belief that the library can play a powerful role within the creative community as well as the larger e-publishing discussion.

Writing Groups and Local Author Events

Princeton Public Library

I spoke to Janie Hermann, the Public Programming Librarian at Princeton Public Library, to hear about the writing groups they host at their main library branch as well as the work they do to support local authors. They have three regular writing groups: one following a very traditional critique format, the Wednesday Writing group that was born out of NaNoWriMo, and a daytime group called Read, Write, Share.

Princeton Public Library registered as a writing location site that offered a quiet space at specified times to writers participating in NaNoWriMo.[6] The writers that used the space also used the opportunity to network and eventually created a writing group that focused on encouragement and support. Like many writing groups that meet at libraries, this one was spurred on by a local author, Beth Plankey, so the library's direct involvement is minimal. With a dedicated volunteer, Hermann says, a library hosting a writing group needs to provide the space, advertise, and communicate regularly with the leader.

The more formal writing group, Writers' Room, meets twice a month and has about 15 members. The coordinators of the group write mainly creative nonfiction, so this has often been the focus, though they encourage writers of any genre to participate. At each meeting two or three participants read about 15 minutes' worth of their work and members take time afterward to share their responses and offer suggestions.

Read, Write, Share has a more informal setup, though the writing in this group is often memoir or nonfiction and the group members also take time to just talk about what they are reading or share passages from books they enjoy. This group is also led by members of the community.

The third group, called the Wednesday Writing group, also focuses on support and sharing. These meetings feature prompts and writing warm-ups. Hermann described it more as an atmosphere of "mutual support" and a place to "develop your inner writer." The total membership of the group is over 30, but the weekly count is usually closer to 10. An online community also complements the weekly meetings and keeps members connected and updated.

---

[4]   LaRue, J. "All Hat, No Cattle: A Call for Libraries to Transform Before It's Too..." The Digital Shift. http://www.thedigitalshift.com/2012/06/ebooks/all-hat-no-cattle-a-call-for-libraries-to-transform-before-its-too-late/

[5]   Coker, M. "Mark Coker: Libraries to Become Community Publishing Portals." http://www.huffingtonpost.com/mark-coker/library-ebooks_b_2951953.html

[6]   "Come Write In: Libraries—National Novel Writing Month." http://www.nanowrimo.org/en/library

In addition to the writing groups Princeton Public Library hosts, they also run a Local Authors' Day to feature and support local and independent writers. Hermann found many self-published authors were requesting readings, and the library tried hosting readings or signings, but without name recognition or a solid readership, it was difficult to bring in a substantial audience. So instead of trying to accommodate many smaller features and readings, Local Authors' Day was created.

Princeton's Local Authors' Day began by hosting 20 authors, and has grown this year to over 70 applicants for 40 spaces. There are simple criteria to qualify: one must live within a certain range of the library and to have published recently. Hermann explains that these criteria keep the content presented fresh and new authors coming in, rather than writers presenting the same book over multiple years.

The program has the flavor of many author fairs. The writers are able to set up a table with their books to sell, and the afternoon is devoted to readings. Fifteen authors are chosen by lottery to read aloud from their work. But on top of these activities, the library also takes the opportunity to make the day just as much about professional development as about providing a space for marketing.

Through the morning of Local Authors' Day workshops are offered to the authors and to the public. The topics range from time management to working on character development and are generally taught by traditionally published or more experienced authors. This year, one workshop focused on novel writing, specifically "Two Important Steps in the Novel-Writing Process: How to Formulate an Idea and How to Plot [a] Story,"[7] presented by Mark Di Ionno, and the other, run by Jon Gibbs, was titled "Recognize and Embrace Your Narrative Voice."[8]

It was important, Hermann noted, in a community with many literary and creative interests, to develop this program as a service to the writers as well as an event for the community. With a successful system in place they are able to have a clear answer and service for authors who have made the effort to market themselves to libraries.

Wirt Public Library

Alice & Jack Wirt Public Library in Bay City, Michigan, supports a program similar to Princeton's Local Authors' Day. In response to many patrons' inquiries about publishing and writing, librarians Cindy Gregory and Amber Hughey created Writers' Night. They invited four local authors or publishers to come give a brief talk and serve as a panel for the attendees to ask questions. For the first Writers' Night they invited authors they knew personally or who already had connections to the library, which included a local historian and a music author.

---

[7]   "Workshop for Writers | Princeton Public Library." http://www.princetonlibrary.org/events/2013/04/workshop-writers

[8]   "Workshop for Writers | Princeton Public Library." . http://www.princetonlibrary.org/events/2013/04/workshop-writers-0

They also relied on suggestions, and later were able to reach out to Wayne State Press to get more recommendations for authors who live and write nearby.

The event was marketed thoroughly through their website, flyers, and e-mails to local colleges, as well as on a local television station. All of these efforts paid off with 65 participants signed up and 10 on a waiting list. Their second Writers' Night in April 2013[9] had a similarly enthusiastic response of around 60 participants, and both the first and the second program had a wide age range of attendees. With many programs' attendance closer to 10–15 participants, after the first Writers' Night it was clear there was a definite interest and need in the community to hear about the experiences of writers, publishers, and self-publishers.

Each author or publisher invited prepared a talk of about 15–20 minutes, with each talking about their writing process or their journey to publication. The following question and answer time further displayed the community's enthusiasm, with much interest in the process of finding a publisher and the marketing of self-published works.

Hughey pointed out that although it was hard work initially to coordinate all the presenters and get the program off its feet (the first Writers' Night was the product of seven months of preparation), each subsequent program has gone more smoothly and the preparation time has been cut down.

Similar to Princeton's Local Authors' Day, the authors presenting at Wirt Public Library's Writers' Night were given a space to sell or market their book during the intermission and after the program. It gave the opportunity for participants to speak one on one with the participating authors and publishers, as well as generating sales.

An exciting outcome of the Writers' Nights is the prompting of a writers' roundtable at the library. With many of the attendees of the Writers' Night interested, Gregory and Hughey set up the Writers' Roundtable to allow interested participants to meet, talk about writing, and form their own writing groups. With the space and the first meeting facilitated by the librarians, the writers who attended the first meeting have created a monthly critique group. Here the library played an important role in offering the space and creating an atmosphere ripe for collaboration and creativity.

Safety Harbor Public Library

Gina Bingham, the Adult Services Librarian at Safety Harbor Public Library in Florida, also coordinates a variety of author and writer services for the community. She describes the small coastal town as a "retreat for the creative" with a community that is immensely supportive of the library and all they do and offer. Safety Harbor has been hosting one writing group, called Story Circle, for four years now and was recently asked by an existing writing group to host an offshoot group as the original group grew too large.

---

[9]   "2013—The Bay County Library Systems." http://www.baycountylibrary.org/wp-content/uploads/Mar-Apr-13-Web.pdf

Story Circle, run by local writer Jan Golden, focuses on memoir and personal experience. Often a prompt is assigned beforehand and writers come prepared to share their writing on themes such as influential persons in their lives or holiday stories. Golden utilizes a blog to communicate with members, remind them of assignments, and share relevant articles.[10] The blog actually serves two writing groups that Golden leads, the other meeting at Largo Public Library, only 20 minutes away. Bingham noticed that having two sessions of the writing group each month has allowed her patrons a choice of where and when to attend. If someone had to miss a meeting in Safety Harbor, they could then attend the Largo meeting on a different night of the week. Having the consistency of one facilitator and a uniform setup and assignments make this arrangement convenient.

The second group began with a start-up meeting at Safety Harbor Library in March as a result of steadily growing interest in a critique group run by Safety Harbor Writers and Poets,[11] which reached its maximum for group members. Laura Kepner, one of the founding members, approached the library to begin a new group with the dual purpose of giving interested parties an overview of what has been successful for their writing group, which has thrived over the last three years, as well as providing a place for sharing and critique. This writing group will continue as a place to meet other writers, learn about participating and facilitating in a critique group, and form smaller groups. Writers also are encouraged to bring work to share and get feedback for improvement. Bingham says that the first meeting was well attended and that many patrons have inquired about the group at the reference desk in the library.

Safety Harbor Writers and Poets Library Group: Thursday, July 25 from 6:00-7:00 pm. This monthly gathering of writers is meant to be a platform for those in search of forming or joining a writers' group, connecting to others with similar writing goals, and as a mentor group for writers in need of constructive tips and ideas on how to make their current or future group successful. Bring something to share (optional) and if time permits, we will discuss the strengths and also how your work may improve. (This group meets monthly on the fourth Thursday.)

The description of the writing group on Saftey Harbor Public Library's events website

While the writing groups are run by community members, Bingham and other librarians are often asked to make appearances in the meetings to share about writing resources the library offers. They have done presentations on NaNoWriMo (National Novel Writing Month), social networking for writers with tools such as WattPad (http:\\www.wattpad.com), and resources found right in the library like the *Writers' Market*. Bingham also shares with authors ways that librarians help writers with research, citing a time that a historical fiction author needed help finding information on the television broadcasting of a rocket launch.

On top of the regular meetings of area writers, the library offers other single-event programs geared towards writers' professional development. In the past they have hosted sessions on publishing novels, how to fund self-publishing ventures with Kickstarter, website building for writers and artists, and journaling. Often the presenters approach the library with a program

---

10   "Jan Golden's Story Circles." http://www.jangoldenstorycircles.blogspot.com/

11   "Learn—Safety Harbor Writers & Poets." http://safetyharborwritersandpoets.com/Learn.html

idea, and after Bingham spends some time looking at the presenters' credentials, the program is set up. Evaluation surveys, which are e-mailed to past participants every few months, have shown positive feedback and interest in more programs that provide resources for and encourage writers.

Armed with the knowledge of what her community enjoys and needs, Bingham is able to work with local authors when they come to speak to urge them to talk about their process, crowdsourcing funds, and other publishing experience, as well as information about the book they present on.

Author Incubator Program: Douglas County Library System

From writing groups, to relatives reading and commenting on chapters, to online forums, to online services that make the steps easier—no writer is an island. Impressing this fact on both the writers that seek to self-publish as well as libraries that are grappling with adding self-published works to their catalogs is key.

For writers, arriving at the self-publishing stage can be jarring. It is a swift transition from the creative, nebulous task of writing to a checklist of often tedious decisions from important to trivial. For those in a position to support self-publishers, a group which hopefully will include more and more libraries, ensuring that the checklist takes the writer on a journey to produce the best book possible serves the best interests of all.

This is the basis of the Author Incubator Services that Douglas County Libraries is in the process of developing. Born out of their trailblazing work in e-book lending and a desire to bring their business to independent publishers and self-publishers of e-books, they are determined to also take part in the creation of the book.

The groundwork was laid in the library system's work in creating its own e-book lending system. In a climate of unsustainable e-book pricing and licensing debates, Douglas County decided to create their own solution to the problem. The idea was to be able to offer e-content to their patrons without sacrificing a huge portion of their budget and still not being able to guarantee the longevity of that content. They also wanted to present a more fluid experience within their catalog to allow print books and e-content to be viewed, previewed, and accessed in one interface without having to exit the library's website and log in at another location.

The development of such an infrastructure was a huge project and investment, but the precedent the project represents is huge. Several other library systems have begun implementing similar programs, including the Marmot Library Network and Califa. More than that, as this system was put in place, alternate ways of acquiring this e-content were being explored. Because the library could now host and manage the digital files with a content server, dealing directly with publishers became possible. This gave Douglas County the opportunity to work with publishers that would not manipulate the pricing of content for libraries and sell the work outright instead of licensing it. Both the discovery interface Douglas County has worked on and information about working directly with publishers is available on the initiative's site: http://evoke.cvlsites.org.[12]

With an investment such as this and the commitment to acquiring independently and self-published works, Douglas County gives us a glimpse as to why it is so important for libraries to take an active role in the publishing process from the point of creation. There is valuable content available through companies and individuals outside of the leading publishers, and libraries have an opportunity to present these options to patrons. As organizers of information, curators of content, and evaluators of resources, librarians are primed for both the challenge of sifting through the increasing amount of content available and helping creators in their local community produce the best work they can.

The resulting Author Incubator Program has two goals. One is to link the library more closely with local authors by providing them with resources for the writing, polishing, and publishing of their work; the other is to connect those authors with readers.

The service, intended specifically for the local community (e.g. Douglas County Library card holders), would begin for writers as a link from the library's webpage that leads to the primary question: "Do you want to write a book? Or do you want to write a good book?" This entry point will lead the author through a publishing roadmap with resources specific to the Douglas County area. There are recommendations for writing centers and groups and lists of freelance copy editors and cover designers, all with interactive features allowing for ratings and comments to keep them relevant and up to date. While this sort of road map doesn't ensure that the writers take advantage of these options, it will certainly get them thinking.

Once the author has used these resources and published the book through a recommended e-book distributor (generally Smashwords, as they provide key services such as ISBNs for free), the next step is to, through the Douglas County Library interface, submit the first chapter and an outline of their book directly to the library. The library is currently working on assembling a group of volunteers, mainly local authors, to participate in the process in a very important way. This group of volunteers, called by LaRue "citizen acquisition editors," will use their judgment and a set of provided guidelines, mainly concerning editing and content, to accept the book into the library's catalog. While this may initially seem like a rigorous process to go through to donate your book to a library, there is a payoff in the end. The initial screening allows the library to enforce basic collection development policies and standards, and the pairing of the volunteer with the author allows for greater discoverability. Once the book has been published as a free e-book through Smashwords and acquired by the library, the volunteer provides a review and rating in the library's catalog. This lends the book credibility with the backing of a local author or librarian, and, with relevant keywords in the review, can bring the book to the tops of searches and increase the author's visibility.

While being connected to readers and some free marketing is a great payoff, LaRue says the plan is to add another motivation to authors. They plan to host a competition of the submitted

12   "Evoke | Creating the Future for Library E-Content." http://evoke.cvlsites.org/

titles and award the best in each genre with a review in a high-visibility magazine. The local author is first introduced to local readers and then is introduced to a national audience.

There are two important factors in this plan. The first is that a group of local authors was involved and consulted through the planning process. A program to support writers and authors cannot be successful if their views are not represented in the planning; to leave them out is to be planning to serve a fictional idea of a writer rather than those that really live and write in the community.

The second is that the program relies almost completely on volunteers. When I asked LaRue if the volunteer-run program would be sustainable, he and the library seemed committed to keeping volunteers engaged. "We know people love to read," LaRue reasons. "Why not ask them 'Would you help us solve a problem we cannot solve by ourselves?'" Libraries are often places that know the value of a dedicated volunteer and in many cases have the communication and infrastructure in place to connect and organize this powerful workforce. More about the proposed system can be read about in an article by LaRue in the June 2013 issue of *American Libraries*.[13]

While all the resources are assembled, the Douglas County Libraries are planning to market their new service over the summer and launch in the fall of 2013.

---

[13]   "Wanna Write a Good One? Library as Publisher | American Libraries..." http://www. americanlibrariesmagazine.org/article/wanna-write-good-one-library-publisher

Self-Publishing and Library Resources by Lisa Petrocelli

New York Rider Magazine

I am a lifelong resident of Colonie, New York, and a patron of the William K. Sanford Town Library in Loudonville, New York. I am the editor of *New York Rider Magazine* (circulation approximately 12,000 throughout New York State), a statewide publication for motorcyclists, which also boasts a small international distribution in France and Italy (through regular correspondents in those countries). In addition to regular monthly columns, including my own (Lisa's Peace), we invite readers to submit their own stories and accounts in the biker world. My job is to attend as many biker events as possible in my area and report on those events, as well as to edit all submissions to prepare for print. I have been involved with the magazine since its inception in 2006, first as a contributing writer, then as the editor beginning in 2008. I also write for an online news site called Examiner.

My self-published book is titled *The Gloves Come Off*. My book focuses on 15 men whom I have met over a span of 10 years who represent the American biker culture primarily, but not exclusively, in the Northeast U.S. The book focuses on the lives of these men, their loves, their passions, and why and how they became part of the biker subculture, in a sense revealing the man under the gloves. Between these chapters are essays which reflect my experiences from attending motorcycle events. There is a very large biker community in my area of New York, but many people are unaware of the existence and influence of this subculture.

I sent my manuscript to publishers that I thought were most likely to be interested in publishing a book on biker culture. After receiving no replies from any of the publishers I queried, I decided to look into self-publishing. The biggest difference between traditional publishing and self-publishing is money and marketing. Traditional publishers assume all financial responsibility and marketing for the book, while self-publishing requires the author to assume the financial responsibility and must market his/her own book.

23

I researched the numerous self-publishing companies and settled on Aventine Press, one of the most reputable, and one that offered the services I needed. I decided on Aventine Press for several reasons. Most important was that their prices were very reasonable and I had the option of purchasing each service separately. In other words, I did not have to pay for services I did not want, such as marketing, editing, cover design, etc. I knew I could edit my own work and I also had one of my brothers (an attorney and legal editor) and a fellow writer review it to check my own editing. I didn't want to pay for unnecessary marketing costs, such as posters, flyers, or additional websites, because I knew that the book would automatically be listed on amazon.com and barnesandnoble.com, which were the most important to me, as well as other smaller venues, such as booksamillion.com. I could produce my own flyers and as a well-known author said to me, "I've published both ways—self-publishing and traditional. The biggest difference is the marketing. And who really markets your book better than YOU?"

I was also impressed with the Aventine Press no-frills website, straightforward contract and explanation of services. Since my husband planned on designing and photographing the cover, I had the option of providing my own cover design and only had to choose one of Aventine's templates. The owner, Keith Pearson, was wonderful to work with. He answered all of my calls and e-mails immediately and was extremely helpful during the entire process. By the way, there is a great website called Preditors and Editors (http://pred-ed.com/), which documents the reputation of companies involved in the publishing industry. I would frequently check that site for reviews as well as the Better Business Bureau to see whether any of the companies I considered had negative ratings. I read through some author forums, such as Absolute Write Water Cooler (http://www.absolutewrite.com/forums/) to see what other authors had to say about the various publishing companies. I searched through the Amazon.com site and looked at other books that were published by Aventine Press, and I thought the quality of the product looked excellent. Last but not least, I loved the Aventine Press logo, which featured a graphic of an open book. Somehow it looked more professional to me.

I visited my library for some of my initial research into American biker culture and later to more closely examine books—paperback and hardcover—for size dimensions, paper quality, and which covers (and colors) quickly caught my eye. I also took note of publishing notations and placement of dedications, acknowledgments, etc. I envisioned my own book on the shelves and knew, after some comparisons, that I would settle on a 6x9 format.

A traditional publisher handles all aspects of format, design, and marketing; however, self-publishing companies do offer these services for a price. I opted to edit my own work and handle formatting and cover design. My husband, Dino Petrocelli, is a professional photographer, so I was lucky to have him photograph the cover. There is a lot of time and work involved with the format of a book (details such as font type, size, and special symbols used), and fortunately I was eager to make my own choices and decisions on all of those details.

I did not use any special software to format the book. Aventine Press requested a Word document on CD, which was easy enough. If I wanted special characters, I inserted them myself (for example, I placed a ~ in certain places in the book). There was a limit as to which characters could be used, which was spelled out in the guidelines provided. With Aventine, I had a choice of five different interior templates and after choosing one, I did all of my own formatting, except for the margins; Aventine took care of getting my manuscript into "book format." The interior photos were also done by my husband. Honestly, my biggest problem was getting all the gloves collected on time!

In retrospect, perhaps I could have consulted an agent to advise and help me submit my manuscript to a wider variety of traditional publishers. I did not want to wait any longer to publish, but that may have been the wiser avenue to take. I have sold over 250 copies of my book online and have sold approximately the same number of copies myself offline. Traditional publishing most likely would have resulted in greater sales. Nevertheless, I completed the self-publishing process and was happy with the outcome.

I have promoted my book through *New York Rider Magazine* and Examiner channels and my connections within the many biker events at which I attend and participate. However, it was extremely important to me that my book be made available in libraries, especially my own town library, where I have been a patron all of my life. I also happen to work at the New York State Library and am very aware of the importance of continuing to provide our residents with helpful and interesting reading materials. I felt that inclusion in Upper Hudson Library System's catalog would provide an educational, informative eye-opener to the "biker world" for the interested public.

The staff at the William K. Sanford Town Library assisted me in the promotion of my book. Immediately following the publication of my book in April 2012, I wrote to Richard Naylor, the director of the William K. Sanford Town Library, explaining that I was a local author and had recently self-published a book. I inquired about the possibility of William K. Sanford adding my book to their collection, enclosing a paperback copy of my book. I received an answer within a week from Joe Nash, Librarian, Adult Collection Development and Programs, who offered to conduct an interview at the library which would then be televised on our local television station. Although I was apprehensive about being on camera for an interview, Mr. Nash made me feel very comfortable, asked all the right questions, and it turned out to be a great experience. The interview was then broadcast throughout the entire month of August (link to my interview: https://vimeo.com/45664090).

In addition, the library offered to host an author night and encouraged me to invite the people who were featured in my book. The William K. Sanford Town Library promoted this by developing a flyer which was posted at the library and on their website and Facebook page, and the event was listed in the library's newsletter. This event was held on August 13, 2012, with approximately 50 people in attendance, including a few of my colleagues from the Division of Library Development (Carol Desch, Statewide Coordinator for Library Services, and Maria Hazapis). The staff of the WKS Library prepared their large meeting room for my presentation and welcomed me and my guests. It is important to note that many people who do not normally frequent the library attended this event.

Author Night was a wonderful experience for all involved and I was very proud that my library was willing to assist in the promotion of my book in this way. I expected to be invited for book signings at local bookstores, and I was; however, the events at the library meant more to me because there was no monetary gain involved on the library's part. I donated two copies of my book to the library and was delighted to learn that *The Gloves Come Off* was added to the Upper Hudson Library System's catalog. Of course, at that time, I published an article on my Examiner page announcing the fact that my book was available in local libraries (http://www.examiner.com/article/the-gloves-come-off-now-available-local-libraries). Bernard Margolis, State Librarian and Assistant Commissioner for Libraries, presented my book, along with other books written by New York State Library staff, at his monthly staff meeting, which was greatly appreciated. In addition, I would also like to mention that Loretta Ebert, Director of the New York State Library, has arranged for my book to be included in the New York State Library's collection.

I hope that other authors will take advantage of this powerful resource and realize the benefit that all libraries in New York State are poised to provide their patrons.

Libraries as Inspiration and Centers of Creation

2

IN THIS CHAPTER

W e can see libraries in transition from consumption to creation in many places: YouMedia in Chicago, 4th Floor Chatt, Fab Lab at Fayette Free Library; makerspaces and digital media labs are popping up all over the place. The way library publishing is manifesting itself in public libraries runs parallel to these endeavors. It goes hand in hand with increased technology and software, providing the education to walk makers through whatever their project is and nurturing and then marketing those projects, be it digital storytelling, a classic printed book, a podcast, or an e-book.

Inspiring Interaction and Creation: Idea Box

Oak Park Public Library

Oak Park Public Library's Idea Box brings people in before creative projects start; it provides the opportunity to experience local art, inspiration, and often a way to contribute their own voice. I think it also helps people overcome the fear of sharing and experience the joy that comes with seeing what happens when a whole community can share stories and ideas with one another. Looking at the success of the Idea Box can give many libraries ideas and inspirations about drawing their patrons into the realm of creation and interaction.

The concept is a simple room that rotates through a variety of interactive exhibits. In her article in the ILA Reporter[14] about the Idea Box, Harris explains it in this way: "We took a 9-by-13-foot space and made it a physical representation of these participatory values we had been exploring as a library. The Idea Box is always open for public participation, creativity, play, and constant change, much like the Web itself." The space had been hosting a café, but when the business closed the library was given the opportunity to reimagine what that space could be. In a community with an interest in art, dedicating the space to exhibits and creation seemed natural. As the new customer service manager, Harris began to oversee and coordinate Idea Box.

At the start the Idea Box had no dedicated budget, but the needs were quite minimal. Ideas, and in some cases a fresh coat of paint, were all that was necessary. Now the project has a built-in budget, and supplies are bought that can be repurposed for other uses in the library after the exhibit is finished.

Suggestions for exhibits, while open to the public, mainly came from staff at the library. Accommodating installations from the community is challenging, said Harris, mainly from a logistical standpoint on details like timeframes; the exhibits the library sets up are on a specific time schedule to match the loan period of their items. This allows more patrons to experience and expect something new from the Idea Box each time they visit. The other challenge is that the space is largely unpatrolled, so installations that are valuable or one-of-a-kind items can't be monitored. Oak Park has been able to collaborate with community organizations. One exhibit brought in students from the American Academy of Art in Chicago, who installed pegboards with extra holes drilled in them and painted golf tees for the patrons to play with like a Lite Bright. Any suggestions, from staff or community, get added to a list for upcoming exhibits. The staff meets quarterly to choose and plan for three months of exhibits. Their system allows for discussion of the merits and drawbacks of each exhibit idea Then the group votes to determine which will be implemented.

All exhibits are geared towards catching people's eyes and getting them to participate. For example, one exhibit asked patrons to write the name of their favorite book on a Post-it and

---

[14] "April 2013—Illinois Library Association." http://www.ila.org/Reporter/April_2013/Reporter_0413.pdf

add it to the wall in the Idea Box. The number of colored Post-its grew and created an organic piece of art, Harris said. People started to add their own instructions, like "Put check marks on ones you like" or answering questions about which author wrote a certain book. "If you give [people] a space and ask them to be creative, they use the space in ways you would never expect," Harris commented.

Oak Park Public Library

The Idea Box brings the opportunity to the patrons at Oak Park to experiment and play creatively, a rare thing for many people. And because collaboration, interaction, and experimentation are built-in aspects of the Idea Box, even a person that visits the library every day is likely to see something new in the space, something generated by their community.

The space was brought into an atmosphere of experimentation and change. Oak Park had a new director with new initiatives. The library was brainstorming ways to provide excellent programming, and when the opportunity to create the Idea Box came along, the library not only embraced it, but gave it a place within a department and job responsibilities.

The Idea Box is advertised on the Oak Park Public Library's website, but beyond that there are not a lot of marketing needs. Harris points out that it's special for patrons that already come to the library, giving "a value to their loyalty." They see something new each time they come, and it draws them in to see the library as a place in which to participate. For new patrons, it sets the tone for their visit, a feeling of "whimsy."

Each exhibit is recorded with pictures and posted on the library's Flickr site for the public to see, capturing those quick, ephemeral creative moments from so many in the community. They have had interest from patrons who would like to see the breakdown of the content that is created through the Idea Box. "It's almost as if they want the data," Harris notes. So far there are no plans to publish the outcome, which seems apt for a space that focuses on inspiration and creativity. Oak Park staff does solicit general feedback from the community through their customer service department to find out what was most successful and get comments about the exhibit.

What's next? The Idea Box continues on, hosting a new idea every month. Other spaces in the library continue to change to encourage participation. The lobby outside of the Idea Box will be redone to accommodate lounge space and what Harris calls "flash programming," an event that may not warrant reserving a space but could be set up for passersby to quickly see or experience.

Creating a Digital Media Community Repository: LibraryYOU

A Talk With Donna Feddern

Donna Feddern, the Digital Services Manager at Escondido Public Library, coordinated the launch of LibraryYOU (libraryyou.escondido.org), a digital collection of community knowledge and expertise in video and podcast format. So far the library has worked with community members to produce almost to 40 videos and four podcasts. The library is also supporting digital media creation with their teen program Pop Up Podcast (http://popuppodcast.org).

Q: Where did the idea of LibraryYOU come from?

A: LibraryYOU was inspired by the YOUmedia project at the Chicago Public Library. I was excited by the idea of expanding a public library's technology offerings to digital media equipment and software. Also, I was redesigning the library website and was looking for ways to incorporate patron-generated content (photos, reviews, testimonials, videos). So providing a digital media studio where patrons could create videos and podcasts for the library's digital collection was a good marriage of those two ideas.

Q: Can you take me through the process of getting the program started—funding, choosing equipment, staff training, etc.?

A: I was encouraged by the administration at my library to submit a Pitch an Idea proposal for the California LSTA grants. My idea was accepted by the state library grant team, so I wrote the LSTA grant for $35,000 in funding. The money paid for two part-time staff, equipment, and publicity materials. The Recording Studio Coordinator and the Digital Services Librarian put together the list of equipment we'd need for audio and video recording. Our first tasks were to purchase the equipment and get the LibraryYOU website up and running. Staff were trained about the goals of the grant and either came to the project with their own skills or learned media recording skills through online courses (Lynda.com) as needed.

Q: What software and equipment do you provide?

A: Our recording studio (or digital media lab) has two iMacs, two high-end HD video cameras, lighting, tripods, (many) microphones, a backdrop, digital storage (hard drives, flash drives, SD cards), iMovie software, and Adobe Audition (sound editing) software.

The recording studio is located in a back office so it is not open to the public right now. We are planning to offer appointments (similar to Book a Librarian programs at other libraries) to help patrons get access to the equipment and spend time with staff learning how to use the software and equipment. Most of our contributors wanted to share their expertise but weren't as interested in learning how to make their own digital media. We offer some basic classes on digital video recording and podcasting but only a few LibraryYOU contributors attended these classes to learn more.

Q: Can you talk about getting the website up and running and the decisions you needed to make throughout that process?

A: I looked into using Omeka for the website since it is open source and made for digital archives. There were some issues with embedding videos, though. And if we hosted it ourselves, we'd need a LAMP server. We didn't have the money to buy one or have them host it for us. I ended up using a Content Management System called mojoPortal. The City of Escondido had chosen it for their new website and I'd used it for the redesign of the library's main website so I was already familiar with it. No learning curve!

I created the website—the architecture, design, content, etc. I've redesigned the library's website three times in the last 10 years so I know how to plan a website and get it up and running. With LibraryYOU, I wanted it to be simple and for the videos and podcasts to be the main content, so it wasn't that difficult to put together. I did hire a graphic designer to create a logo, business cards, and the website header image for the LibraryYOU so the color scheme and identity came from his work.

We went with Vimeo because it seemed to be a more positive site. I didn't want to ask our community, many of whom were new to online video, to put themselves out there just to have their video filled with negative comments. I realize there is more visibility on YouTube since they have far more viewers, but that didn't bother me. I made sure to use search engine optimization tools to make sure the LibraryYOU content was visible through Google searches, and that worked well.

I think with more money and expertise on staff, we could have had a better LibraryYOU site. I am of the opinion that you should just do and try with what you have. Maybe in the future we can make the content accessible through our ILS using a digital archive add-on. ILS

*databases are not visible through Google (unless you pay to have your holdings on OCLC),
but I hope that changes soon. Right now, I'm not willing to move the LibraryYOU collection
and lose our visibility on Google.*

Q: Are the videos and podcasts completely patron-driven or does the library solicit any participants?

*A: One of the commitments I made for the grant was to speak to 10 organizations in order
to find contributors. We found several participants through these presentations. Others
saw posters in the library or read newspaper articles and contacted us about becoming
contributors. The rest of the contributors were people who were doing events at the
library and were encouraged to create a video or podcast as well. Any time I meet someone
interesting, I ask them if they would like to be part of the project.*

*Although it wasn't part of my initial plan, I did work with a local Toastmasters group
to find our first LibraryYOU contributors. Since Toastmasters groups are usually full of
interesting, accomplished people who are looking to improve their public speaking skills,
several of the members were happy to participate in LibraryYOU.*

Q: What has been the most memorable outcome of this service?

*A: I think it is amazing that content created by an expert in the Escondido community, in
collaboration with the library, has such reach on the Internet. We have had people from 85
countries visit the LibraryYOU site through search engine keyword searches.*

*Also, I see our patrons differently. It used to be that they came into the library for our
expertise. Now, I look around the building and see a community of experts. Knowledge
isn't just found in the staff or in the books. Knowledge can be found in every member of our
community.*

Q: Now that LibraryYOU is underway is there anything you would have done differently or changed the design of? Or have any adjustments been made as the program goes on to increase the effectiveness?

*A: I would have allocated grant funds to creating a media lab in a publicly accessible area.
The biggest challenge has been not having the public space for the digital media lab so that
patrons may use the equipment on their own. Also, due to our limited budget, we will not
be able to have staff that are dedicated to the media lab. We will need to recruit dedicated
volunteers. We also need to look into digital asset management for the long-term storage of
our content.*

Q: What advice would you give to other libraries that want to start a similar program?

*A: There are a lot of options for doing this kind of project on a smaller or larger scale. It is
good to determine your goals—Do you want to add to your digital collection? Or is your
aim to educate patrons about using digital media? Would you be willing to compromise on*

quality of production? Lower-cost equipment and storage options are available for libraries with smaller budgets. The most important piece is finding the staff or volunteers who are excited about creating with digital media and are willing to keep learning and improving their skills.

Q: Are there other libraries that you look to for inspiration and ideas?

A: I still look to Chicago Public Library's YOUmedia project for inspiration. Skokie Public Library is doing great things with their digital media lab. Also, the Anythink Wright Farms Library got a YOUmedia-like grant to set up a digital media lab they are calling The Studio, and I know they'll be doing some exciting programming.

I have done other webinars and blog posts about LibraryYOU. There are a list of links at this address: http://claimid.com/donna.

Library YouTube Channel by Kara Stock

Buffalo & Erie County Public Library (B&ECPL)

The Buffalo and Erie County Public Library (B&ECPL) strives to provide quality services while remaining relevant to meeting the ever-changing needs of library users. With demand for classroom-style technology training at an all-time high, staff recognized the need to supplement the traditional in-library formats. YouTube videos provided an excellent opportunity to attract new library users while meeting the growing virtual technology needs fueled by the shift to digital devices.

On May 5, 2011, the *BECPL TrainingLab* YouTube Channel (http://bit.ly/KdRNzH) was created. The initial motivation was to provide brief instructional videos based on popular questions generated during the public computer training classes. Topics included how to use *Consumer Reports* online, how to search for e-books, and how to send an e-mail attachment. The average length of these videos is three minutes, based upon analysis revealing that people are more likely to watch brief rather than longer versions.

Capitalizing on the success of these instructional videos, the next venture involved the production of more entertaining videos designed to educate as well as publicize free services and programs offered by the library. One example is the U.S. Marine Corps Brass Band performing at the Central Library during Buffalo Navy Week (http://bit.ly/10XKp2M). "How To Clean a Touch Screen Monitor" (http://bit.ly/Mp8Obn) takes humor to a new level and the documentary "Behind the Request" showcases the staff who get materials transferred to local libraries for patron pick-up (http://bit.ly/U4xVEl).

To date we have 27 public videos posted on our site with a total of 22,822 views, according to YouTube's analytics. The most popular has been "Using the e-Library Catalog's My Account Feature" with 3,574 views, followed by "How to Open and Save E-Mail Attachments" with 2,220 views, and "How to Set Up an iPad to Download eBooks and Audiobooks" with 2,008 views.

Creating a YouTube Channel has many advantages. YouTube is a popular site, which affords the library the opportunity to reach a larger and virtual audience. It allows us to educate using social media as an alternate platform and it puts the library where our users are, 24 hours a day, 7 days a week. The format increases the media coverage for the library and provides us with free analytics. YouTube users can interact by commenting on and liking our videos as well as sharing them with their friends.

Buffalo & Erie County Public
LIBRARY

Using the Freegal App

Free mp3 downloads on your
tablet or mobile device

Buffalo & Erie County Public
LIBRARY

Thank you for watching this video on Freegal.

Need More Help?
Click the 'Contact Us' link at:
www.BuffaloLib.org

Intro & End Slides for B&ECPL Video on Freegal

B&ECPL Librarian Andrew Aquino has produced several instructional videos for our YouTube Channel during the past two years. When he first started he would create an outline of the topic and then begin recording. Through trial and error, he eventually began to write a more detailed script before recording to ensure that all relevant information was included. The fully fleshed-out script also gave him a better idea of how long the video would last, with the goal for a three-minute length. Once he finished a recording, using Camtasia Studio 8 software, he moved into the editing phase, removing any long pauses or errors. Next, he added zooming and text callouts such as the library website address. To finish the process, he rendered the video into a YouTube-compatible format and uploaded it to YouTube. Once uploaded, a description, tags, and closed captions were added.

Jordan Smith, another B&ECPL librarian, produced the previously mentioned short documentary "Behind the Request." Jordan began with a library-related theme, patron requests for materials, and then thought about ways to include the human story. He also researched the request procedure in detail. Jordan then tracked down staff members to talk about their role in the process. As part of the interaction, he often had to first convince them to be on camera. When filming, Jordan tried to help them feel natural and comfortable, not awkward. He asked them questions to get the story he was looking to cover. When the filming was finished, he edited all of his footage into a narrative. This involved watching a lot of video tape and finding naturalistic moments within the theme.

Once a new video is made public, it is promoted in several ways. It is highlighted on the B&ECPL homepage promotional scroll (www.buffalolib.org) and added to other sections of the library's website, including e-Community (http://bit.ly/VBLKIQ) and e-Content Pages (http://bit.ly/IskveQ). The video is also posted on the library's Facebook page, tweeted in the library's Twitter account, and pinned to the library's Pinterest page. The training lab YouTube Channel also has an icon on the computer training section of the library's website (http://www.buffalolib.org/content/computer-training).

It is important to monitor the content and ensure the accuracy of all posted videos. Some videos have been removed from our YouTube Channel due to software updates. For example, we deleted "How to Download and Install Adobe Digital Editions" and quickly replaced it with an updated video, "How to Download and Install Adobe Digital Editions 2.0." A more recent example is when our e-book vendor, OverDrive, rolled out their next-generation user experience. The process for searching and borrowing e-books changed so radically that all related videos needed to be immediately removed. We are currently working on updates.

The cost for video production has been minimal. In 2011, Central Training Lab librarians attended a three-hour workshop on "Screencasting in Your Library" at the Western New York Library Resources Council (WNYLRC). The cost was $15 for each attendee, and the focus was on Camtasia Studio, a recording and editing software program. Staff returned from the training enthusiastic and motivated, which resulted in the library purchasing three Camtasia Studio software licenses as several staff members would be involved in creating the videos. Each license was $299. Some alternatives to Camtasia are Adobe Captivate and Jing. The Adobe product offers a free trial and can be purchased for $359. Jing is free but is more limited because it doesn't allow for editing; its focus is instant sharing. Camtasia also offers a free trial, which provides a great opportunity to give the software a test drive.

To capitalize on the success of the simple screencasts and expand video capabilities, we next acquired a Canon Vixia camcorder, a camcorder case, and a tripod. We soon noted the need for an extra battery for the camcorder and a charger for that battery. We bought two Logitech headsets with microphones for recording purposes and a 16 GB flash memory card. Lastly, we purchased an external hard drive in order to back up and save our large video files. The cost for these purchases was $725.

The total cost so far has been approximately $1,700. We identified the need. The administrative staff of the library evaluated the proposal, along with the potential benefit, and recognized this as a valuable initiative. The funding for the software and equipment were then allocated from the operating budget. The library continues to look for appropriate technology support and community grant opportunities to supplement and expand the project.

The *BECPL TrainingLab* YouTube Channel has allowed us to reach more people regardless of distance or time of day. It has provided instructional and training opportunities beyond library buildings and beyond traditional service hours. It has brought the Buffalo & Erie County Public Library to our patrons 24 hours a day, 7 days a week and is available for unlimited viewing. Although the videos are geared toward library users, they can also be beneficial for staff.

The B&ECPL is fortunate to have dedicated and talented Central Library training lab staff members who were willing to experiment with the alternative technologies. They were interested in learning something new and embraced formats which incorporate creativity, bringing training opportunities to a new level. And although we have not reached the popularity of YouTube's 2012 "Gangnam Style" or "Carley Rae Jepsen," we're pleased to have 22,822 views supplementing our in-house classes. We plan to continue to generate educational and entertaining content, and you never know, there's always the possibility that a viral video is in the Buffalo and Erie County Public Library's future.

Appendix: Sample Video Script

Consumer Reports
Andrew Aquino

[Music]

Hello and welcome to this online tutorial on accessing *Consumer Reports*, via the Buffalo and Erie County Public Libraries databases. In this lesson, you'll learn how to access *Consumer Reports* via the libraries databases, how to browse the issues and how to search for a specific article.

So did you know that you can get full-text of *Consumer Reports* magazine including graphs and pictures through the libraries' databases? Just for being a member of the Buffalo and Erie County Public Libraries, you have electronic access from any computer to over 20 years of Consumer Reports, including the most recently published issues.

A screen will pop-up and take you to the *Consumer Reports* page contained in a database called *MasterFILE Premier*. You can see the dates that full-text of this magazine is available.

There are two ways you can access articles from this screen. If you know what issue of the magazine you wanted to look at you can use the browse function. If a friend of yours told you there was a good article on credit cards in the November 2010 issue, all you would do is click on the year 2010, then pick the November issue.

At this point a list of articles will appear, much like a table of contents, from which you can pick your article. In this case we see the article we are interested in on the second page of results. From here we can click on "PDF Full-text" to see the article. As you can see it looks just like it does in the print edition of the magazine with full-text, color photos, illustrations, and charts.

Now if you're interested in doing a search for information on a particular subject then there are a few different steps to take. You would want to start at the *Consumer Reports* page once again. However, this time you'll click on 'Search within this publication.' Now we'll suggest you click on the "Advanced Search" link.

At this point we are going to search *Consumer Reports* for information on refrigerators. Our results list will be in order of post popular and relevant articles. You can order results by clicking on "Relevance Sort." Now you can click on "PDF Full Text" to see the contents of the article.

Thank you for watching this online tutorial on accessing *Consumer Reports*.

The Library as a Community Publisher

Print on demand technology and the introduction of the Espresso Book Machine introduced an easily accessible alternative to the traditional publishing model. While some speculated whether the trend would take over or harm the traditional printing and distribution of books, over the years companies that provide print on demand seem to have found a niche in the publishing market. Small and self-publishers take advantage of only paying to print books that are ordered, eliminating some upfront costs and the waste and hassle of overproduction. Similarly, the barriers to developing e-books are quickly disappearing with free and affordable services and platforms.

By now, none of this is new or news, but we are beginning to see the creative ways this technology is being used—the power of the local, community-oriented, and self-published.

Public Libraries Utilizing Print-on-Demand Technology

I Street Press, Sacramento Public Library

The Sacramento Public Library is one place these possibilities have taken root. With the purchase of an Espresso Book Machine (EBM) thanks to a grant, dedicated staff, volunteers, and a creative community, I Street Press was born.

A member of the community and volunteer who had seen the Espresso Book Machine in action brought forward the possibility, and from there the ideas kept coming. Being the publisher of choice for the community held enormous possibility, as Director Rivkah Sass put it. In addition, a nearby college's creative writing program was closing down, and the library began to imagine other components to the new service to make up for the loss of writing instruction in the community. While not every detail of the original plan was realized (e.g., the idea for six-week writing courses has been revised to envision half-day writing workshops in the future), it turned out the community had been waiting for this sort of responsive, personal, and local option for publishing.

IDb SACRAMENTO PUBLIC LIBRARY

home > services > **i street press**

A COMMUNITY WRITING & PUBLISHING CENTER

Jump into the world of print-on-demand, self-publishing and writing/publishing classes. We hope that I Street Press will become the go-to destination for all things writing and publishing. Do you have a book inside? We can print it for you!

LEARN

View our **Events calendar** for classes on writing and publishing for I Street Press.

PUBLISH

1. Read the how-to guide, **I Publish at I Street**

   o **Welcome to I Street** Press

   o **Quick Guide**

   o **Pricing**

   o **Submission and Formatting Guidelines**

   o **Formatting Hints and Other Tips**

The service was launched with informational sessions and the printing of a sample book, a compilation of librarian Gerald Ward's series of blog posts. A year and half into operation, the press has printed over 6,500 books, often totaling more than 500 per month. And while one selling point of the EBM is that it provides access to millions of titles available for immediate download and print, Ward indicates that 99% of books printed at I Street are original or self-published works. Just this past May the press printed 557 books, which included 15 original titles by 12 different authors, four student projects from the local high school, and three compilations of student work. I Street's clients range from local professional booksellers and writers with selling licenses to community organizations printing anthologies of student work to local transients. The people and stories that have found their voice through I Street Press are diverse and inspiring. A group of volunteers funded the publication of a local homeless man's poetry, a volume entitled *The Hobo Speaks*. The

40

first information session I Street ran brought in an Afghani woman from over an hour away in the Bay Area who was looking to print her memoir.

Beyond initial press releases and cultivating a Web presence, the library has not had to do further marketing or promotion. Director Rivkah Sass noted that, "Word of mouth has treated us very well." It seems there certainly was an advantage to the physical presence of the machine and service and that library patrons found publishing and printing their work far more approachable in a familiar environment with a friendly face to introduce them to a new opportunity. The initial grant covered the machine's purchase and hiring of a part-time assistant. In developing the service, the library also hired a designer to produce their resource book.

When asked about the challenges, Gerald Ward pointed out, "It was a hard transition to charging [patrons for services] as a librarian." But of the three tiers of pricing and service on offer, the most popular are the more expensive with more service, support, and one-on-one attention. Tier 2, with a $99 setup fee and printing costs of $6 per book, offers the assistance of the press' publishing assistant, a free proof copy, one free revision upload, and the files saved on the server for future printing. With a $300 setup fee, the Premier Tier 3 adds on an ISBN number, barcode, Library of Congress Control Number, and copyright registration, as well as registration with On Demand Books' database of printable books.

Personal attention and encouragement, Ward says, is the biggest advantage they can offer that online POD platforms cannot. Sass describes Ward, who oversees the press and the part-time publishing assistant they employ as a "book therapist" and a "creative therapist," as he works so closely with the authors, even in the writing process before the books are submitted for print. This image of the librarian as champion, encourager, and therapist for writers is an inspiring one, probably because it is so close to the role a librarian plays in learning, discovery, and research.

Example of an anthology published at I Street

As with introducing any new service, there were procedures and challenges to address. The EBM, unlike a simple printer, needs to be attended while any book is being produced and so requires a dedicated staff member. While it is true that one book can be produced in about five minutes, the library can only reasonably produce 40–50 titles a day. Sass says this is one of the biggest hurdles as I Street, as a community publisher, forges relationships with local groups and schools, but sometimes cannot accommodate tight schedules for large orders.

For now the supporting programming for I Street is a consistently run informational session that introduces interested parties in the service, setup options, and file requirements. These sessions regularly attract about 10 participants. The computer labs are equipped with basic tools like Microsoft Word that can support patrons looking to produce PDF files to submit to I Street. Ward notes, "We can't do it for [them], but we can help." The I Street guide, written and adapted by Maryellen Burns, I Publish at I Street, also provides resources for choosing trim size and setting up a book file, as well as some local resources for editing and design services.

The impact of the press is powerful. In the growing world of e-books, the draw of a physical book is strong for many. For I Street staff and many other libraries that host the book machine, the highlight is giving the book to the writer or seeing the writer watch their book come into being after all of their hard work. "You should see their eyes when they see their book," Ward says. Sass described a patron holding their newly printed I Street book, marveling over its warmth, and comparing it to fresh bread out of the oven. There has always been something satisfyingly tangible about a printed book, and bringing the creation of the book to the author is enriching both for the librarian and the writer.

So where do these works go once I Street has joined the authors and helped them publish their books? Some books are simply gifts for friends or family, some return to the students whose work is featured for the pleasure and pride of seeing their works in print, and some local authors go on to sell the books themselves. The books printed also get evaluated by Gerry Ward for addition into Sacramento Public Library's collection. For inclusion they must be final printed copies, not proofs, and have an ISBN or LCCN. The library has a local collection to

which many of the books are added, or sometimes the books are put in the general collection.

Interest in and use of the service has continued steadily past the initial development of I Street Press. Their model of publishing reflects the focus and scope of the community publisher they set out to be. I Street has put considerable effort into engaging community partners, a high level of customer service, and smooth running of a publishing and printing service, meeting patrons at their comfort level and guiding them to a finished product. The press has also been used to expand their local collection as well as the library's personal collection to community content creators.

Flash Books!

Flash Books! is another example of the Espresso Book Machine being used by a library to develop publishing services. Grace Mellman Community Library in the Riverside County Library System in Temecula, California, was among the first libraries to house the machine and originally envisioned its role in interlibrary loan as an alternate method to locate and print hard-to-find titles. However, the orders for self-published titles far outnumbered this original purpose. This library also bought the machine with grant funds secured by Deputy Administrator Cindy DeLanty.

With resources from On Demand Books and some on-site training, the library developed their own website, structure, directions, and guides. Flash Books! is staffed with one library employee, Krissie McMakin. "My roles are to assist clients with placing first-time orders or reorders (we have some clientele who come back years later for reprints), double-check formatting for manuscripts to see if it will print well on the machine, create cover design digital art, meet with clients for consultation appointments, perform maintenance on the machine as needed, as well as holding and attending outreach programs for Flash Books!" The branch manager, Ivorie Franks, oversees the program and handles policy changes and relevant documentation.

Like I Street, Flash Books! does not offer formatting services, although they do offer in-house cover design services for $20 per hour. Depending on the books' sizes, they have the capacity to process 12–30 books per day or up to 700 per month. On average, they work with three to six unique titles per month. The order sizes vary, but many customers show a preference for Flash Books!' discounted order size of 25 copies.

FLASH◈BOOKS

What's your story?

Do you have a story to tell? Fiction, non-fiction, memoirs, poetry and more... let the Espresso Book Machine at Flash Books! help bring your story to life. Please feel free to visit our web page to learn more about our services and when you're ready, give us a call or an email - we're here to help.

Steps to Self-Publishing:
1) Have your manuscript formatted to a 5x8, 6x9 or 8x10 size and in a PDF format.
2) Have your book cover design ready to go in a PDF format OR have any images, photographs to be used ready for Flash Books! if you wish to use our cover design services.
3) Contact us. Make an appointment, if needed. Order one proof book.
4) Review your proof book and when you're ready, place an order for up to 25 books at a time. (With 25, you'll recieve 10% off)
5) Congratulations... you are now a self-published author!

To market the service, McMakin contacts as many writing groups and other interested organizations as possible and offers to speak at their meetings about what Flash Books! offers, or she hosts them for private demonstrations. The library has also hosted one information and author-signing event in which around 10 local authors who had printed with Flash Books! presented their books at information tables. An informational program outlining the printing service was also presented. McMakin says they hope to hold another one again soon.

As the library receives more donations of books printed through Flash Books! they will assemble them into a mini-collection and keep them on a specified shelf for patron browsing and borrowing.

The service continues to garner interest from the community. McMakin comments:

> My absolute favorite part is seeing an author's face when they hold their book in their hands for the first time. It's magical. Their face lights up instantly.

> In general, I love seeing people getting excited about this project. Sometimes we get people who have heard of the machine and once they actually see it, it's easy to see the wheels turning in their minds (as if... "I can write a book, I can do that") and that's a truly wonderful part of this job—seeing the community get excited about writing books.

More information about the Riverside County Library System and Flash Books! can be found at their websites: http://rivlib.info and http://flashbooks.weebly.com.

Brooklyn Public Library

Brooklyn Public Library brought an Espresso Book Machine in 2012, advertising it as a "Print Your Own Book" service. Instead of buying the machine outright, Brooklyn had the opportunity to enter into a contract with On Demand Books wherein the library acted as a landlord to the machine. On Demand would cover all operational staffing, support, and outreach, and the library would receive a commission from any transactions. This allowed the library the chance to offer the service with little risk. The library provided a prominent location for the service, and the transition into operation ran smoothly.

Richard Reyes-Gavilan, the chief librarian at Brooklyn Public Library, speculates that it is this separation in staffing and ownership that has kept the library from fully integrating the machine into their services. The machine saw a fair amount of business, mainly independent and self-published works much like I Street and Flash Books! However, with staffing and operation out of the library's control, lack of consistency has been a struggle for both parties. Currently the machine is unstaffed and service suspended while both Brooklyn and On Demand evaluate the options. Reyes-Gavilan says hosting the machine is "an idea [they] are committed to" and do still see the machine and potential services surrounding it as playing an important role in the library's strategic plan and commitment to serve the community.

The future plan is for Brooklyn to follow I Street's example; even if the machine is not purchased outright, the library will take more intellectual ownership of the machine. Ideally, funding would be secured through a grant proposal to allow the hiring of a full-time staff member to operate and market the service, although at this point they are still waiting for final decisions on funding. They hope that rebranding the service, which they will call "Plaza Publishers" because of the central branch's prominent location in Grand Army Plaza, with a more holistic service strategy will enliven the service. Reyes-Gavilan sees the opportunity for the service to morph from simply printing to a suite of publishing resources. They will be able to incorporate their new information commons to support programming and education, which is already the host to many writing and creation-focused skills programs. The other related project on the horizon is opening a Brooklyn Writers' Room, which will house a collection of locally created material. This space will aim to "engage the people that make use of the space to create content [and] make sure [the library] acquires their works."

In the meantime, the related project is Brooklyn's InfoCommons. This newly renovated suite of 5,500 square feet features a main lab that can accommodate classes or "hackathons," a large general workspace with bar-style seating and laptop plugins, individual meeting spaces (one housing an amateur recording studio), and another lab with high-end software that is not available freely elsewhere. The space opened in January 2013 and the library has done a lot of work to leverage this space to provide creation-centered education. Two important community partners are the New York Writers Coalition, which hosts workshops and classes in the space, and BRIC Arts Media, which hosts classes and training in various forms of digital expression, from audio recording to digital literacy. The library provides space and visibility to these organizations, and the organizations provide a much-needed service to the library community.

Reyes-Gavilan sees this space as especially important in Brooklyn where so many in the community engage in writing or digital media creation as their livelihood. Simply providing the space for them to work as an alternative to working from home or from a coffee shop is the first step in forging a positive relationship with this portion of the population.

The space is staffed with two full-time librarians funded through the federal broadband initiative program who manage the space and do outreach, as well as interns who perform the front line customer service and assist with procedures and technology.

The plan for the future is to connect the programming and space in the Info Commons to the Espresso Book Machine in order to provide a more holistic service. In the meantime, the space is hosting important author and creator services, both formally through programming and informally just by being a viable and accessible workspace.

A Library That e-Publishes: Provincetown Public Press

Provincetown Public Library is an example of a library straddling the line between the traditional publishing model and the self-publishing trend. Director of Marketing and Program Development Matt Clark and Library Director Cheryl Napsha see their library as playing an important role in the creation and curation of digital content. Instead of directly assisting the creation of self-published works, they have created Provincetown Public Press. To authors they offer technical and production service, access to worldwide digital distribution, and the branding of the press—all elements that can be challenging when it comes to self-publishing. For readers they offer well-crafted, well-presented local content.

The impetus came from Matt Clark's experiment with iBooks Author. He created a book as proposal that demonstrated both to him and to the library board that with the right tools, the library could create and offer a great product. Pairing their newly discovered capabilities with a rich artistic community furthers Provincetown Public Library's role in support of local creators. The library already plays an active role by hosting open mic nights, art shows, and relevant educational programming such as "Getting Published in 2013 With Jeannette de Beauvoir."[15] Napsha noted, "A lot of residents cobble together a living to be able to write. The facility itself is a haven for writers."

It is the library's role as a respected curator that Clark and Napsha are interested in promoting. Between patron-driven acquisitions and often outsourced collection development, adding in the total overwhelming amount of material available digitally, Provincetown Public Press is their way of offering their patrons a trusted source of content. As bookstores' traffic dwindles, they see the library as the place people can turn to to find the "hottest new books."

With content creation, general "making," e-book quandaries, and self-publishing coming to the forefront of library discussion, it is the perfect climate to experiment with different

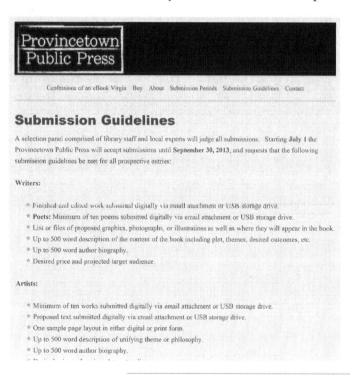

ways a library can be involved in local publishing as well as enter into a larger conversation. Clark mentioned in his interview with *Library as Incubator Project*[16] that there has not only been a large amount of interest from writers all over the country and the media but also from library professionals who want to watch how they are managing this press and evaluate if they too can offer a similar service to their community.

Since national news blogs picked up the original story from the *Cape Cod Times*, the responses to a call for submissions were overwhelming. Napsha and Clark both noted that while they do want the press to be generally

---

[15] "Events From This Venue—Provincetown.com." http://www.provincetown.com/finders/event/event_detail/?finder_month=&finder_day=&finder_year=&finder_end_month=&finder_end_day=&finder_end_year=&eazy_finder_clicked=Find%20an%20Event&finder_u=292dd91669867c6a9d216e504cfed1f6

[16] "Featuring: Provincetown Public Press | Library as Incubator Project." http://www.libraryasincubatorproject.org/?p=10143

focused on the local community, they would be considering manuscripts from all over. They also hope to represent many different genres as well and are more concerned with quality content than finding books that fit into a certain theme or idea. Their submission guidelines reflect this as well as their aim to keep the author involved in many important decisions, such as price point.

The selection committee they assembled for their first submission period consists of the library director, two directors of local art organizations, and two freelance writers. There are plans to expand the committee for the next submission period, however, as the volume of manuscripts has been difficult for the team of five to read in a timely manner. Their process this year was to divide up the submissions for first reading and select quality works from those groups for the entire committee to review.

For Provincetown Public Press, editorial steps leading up to production stay in the author's hands. They are expected to present fully developed and edited works, allowing Clark to focus on the layout, design, and functionality of the digital work. This requirement has weeded out many manuscripts that do not meet the minimum requirements simply because of an abundance of spelling and grammatical errors. Clark commented, "Works worth publishing have stood out immediately." Distinguishing itself more as an imprint than a full-service publisher, Provincetown Public Press in this regard truly sits between traditional and self-publishing. In this model the author is able to concentrate on the writing instead of the technical aspects and marketing, as well as raising awareness of a minimum standard of writing.

Clark uses iBook Author to publish through iTunes and Calibre to optimize the text for platforms of the author's choosing. As it was the ease and functionality of iBook Author as well as the ability to incorporate multi-media that attracted Clark to the idea, the iBookstore is the main mode of publication. Their first publication, released April of 2013, is available through iTunes, Amazon, and Kobo.

Getting a feel for the publishing process, how the community can be involved, and reimagining the relationship between the library, publisher, and author seem to be the focus of Provincetown Public Press for the moment. With e-book sales to libraries and the problem of streamlining lending processes without too many middlemen being at the forefront of public librarians' discussions, it does need to be asked why a library might choose to publish, especially through distributors that do not directly allow library acquisitions. Clark responded:

> I feel that it is important for libraries as a whole to get involved in publishing before an ideal infrastructure is in place because it gives us a chance to determine how this next chapter in publishing history will unfold. Through calculated trial and error, libraries will be able to determine what works as a sustainable publishing and business model. With major bookstores struggling to keep their doors open or turn profits, libraries will be the last brick-and-mortar outlet of literature left standing, so it's essential that they weigh in on an industry that they will play a large role in as time moves on.

The setup is not ideal—from what I can tell, Provincetown Public Press' first e-book publication is not yet available through their own catalog, only for purchase through commercial outlets. But the association of a library with the creation of literature is powerful, and it looks like the partnership will benefit both the library—with press, raised awareness, and a highlighting of an already very artistic community—as well as the authors, who gain the vote of confidence from what may become a trusted imprint and increased production and marketing support.

A Partnership in Publishing: Los Gatos Public Library & Smashwords

I had the chance to speak with Henry Bankhead, Library Director at Los Gatos Public Library, and Mark Coker, the founder of the e-book publisher and distributor Smashwords, about their co-branding pilot to bring library patrons to an easy e-book publishing platform under the library's brand.

The idea is simple: Los Gatos' main library webpage advertises the partnership, and the advertisement provides a link to Smashwords' login page. As the library user works through Smashwords to publish his or her e-book, the library logo is present along the way. Coker, who has written about the potential power of the library in terms of publishing,[17] explains, "I see an exciting opportunity for every library in the world to marshal and coordinate authors. Libraries do a great job at promoting the culture of reading and there is a new role for them to facilitate the writing of books." Los Gatos Library is indeed utilizing the partnership to seize the opportunity to explore programming and services for writers and authors as well as the complicated issue of e-book access.

Furthermore, the partnership exemplifies the power of a community. Even though the hallmarks of e-publishing and a distributor like Smashwords are their ability to reach a worldwide audience, Coker has an interest in Los Gatos because it's his local library, and Bankhead has an interest in Smashwords because it is a local company. Because the two are physically located near each other, the library also gets the benefit of hosting programs run by Smashwords staff to further educate their patrons about e-books, e-readers, and the process of publishing.

At the time of the co-branding's launch, Los Gatos ran three information sessions geared to educate patrons at different levels of e-book consumption or creation. The first dealt with basic e-book trends, borrowing e-books from the library, and related issues. The second provided an overview to the e-book publishing process. The third went more in depth, covering publishing best practices based on Mark Coker's free e-book, *The Secrets to Ebook Publishing Success.*

---

[17]   "Smashwords: How Libraries Can Launch Community Publishing..." http://blog.smashwords.com/2013/03/how-libraries-can-launch-community.html

Los Gatos library patrons who write and publish e-books through Smashwords and would like to donate their e-book to the library are asked to set their library price to free and notify Los Gatos so they can acquire the book through their e-book distributor, Overdrive. This does require that the patron fulfill higher metadata and layout standards as defined by Smashwords to be accepted into their Premium Catalog, which makes the e-book available to the full list of retailers to which Smashwords distributes. The higher requirements include formatting as defined in the Smashwords Style Guide,[18] an .epub file (produced by Smashwords) that passes the industry standard epubcheck, an ISBN, title, description, cover, copyright page, and the fulfillment of Smashwords' Terms of Service (mainly confirming materials as complete and original works).[19]

The partnership touches on two issues that are becoming increasingly important in the discussion of e-book publishing and access. First is the general availability and method of acquiring independently published and self-published works. Smashwords, as one of the main distributors of these types of works, has worked with libraries to develop the Library Direct model, which Douglas County and Califa have taken advantage of, as well as working with e-book lending platforms like Overdrive, 3M, and Baker and Taylor, which allow libraries to purchase select Smashword titles or bulk lists alongside e-content from other publishers and distributors. While it is unfortunate that an author must still go through two middlemen (the distributor and the aggregator) to make an e-book available to a library, it is at least on par with traditional print publishing, where the publisher and the distributor handle the book before it reaches shelves in libraries or retail locations. It seems that this will continue to be the model until more independent hosting and lending systems are developed and libraries can purchase files that they store and distribute themselves.

The second issue is selection; now that more independent publishers and self-publishers are available to libraries and library patrons, the question becomes which titles to buy. Even when it comes to printing self-published books, libraries often do not have policies or simply do not accept such titles. More often the titles are submitted to libraries by the author and evaluated on a case-by-case basis, presumably on the relevance of the subject matter to the community and overall professional appearance of the book. With e-books, this sort of case-by-case handling of self-published titles becomes problematic because of the sheer volume of available titles and authors looking for readership. Also, with self-published titles the library has neither the benefit of interacting face to face with the author nor knowing that by accepting the work into the collection they are supporting a local author. This is where the Los Gatos/Smashwords pilot hopes to supply a way to keep the digital publishing process close to home.

Still, the newly found access to these much cheaper titles can be intimidating and represents the need for more hands-on collection development than is typical. Henry Bankhead, when asked about the issue of selection beyond the titles written by local patrons, acknowledged

[18]   "Smashwords—Smashwords Style Guide—A book by Mark Coker." http://www.smashwords. com/b/52

[19]   "Smashwords—Distribution." http://www.smashwords.com/distribution

the difficulty but pointed out that the process does not need to differ greatly from choosing any other book to add to the collection. "We hide behind the idea that we buy things based on reviews, but we really buy things based on their popularity. We are beholden to the public. So it follows that the more popular books on Smashwords would be bought and local authors would be bought."

Bankhead also made the point that some of the most popular genres for e-book borrowers, such as romance novels, show the often consumable nature of the most popular types of e-books. The format lends itself to content that is read once and returned or passed on, so logic follows that more titles for the same price, which is what Smashwords offers, is a win-win situation. Similarly, the owning of content is a less pressing issue when the reality of how we consume the content is short term and fleeting, so accessing these titles through a third-party lender can be seen as a good option for many consumers.

Libraries that purchase Smashwords titles through their Library Direct program are offered curation services very similar to those of the acquisition policy Bankhead describes. Mark Coker described a very hands-on, thoughtful process when he talked through how his team put together a proposed catalog for Douglas County Libraries. They did a lot of experimenting to determine how best to calculate bestsellers. Because the prices vary, or authors publish anywhere from one to one thousand titles, simple downloads and dollar amounts didn't always reflect which books were most popular. They ended up formulating the aggregate dollar sales of an author over the number of titles those authors had available to come up with a workable list. From there the list was filtered according to some specifications from the customer, such as weeding out erotica and titles priced over a certain amount.

This service, as well as book lists of popular genres and authors, are all similar to the collection development resources offered by aggregators like Overdrive, 3M, and Baker & Taylor. The library has the ability to handpick titles from the distributor's catalog, but because of the volume of titles, they rely on recommendations, ratings, and popularity.

"We are fighting against the negative perception of self-publishing," Bankhead comments. Los Gatos represents simple ways a library can involve themselves in publishing, by linking themselves with a method of self-publishing and offering some classes that support it and making a commitment to acquire those works alongside traditionally published work.

Author Support Starter Kit

Compiled here are resources and general checklists for the writing, design, and production of a book or e-book. This section is meant to both give librarians an overview of what patrons may be looking for as well as content that all are welcome to recommend, distribute, or repurpose.

Craft Books:

General:

- Elements of Style by Strunk and White (Illustrated Edition featured): Strunk, W., & Kalman, M. (2007). *The elements of style.* New York: Penguin Press.

- Writing Down the Bones by Natalie Goldberg, Goldberg, N. (1986). *Writing down the bones: Freeing the writer within.* Boston; [New York]: Shambhala ; Distributed by Random House.

- On Writing by Stephen King: King, S. (2000). *On writing: a memoir of the craft.* New York: Scribner.

- Robert's Rules of Writing by Robert Masello: Masello, R. (2005). *Robert's rules of writing: 101 unconventional lessons every writer needs to know.* Cincinnati, Ohio: Writer's Digest Books.

- The Writing Life by Annie Dillard: Dillard, A. (1989). *The writing life.* New York: Harper & Row.

- Bird by Bird by Anne Lamott: Lamott, A. (1995). *Bird by bird: Some instructions on writing and life.* New York: Anchor Books.

- On Writing Well by William Knowlton Zinsser: Zinsser, W. K. (2006). *On writing well: The classic guide to writing nonfiction.* New York: HarperCollins.

Fiction/ Plot:

- Save the Cat by Blake Snyder: Snyder, B. (2005). *Save the cat!: The last book on screenwriting you'll ever need*. Studio City, CA: M. Wiese Productions.

- Plot & Structure by James Scott Bell: Bell, J. S. (2004). *Plot & structure: Techniques and exercises for crafting a plot that grips readers from start to finish*. Cincinnati, Ohio: Writer's Digest Books.

- The Art of Dramatic Writing by Lajos Egri: Egri Lajos. (2009). *Art of dramatic writing*. [S.l.]: Wildside Press.

- Making a Good Script Great by Linda Seger: Seger, L. (1994). *Making a good script great*. Hollywood: Samuel French Trade.

Poetry:

- Triggering Town by Richard Hugo: Hugo, R. F. (1979). *The triggering town*. New York; London: Norton.

- Poetry Home Repair Manual by Ted Kooser: Kooser, T. (2005). *The poetry home repair manual: Practical advice for beginning poets*. Lincoln: University of Nebraska Press.

- i by e.e. cummings: Cummings, E. E. (1953). *I: six nonlectures*. Cambridge: Harvard University Press.

---

8 Tips for Holding an Author's Night from Cindy Gregory and Amber Hughey at Wirt Public library

1. Review potential presenters and their books before approaching them.

2. Look outside the immediate geographic area for presenters.

3. Try to find authors who've recently been published and authors from multiple genres.

4. Utilize all possible resources to advertise the event: Internet, listservs, local TV, websites, etc.

5. Allow presenters to market their books/materials before/after the program, especially if you're not able to pay them to present.

6. Have authors do their presentations, then facilitate a Q&A panel with all presenters.

7. Rotate presenters - try to find new presenters for each event to draw repeat patrons.

8. Be prepared to create a writing group if there's not one already in the area.

Starting a Writing Group

If you don't find an existing writing group—start one. Maybe you're a librarian who was asked to coordinate or host a writing group but haven't had prior experience. Either way, here are some details to consider and discuss as the group gets started:

- Mission: It is helpful to have a mission statement that addresses some of the processes of the group so that newcomers can be welcomed and integrated easily.

- Guidelines: Come up with some standards and guidelines that will keep some order to the group. Answer the questions like "What are we hoping to get out of this group?" but also address the details like:
    - What genres will you focus on?
    - What is the page limit for works that will be read?
    - Will the discussion be free-flowing or have a moderator?
    - How does your group define constructive criticism?

- Structure: Having a plan for the order of events helps with transitions and keeps the discussion moving and productive. Come up with a plan that works for your group and stick to it. Think about these possibilities:
    - Beginning the meeting with a free write. *Tip: If you are meeting at a library, ask your librarian to recommend some resources from the collection about writing assignments and warm ups*
    - Providing prompts or assignments to complete and share them at the beginning of the next meeting
    - Planning a specified amount of time to dedicate to each writer, and if the group is large enough how many and which writers will share each week
    - Will the works be read ahead of time or together at the meeting?

- Delivery: If the writing will be read ahead of time, make plans to either distribute paper copies the week or month previous or set up a group e-mail so the documents can be accessed electronically.

Here is an example of a blog an author uses to keep her writing groups updated and to provide assigments for participants to complete before each meeting: http://www.jangoldenstorycircles.blogspot.com/

Online Writer's Communities

Collaborative writing and web services that allow writers to glean feedback from readers and other writers are becoming more prevalent. If you'd like to get an idea of how people react to your work or what might need more development but don't have the time, means, or desire to participate in a writing group, these are some great options to consider:

- Good old-fashioned blog: this will require simple set up, as well as some networking and marketing to connect with people to read and give you feedback. This is a good option for existing writing groups that can't meet regularly or don't live near each other. Blogger and Wordpress are free and user-friendly.

- Authonomy.com: http://authonomy.com/

- Redlemonade: http://redlemona.de/

- LeanPub.com: https://leanpub.com/authors

- figment.com: http://figment.com/

Collaborative Writing Tools:

- Google Drive: I've enjoyed using Google Drive to collaboratively edit or write. It has especially been helpful with a long distance writing group—with Google Hangout we can group video chat, add relevant documents, and read and comment together face to face.

- Draft (https://draftin.com): Draft offers an 'Ask a Professional' feature. The click of a button will send your work to reviewers for editing at a reasonable price.

Editing/Revising Resources:

- Revising Prose by Richard Lanham: Lanham, R. A. (2007). *Revising prose*. New York: Pearson Longman.

- Manuscript Makeover by Elizabeth Lyon: Lyon, E. (2008). *Manuscript makeover: Revision techniques no fiction writer can afford to ignore*. New York: Perigee Book.

- Revision and Self-Editing by James Scott Bell: Bell, J. S. (2008). *Revision & self-editing techniques for transforming your first draft into a finished novel*. Cincinnati, Ohio: Writer's Digest Books.

Hire a copy editor or proofreader:

- Media Bistro's Freelance Market: http://www.mediabistro.com/fm/

- The Freelancer's Union: http://www.freelancersunion.org/

- Freelancer.com: https://www.freelancer.com/d/United_States/Proofreading/ (Set filter to proofreading and the US)

- More generally:
  - https://www.taskrabbit.com/ Available in major cities.
  - Craigslist.org

Design & Production Checklists

Copy Editing/Proofreading Checklist

Read for:

- Spelling
- Grammar
- Word choice (you're/ your)
- Punctuation
- Consistency
- Fact checking

Interior Design Checklist:

- Choose appropriate trim size
- Account for minimum margins (check with your printer). Safe bet estimates would be: <150 pages: 0.5 in., >150 pages: .75 in., >400 pages: 1 in.
- Choose a standard readable font & size: 10pt–12pt at single or 1½ line spacing
- Identify and categorize document elements for styling (e.g. chapter titles, subtitles, body text, captions)
- Customize your styles

Interior Layout Checklist:

- ☐ Style (format) main body text elements
- ☐ Insert pictures, tables, or illustrations
  - ○ Formatted & captioned consistently
- ☐ Compile & insert front matter[20]
  - ○ Title page
  - ○ Copyright
  - ○ Dedication
  - ○ Table of Contents
  - ○ Foreword/Preface/Acknowledgments/Introduction
- ☐ Compile & insert back matter[21]
  - ○ Appendixes
  - ○ Endnotes
  - ○ Glossary
  - ○ Bibliography or Reference List
  - ○ List of Contributors
  - ○ Index

---

[20]   "The Parts of a Published Work - The Chicago Manual of Style Online." http://www.chicagomanualofstyle.org/ch01/ch01_toc.html

[21]   "The Parts of a Published Work - The Chicago Manual of Style Online." http://www.chicagomanualofstyle.org/ch01/ch01_toc.html

Cover Layout Checklist:

- ☐ Consider printer specifications
  - ◦ Spine width
  - ◦ Bleed space
  - ◦ Colorspace (sometimes CMYK is required)
- ☐ Obtain photos
  - ◦ Appropriate permissions & acknowledgements
  - ◦ Resolution (300–600dpi)
- ☐ Insert content
  - ◦ Title, author, illustrator, editor
  - ◦ Publisher
  - ◦ ISBN
  - ◦ Blurbs and/or summary
  - ◦ Author biography & photo

Proofing Checklist:

- ☐ Check for formatting errors
  - ◦ Headers & footers
  - ◦ Page numbers
  - ◦ Spacing
  - ◦ Widows & orphans
  - ◦ Table of contents/index
- ☐ Check your images, graphics, tables, and illustrations
  - ◦ Quality
  - ◦ Placement
  - ◦ Captions
- ☐ Read your text: TIP: Print out a copy or proofread it on a different device! Looking at your work in a different format helps you notice more.
  - ◦ For grammar
  - ◦ For spelling
  - ◦ Compared to the original text

Part 2

Trends & Essentials in Scholarly Publishing

The Development of Library-Led Publishing Services at the University of Utah

Valeri Craigle, John Herbert, Anne Morrow, & Allyson Mower

University of Utah

1 IN THIS CHAPTER

Theme

Assessment & pilot publishing projects

Highlighted Services

Print, multi-media e-content, web-hosting

Software/Platforms Utilized

Booktype, Omeka, OmniUpdate, Pressbooks & Wordpress

Resources

Assessment model & online publishing platforms compared

In the last decade, scholarly communication has shifted. A lot. Not just from digital and networked technology, new information policies, or the open access movement, but also from a rise in publishing programs in academic libraries. As noted in a series of reports from the Association of Research Libraries (Hahn, 2008), ITHAKA S+R (Brown et al., 2007), the Scholarly Publishing Academic Resources Coalition (Crow, 2009) and the Institute of Museum & Library Services (Mullins et al., 2012), libraries "have begun to expand their role in the scholarly publishing value chain by offering a greater range of pre-publication and editorial support services" (Mullins, p. 5). This represents a new role for librarians as curators of traditional content and collections. However, when you think of them as builders of digital libraries, similar skill sets and tools are more obvious: market analysis; needs assessment; project management; web design; layout; proofreading; robust technical infrastructure; metadata standards; good relationships with authors, creators, and vendors; copyright; and contract expertise. This chapter will describe the experiences at the Marriott and Quinney Libraries at the University of Utah in developing library-led publishing services.

Publishing Services Model

In the IMLS study *Library Publishing Services: Strategies for Success*, more than half of ARL-member libraries indicated they offer, or are interested in offering, publishing services (Mullins et al., 2012). According to the study, "the vast majority of library publishing programs were launched in order to contribute to change in the scholarly publishing system, supplemented by a variety of other mission-related motivations" (p. 6). Mission-driven rationale depends on sources of funding. Most publishing service units in libraries report the following as primary funding sources: library budget allocation, temporary institutional funding, and grant support. Many of these library publishers, however, expect a "greater percentage of future funding to come from service fees, product revenue, charge-backs, royalties, and other program-generated income."

At the University of Utah, we established a theoretical publishing services model based on these potential sources of revenue and funding, as well as the changing scholarly publishing landscape. Our model has three main components:

- Faculty needs

- Reader demand

- Feasibility

Faculty Needs

One example of change in scholarly publishing is supporting the scholar whose book does not have popular appeal or high sales potential. Some publishers have argued for a two-tiered scholarly publishing system in order to address the low-revenue-producing book. In a 1997 interview with August Fruge, long-time director of University of California Press, this idea emerged (Riess & Fruge, 1997). Fruge argued for on-demand publishing, envisioning the traditional book trade as one level of scholarly publishing, combined with a second, lower level of on-demand trade. This second level of publishing would be limited to brief prose and a bibliography and handled in the same way as dissertations. The publisher would prepare camera-ready copy, print a small run, and maintain the film so that "if somebody wanted one they could always print [it] off" (p. 107). Fruge argued that this is "really [...] closer to a library service than it is to publishing," pointing out that "you have to make some effort to sell it" (p. 108). Our model focuses on this second level of book and seeks to address these two elements: on-demand publishing as a library service and making an effort to sell it.

Reader Demand

Making an effort to sell something, as Fruge phrased it, means understanding its target market and estimating potential reader demand. While library services may not be at the same level as the traditional book trade, determining reader demand remains an important element to any publishing venture. After all, if there is no readership, justifying the effort and expense to create a product becomes very difficult. Having not yet discovered how to accurately estimate reader demand, we rely on our experiences and common sense. Despite this, it serves a primary role of counter-balancing faculty need and informs our scoring model.

> ...determining reader demand remains an important element to any publishing venture

Feasibility

Library publishing services require the right skills, expertise, and technological infrastructure, especially when offering on-demand services. Many traditional library processes can translate to publishing: acquisitions, contracts, risk-taking, production workflow, distribution, and preservation.

In order to ensure success, we chose projects where we had existing expertise and infrastructure. For example, our competency in video digitization allowed us to address multimedia publishing needs. For print-on-demand that Fruge discusses, we already operate an Espresso Book Machine (Riess & Fruge, 1997). For long-term preservation, we can utilize our recently launched digital preservation program. And for web interfaces needed in publishing projects, we can rely on a web development team within Library IT.

Fruge indicated that the "dividing line between the author and the publisher—what they do—has to move over a step" (p. 108). This means the author, using today's word processing tools, develops a manuscript nearly good enough for immediate publishing. While libraries may have limited editorial expertise, they can use freelance editors to prepare final manuscripts, and using existing digital library infrastructure, publish and widely distribute the work in various formats.

Faculty Needs Assessment at the University of Utah

In order to ground our model and establish a foundation for publishing services, we conducted a faculty needs assessment on our campus. First, faculty received an email inviting them to a web survey on publishing activities. The survey addressed past publishing practices, identified current publishing activities and needs, and gauged their interest in partnering with us. Fifty-seven faculty members from social sciences, sciences, law and the humanities participated. Survey results indicated the majority published journal articles more frequently than invited chapters, book-length monographs, or textbooks (see Figure 1). Over three-quarters identified their research as interdisciplinary. When comparing their colleagues' publishing needs to their own, a majority described their colleagues as "maybe" having similar needs while others identified their colleagues as having needs similar to their own.

Figure 1

Types of Publications

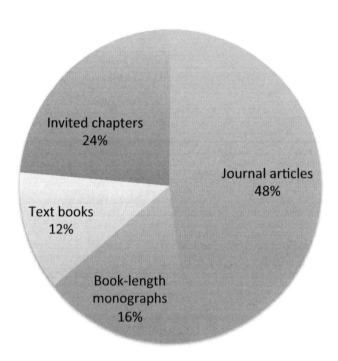

Figure 1: Type of publication most frequently produced.

Nearly half of the respondents expressed interest in having their work available on the Web (see Figure 2). When asked if there were additional materials not currently supported by traditional publishing with their published work, a little over a third of respondents indicated there were. When asked to rank additional materials and/or services they would like to have included with their published work, a third of respondents indicated long-term preservation, closely followed by print-on-demand and the ability to add content over time as other top priorities (see Figure 3). Two-thirds indicated that they would consider taking advantage of platforms for web publishing provided by the library (see Figure 4). See Appendix A for the full survey results.

Figure 2

Interest in having work on web

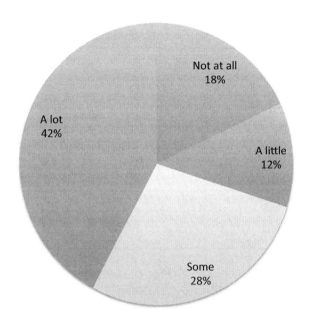

Figure 2: Interest in having work available on the Web.

Figure 3

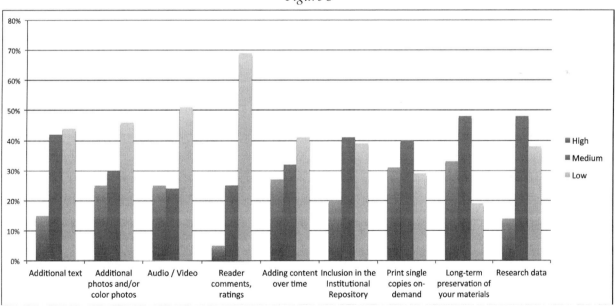

Figure 3: Need for additional services and materials.

Figure 4

Would you use library publishing services if they were available?

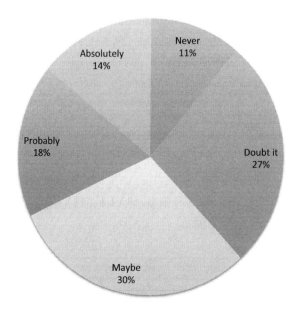

Figure 4: Likelihood of using library-based publishing services.

Forty percent of respondents were interested in a follow-up interview. These interviews became the basis for the second phase of our needs assessment. During this phase we provided each interviewee with more details about the library's interest in publishing services. We also asked them about their research interests and current publishing projects. Our questions addressed publishing trends in their discipline, determined if they had research results that were not being published but they wished could be, and asked what support they needed for publishing and for long-term preservation. Several faculty delved into the many possible angles of presenting their scholarly communications in a digital environment. The role of copyright in student and faculty works' accessibility on the Web was another area of heightened interest.

Through the course of the interviews, several opportunities for pilot projects emerged, each of which could address a specific need or set of needs. We selected a range of pilots to assess our capabilities to support different types of publishing projects. Whether the pilots succeeded or failed, they would collectively serve as a litmus test of our ability to provide independent publishing services.

We initiated a series of five pilot projects that utilized library resources, personnel, and expertise. The pilots included an online text-based sourcebook, choreographed dance pieces, an architecture thesis with supplemental multimedia, and an e-anthology of mixed media (text, image, video). Combined, they addressed the amalgamated types of publishing we saw ourselves offering: print-on-demand, web hosting, design, organization, metadata, and access.

Once the projects were launched, we examined several technological platforms that could provide infrastructure for publishing services. We assessed Booktype, Omeka, OmniUpdate,

Pressbooks, and Wordpress. We created small-scale prototypes for each and ultimately decided on Wordpress because it performed best in presenting the pilot projects and was scalable, extensible, and intuitive to use. For a summary of our findings on the software evaluations, please see Appendix B.

Reader Demand and Feasibility: The Scoring Model

In order to address reader demand and feasibility, we created a project assessment, or scoring, model based on the following criteria:

- Service to the university
- Alignment with future direction
- Revenue-generation potential
- Feasibility
- Longevity
- Audience/marketing plan/needs assessment
- Staff-time and resource commitment
- Equipment and software required

Design

These eight criteria were thoroughly reviewed and consolidated into four broad categories: Audience, Innovation/Risk, Feasibility/Cost, and Longevity/Impact. The categories were then weighted by assigning percentages to each in order to reflect its relative importance.

The weighted-average scoring model (Weighted Mean, 2013) is illustrated in detail below. The categories, listed in order of importance, assess the value of each project, based on the scores they received.

> Most important were new and innovative projects that address an unmet need within the community. We realized that these types of projects were inherently risky, but believed that innovation and originality generally outweigh any risks involved.

<u>Audience</u>   45%

- Marketing plan /needs assessment
- Service to the university
- Revenue-generation potential

<u>Innovation/Risk</u>   25%

- Novelty/unusual/creative/inventive/not something that libraries normally do
- Setting a new standard/delivering a new product or service/finding new customer groups

<u>Feasibility/Costs</u>   20%

- Staff time and resource commitment
- Equipment, software, purchases required
- End-of-project costs

<u>Longevity/Impact</u>   10%

- Sustainable over time or one-time impact
- Capacity-building/ability to lead to future projects

Audience: We defined audience as any member of the university community or the public as a whole. We considered Audience to be the most important of the four categories, as community engagement and revenue-generating potential were key factors to the success of a project.

Innovation/Risk: Most important were new and innovative projects that address an unmet need within the community. We realized that these types of projects were inherently risky, but believed that innovation and originality generally outweigh any risks involved.

Feasibility/Cost: Institutional resources, including staff time, equipment, and facility costs, were included, as were the resources required to carry the project into the future

Longevity/Impact: Too often, projects are undertaken without considering long-term sustainability, or the project's potential to build capacity among its stakeholders. We considered the project's impact beyond the present, favoring those with the potential to meet these criteria.

To "score" a project, we simply rated each category on a five-point scale (1 being low and 5 being high), multiplied that rating by the category's percentage, and added up these individual category scores for the total project score, which is also on a five-point scale.

Implementation

We implemented the model by scoring each of the five publishing services pilots. From that point, we expanded the model's application to assess a larger number of revenue-generating projects being considered by a separate library committee. Our general project evaluation process is as follows.

Each pilot receiving a score of 2 or higher progressed to the expanded assessment phase. Anything with a score of less than 2 was rejected from further consideration. A score of 2 to 3.7 placed a pilot in the "maybe" category. In certain circumstances, these projects may be scored more competitively, depending on the overall quantity and quality of the projects being assessed at the time. Pilots with a score of 3.8 or higher were considered to have greatest potential for success and were moved into the development phase.

Each project needs a facilitator—referred to as a "wrangler"—from the committee to shepherd it through the scoring process. The project's author, or client, communicates the initial project idea via posting to an online "Idea Wall," which all committee members check regularly for new submissions. The appointed wrangler claims the project and facilitates committee meetings and scoring model activities. Clients meet with the committee and are informed of the scoring model results and the criteria used for assessing the project's potential. The wrangler keeps the client informed of the group's decisions and facilitates all communications.

If the project scores highly enough, it continues along a path to development and moves into a work queue. If the project has a low score, clients may address the project's deficiencies and submit it for a second scoring. If there is a disagreement between the client and the committee about the scoring, clients have the option to present their case to the library's Executive Committee.

Conclusion

In the near term, we plan to complete our pilot projects, some of which need finishing pieces from the authors. Two key learnings from our pilots have been to start with finalized content, rather than works-in-progress, and to have service-level agreements in place to guide our progress and contain the project's scope. This aspect will be reflected in our longer-term goal to move towards a tiered service model as described in the Publishing Services Model section.

The theoretical publishing services model, along with the scoring model, allow the Marriott and Quinney Libraries to strategically move forward with providing a relevant service to faculty, innovative products, and quality scholarly materials for readers.

References

Brown, L., Griffiths, R., Rascoff, M., & Guthrie, K. (2007). *University Publishing in a Digital Age.* New York, NY: ITHAKA S+R. Retrieved from http://www.sr.ithaka.org/research-publications/university-publishing-digital-age/

Crow, R. (2009). *Campus-Based Publishing Partnerships: A Guide to Critical Issues.* Washington, DC: SPARC. Retrieved from http://www.sparc.arl.org/bm~doc/pub_partnerships_v1.pdf

Hahn, K. (2008). *Research Library Publishing Services: New Options for University Publishing*. Washington, DC: ARL. Retrieved from http://www.arl.org/storage/documents/ publications/research-library-publishing-services-mar08.pdf

Mullins, J. L., Murray-Rust, C., Ogburn, J. L., Crow, R., Ivins, O., Mower, A., Nesdill, D., Newton, M. P., Speer, J., & Watkinson, C. (2012). *Library Publishing Services: Strategies for Success: Final Research Report*. Washington, DC: SPARC. Retrieved from http://docs. lib.purdue.edu/purduepress_ebooks/24/

Riess, S. (interviewer) & Fruge, A. (interviewee). (1997). *A Publisher's Career With the University of California Press, the Sierra Club, and the California Native Plant Society* [Interview transcript]. Retrieved from the Regional Oral History Office, University of California http://content.cdlib.org/ark:/13030/kt596nb0t2/

Weighted Mean (April 7, 2013). *Wikipedia*. Retrieved April 22, 2013, from http://en.wikipedia. org/wiki/Weighted_mean.

APPENDIX A – Full Survey Results

1. Are your academic publications typically: (click all that apply)

Journal articles		51	89%
Book-length monographs		17	30%
Text books		13	23%
Invited chapters		25	44%
Other, please specify		6	11%

2. Do you consider your research field interdisciplinary?

Yes		44	79%
No		12	21%
Total		56	100%

3. Are there additional materials, not currently supported by traditional publishing, that you would like to include with your published work?

Yes		19	36%
No		34	64%
Total		53	100%

4. How interested are you in having your work available on the web?

Not at all		10	18%
A little		7	12%
Some		16	28%
A lot		24	42%
Total		57	100%

5. How high/low is your need for including each of the following as additional materials in your publications?

Top number is the count of respondents selecting the option. Bottom % is percent of the total respondents selecting the option.	High	Medium	Low
Additional text	8	23	24
	15%	42%	44%
Additional photos and/or color photos	14	17	26
	25%	30%	46%
Audio / Video	14	13	28
	25%	24%	51%
Reader comments, ratings	3	14	38
	5%	25%	69%
Adding content over time	15	18	23
	27%	32%	41%
Inclusion in the Institutional Repository	11	22	21
	20%	41%	39%
Print single copies on-demand	17	22	16
	31%	40%	29%
Long-term preservation of your materials	18	26	10
	33%	48%	19%
Research data	8	27	21
	14%	48%	38%

6. Are you currently researching/writing a work for publication?

Yes		50	89%
No		6	11%
Total		56	100%

7. If "yes" on question 6, do you need technical assistance, equipment, or facilities to create multi-media materials?

Yes		12	24%
No		37	76%
Total		49	100%

8. If "yes" on question 6, would you take advantage of a technological platform and/or other services for web publishing provided by the University Libraries?

Never		5	11%
Doubt it		12	27%
Maybe		13	30%
Probably		8	18%
Absolutely		6	14%
Total		44	100%

9. If "yes" on question 6, would you be willing to offer your publication as a pilot for new services offered by the University Libraries?

Yes		21	50%
No		21	50%
Total		42	100%

10. What is your academic department?

57 Responses			

11. Are your publishing needs typical of other colleagues in your department?

No		7	12%
Maybe		33	58%
Yes		17	30%
Total		57	100%

12. Would you further assist us with a face-to-face interview?

Yes		27	47%
No		30	53%
Total		57	100%

APPENDIX B: 5 Softwares Assessment, January 2012

Omeka: http://omeka.org/

Although Omeka has features for managing exhibits, videos, images, and document viewing, it is not that intuitively designed. It's not readily apparent how to integrate its features in a seamless way. In the production workspace, features appear in separate tabs/functions so it isn't obvious how one coordinates and manages the blending of these features to produce an object containing multiple file types. Omeka has a learning curve. It's simple to add files; however, the trial and error would come in experimenting with the variety of displays. It would seem that this flexibility would be a good thing, but it only served to make Omeka even less intuitive.

Pressbooks: http://pressbooks.com/

Pressbooks is designed with a book format in mind and handles image files relatively well with some minor caveats. The layout favors a portrait- as opposed to landscape-oriented book, which works better with displaying images. There are multi-faceted options available for customizing individual images that would assist in improving image display. However, for the purposes of the pilot, no image adjustments were performed. As Pressbooks is meant for the traditional text-heavy book, it is not quite as versatile as one would like when it comes to representing interactive multimedia. A bonus of Pressbooks is its ability to export to mobile devices, including the iPad and iPhone, and (with a little extra effort) adding it to a Kindle library.

OmniUpdate: http://omniupdate.com/

OmniUpdate has six or so basic display templates to work with. It has the versatility you would want for a website but wasn't adequate for presenting a non-traditional publication. We ran into issues with using images and videos. Due to these constraints, the pilot in OmniUpdate was cut short.

BookType: http://www.sourcefabric.org/en/booktype/

Booktype does not currently manage videos, although it has been reported this functionality is under discussion in Booktype's user forum. Booktype includes five different "publish this book" formats: Book, e-book, Lulu.com, Screen PDF, and Open Document Text. Each publication method includes additional configurable settings. E-book was selected, and among the setting options were iPad, Kindle, and General. General was used as a default for the pilot. Booktype has the ability to customize headers, fonts, etc.; adds a custom CSS; and retains basic formatting in Word documents but not in PDF text documents.

Wordpress: http://wordpress.org/

The Wordpress pilot included text, images, and videos. Because of the Web version's 250MB file limit, Wordpress was installed on a local server. The Wordpress platform is intuitive, extensible, and stable. Wordpress plugins have been useful in managing different aspects of the pilot, including producing printable PDFs and screening spam aimed at comment strings. There are several plugins that support adding, organizing, and presenting images in galleries and slideshows. Wordpress allows for the .mp3 filetype and is compatible with YouTube.

The University Library System, University of Pittsburgh: How & Why We Publish

Timothy S. Deliyannides & Vanessa E. Gabler

University Library System, University of Pittsburgh

2 IN THIS CHAPTER

Theme

Elements & workflow of a multi-faceted publishing program

Highlighted Services

Journal hosting, training, website customization, metadata & indexing

Software/Platforms Utilized

Open Journal Systems

Resources

Proposal forms, service agreements, and OJS training materials

The University Library System (ULS), University of Pittsburgh has provided publishing services to the scholarly research community for nearly 15 years. The ULS launched its e-journal publishing program in 2007 and in six years has quickly grown to publish 35 peer-reviewed scholarly research journals. Here, we offer insight into the rationale for this program to publish new original content, describe how the program evolved, and explain why the library sees this program as a logical and necessary investment in improving library service and creating positive change in scholarly communications. We also detail the services we offer and describe the specific tools and processes we have developed to launch a new academic journal.

Origins of the ULS Publishing Program

The University of Pittsburgh is a state-related research university founded in 1787, and in recent years, it has consistently ranked among the top cluster of the nation's research institutions (Capaldi, Lombardi, Abbey, & Craig, 2010). In addition to supporting the general research needs of the university, the ULS has built a strong digital publishing program over the past two decades. The Library D-Scribe Digital Publishing (http://www.library.pitt.edu/dscribe/search.php) program contains nearly 200,000 digital objects in over 100 thematic digital collections, including photographs, manuscripts, maps, books, journal articles, electronic theses and dissertations, government documents, and other gray literature such as working papers, white papers, and technical reports. Almost all of these materials are offered via open access to the global research community.

D-Scribe grew out of a series of digitization projects beginning in the middle 1990s designed to reformat works from the ULS' rare or unique print holdings. In the year 2000, the ULS began for the first time to make available new research born in electronic format. Working with faculty from the Department of History and Philosophy of Science, one of the university's flagship departments, the ULS developed the PhilSci-Archive, an author self-archiving repository for preprints, which has now become the world's primary repository for rapid dissemination of new research in its field. Many articles first disseminated in PhilSci-Archive are later published in refereed scholarly journals. Early in the last decade, a number of additional repositories of original research material were added, including the university's mandatory electronic thesis and dissertation submission system, D-Scholarship@Pitt, the University of Pittsburgh's institutional repository, and several subject-based repositories for gray literature, including the Aphasiology Archive, the Archive of Essential Limb Care, the Archive of European Integration, the Industry Studies Association Working Papers, and the Minority Health and Health Equity Archive.

Having gained experience in disseminating preprints and other original scholarly content online through open access, the transition to publishing scholarly journals with peer-reviewed content seemed a logical next step. Initially, the ULS reached out to established print journals, primarily in the humanities, that were edited at the University of Pittsburgh and had not made the transition to electronic publication. With a small subscription base and faced with rising printing and mailing costs, a free platform for journal publishing seemed an attractive means to gain entrée to electronic publishing, a domain that some academic editors, rooted in the tradition of print publication, found mystifying.

> **Emphasis is placed on leadership in transforming the patterns of scholarly communication and supporting researchers not only in discovering and accessing scholarly information, but in the production and sharing of new knowledge and the creation of original scholarly research.**

Why We Publish

First and foremost, the development of the ULS publishing program has been driven by a strong and enduring institutional commitment to open access to scholarly information. Innovation in scholarly communication is a core value of the ULS and one of five strategic goals in the ULS Long-Range Plan. Emphasis is placed on leadership in transforming the patterns of scholarly communication and supporting researchers not only in discovering and accessing scholarly information, but in the production and sharing of new knowledge and the creation of original scholarly research. Desired outcomes are rapid dissemination of new research, broader access to scholarly information worldwide, and the opportunity to advance a new business model as an alternative to unsustainable serials price increases.

Second, by employing innovative electronic publishing technologies, we believe that libraries can leverage their traditional strengths in organization, presentation, and preservation of content with their newer roles of teaching, training, and assisting researchers in using online information systems. These modes of interaction with scholars are very similar to those employed by liaison librarians, and these roles come naturally to libraries in a way that may not be true for a traditional university press.

Finally, today's Web-based publishing systems offer the perfect environment for building collaborative partnerships with faculty and research communities within the university and around the world to improve the production and sharing of scholarly research. By becoming a publisher, the library can meet researchers on their turf and offer a service that can help improve the impact of the research. We have found that this new service is at once relevant to faculty, well understood, and deeply appreciated.

How We Publish

The ULS has developed a suite of specific tools and techniques to build a highly cost-efficient e-journal publishing program. By following a defined process to work with our publishing partners, we have developed the capacity to launch many new titles each year with a small staff.

At the core of the ULS' journal publishing program is the open source Open Journal Systems (OJS) software developed by the Public Knowledge Project, a nonprofit research initiative originally funded by the Canadian government. OJS is now the leading open source journal publishing platform with over 12,000 journals in publication worldwide. The software allows for a highly customizable management of all stages of editorial workflow. In addition, OJS sports a number of reader tools to enhance content discovery and use. These tools include multilingual support for both online interfaces and content in many languages, persistent URLs, RSS feeds, tools for bookmarking and sharing articles through social networking sites, full-text searching, compliance with the Open Archives Initiative Protocol for Metadata Harvesting, and online usage statistics.

Additional services offered by the ULS include consultation on editorial workflow management, software configuration, graphic design services, initial training, review of all new published issues for metadata quality, and ongoing systems support. The ULS also provides ISSN registration, assigns digital object identifiers (DOIs), and assists in promotional efforts to establish the journal. The ULS uses OJS' built-in integration with the LOCKSS (Lots Of Copies Keeps Stuff Safe) system to create a distributed archiving system among participating libraries that use LOCKSS to register and cache journal content in geographically dispersed locations to ensure a secure and permanent archive for the journal.

The ULS is named as the official publisher of record, and the University of Pittsburgh Press is typically named as a cosponsor of the journal, provided that the journal adheres to a rigorous peer-review process for its content. The ULS enjoys a highly collaborative relationship with the University of Pittsburgh Press. Through a joint program, the ULS has digitized and made available online via open access over 745 monographic titles published by the University of Pittsburgh Press. The University of Pittsburgh Press Digital Editions program includes both in-print and out-of-print books. The press continues to focus on monographic print publications, whereas all material and technical support for e-journal publishing is provided by the ULS.

The editorial staff of each journal determines the content of the journal and controls all editorial decisions. Using the OJS platform, the editors are responsible for all editorial workflow management, including the work of soliciting submissions, conducting peer reviews, copyediting, layout, publication scheduling, and all correspondence with readers, authors, reviewers, and editorial staff.

Each new relationship with a potential publishing partner begins by asking them to complete a Journal Proposal Form. The data collected on this form are geared toward determining whether the proposed content will meet the ULS selection criteria, the credentials of the editorial team, the nature of the peer review process to be employed, whether the editorial team has adequate support and resources to maintain publication of the journal in the long term, and also basic information such as the focus and scope of the journal, frequency of publication, and information about existing content for journals that have an established publication.

The chances for a smooth implementation are greatly improved by establishing shared expectations with our publishing partners. Early in the engagement process, we review with each partner, using a PowerPoint developed for this purpose, our basic services and the steps to setting up a new journal with our program. Our partner will then know what to expect from the process and can plan accordingly. This also consists of a list of early decisions the journal will need to make, such as the desired URL, projected date of first publication, publication schedule, and the key journal team members.

We created our selection criteria to ensure that we are partnering with journals of high academic quality. We accept journals that use a rigorous peer-review process, have an editorial board of internationally recognized scholars in their field, possess the staff resources needed to ensure timely publication, solicit new original scholarly research through an open call for papers, and practice selectivity regarding published content. We then evaluate the Journal Proposal Form and submit it to our Publications Advisory Board for their review with a recommendation to accept or reject the proposal. This board comprises key stakeholders in open access publishing from within and outside of the University of Pittsburgh.

For journals with student editorial teams, we take care to evaluate whether the journal has a clear plan to maintain continuity by continually recruiting members who are at an early stage in their degree program and can make a multi-year commitment to the journal. We also require that a faculty advisor be appointed to oversee the editorial team, which provides continuity as well. Outgoing student editorial team members are expected to train incoming members in the workings of the journal and the OJS software each year.

Once the Publications Advisory Board has accepted a new journal, we will sign a Service Agreement with the journal. This document outlines the roles and responsibilities of both parties, the terms of service, the terms of the author copyright agreements, and the fees for services. The term of the Service Agreement is for a period of one year and renews annually automatically unless the journal notifies the ULS of termination 180 days prior to the expiration date.

To establish a system of clear communication among the journal staff and the ULS team, we have developed a Communications Protocol that uses a group distribution e-mail address for every journal. This becomes the main contact address for the journal and includes the necessary ULS staff, as well as any key individuals the journal determines should be involved in regular communications. The Communication Protocol requires that the journal designate a first responder for all external inquiries. The system is designed to ensure that everyone involved is aware of journal activities and that messages do not go unanswered.

At the time we send the Service Agreement and Communication Protocol to the journal, we also share a Website Design Brief so that they can prepare to provide feedback about the graphic design of the journal's website. This document explains what elements of the OJS software can and cannot be changed. A cascading style sheet can be used to customize many of the features affecting the look and feel of the website. However, it is important to explain at the beginning that certain features, such as the navigation bar, are tied to key functionality in the software and can't be changed or removed without damaging that functionality. The Website Design Brief gives instructions for what elements can be changed; how to submit image files a journal would like to be included in the design, such as logos; and an outline of the timeline for the design period. It also suggests that the journal provide examples of other website designs they like and what specifically about those websites they like. A design meeting is held with a graphic designer during which the journal can provide feedback based on the guidelines in the Website Design Brief. Typically, an initial website design is ready for presentation to the journal in about one month. A one-month review period follows during which the journal can request changes to the design. At the end of the one-month period, the website design is closed.

Once the website design is finalized, we ask the journal to complete an Article Template Questionnaire, which includes a series of questions that will determine the final look and layout of the articles. The look of the articles will also be informed by the final website design. The graphic designer will create an article template in Microsoft Word that the editorial team will use to format their articles. Unlike the website design period, there is no strict moratorium on changes once the article template has been completed. Many situations can arise where the content being formatted for a particular article is unique and the template needs to be adjusted. The ULS chose to create templates in Microsoft Word because it is a familiar program with a gentle learning curve for our publishing partners, many of whom have no prior experience with graphic design or document layout, and also because the cost barrier is relatively low compared with other layout software. When we present the template to the journal, we also provide a help guide that explains how to apply the styles and lay out an article using the template. We then provide ongoing support while the journal works with the template to format articles for each issue.

Whereas the publishing partner may select options for dozens of design features, we require a number of standard elements to appear on every article or every page. Every page, in either the header or footer, must contain the journal title, URL, publishing enumeration and chronology, and the DOI. On at least one page of each article, the ISSN and statement of the Creative Commons licensing terms must appear. These requirements are largely to ensure that if an article is printed by an individual, given only one page a person has all of the necessary information to create a citation and also has the information needed to drive traffic back to the journal's website.

The ULS takes responsibility for registering the ISSN with the Library of Congress on the journal's behalf. Also, through a membership with CrossRef, the ULS assigns DOIs for each journal article and deposits the metadata with CrossRef at the time of publication of each journal issue. DOIs are unique persistent identifiers that are assigned to each article.

While the graphic designers are working on the design of the website and the article template, we provide training to the journal in using the OJS software. We provide two primary training sessions. The first training session focuses on the initial setup of the journal, such as entering information about the focus and scope of the journal, the masthead, author guidelines, homepage content, and other information that will display to the public on the website. Also, we train them in how to configure the editorial workflow, such as creating custom review forms, setting the intervals for automated reminder e-mails, and managing user accounts. In the second session, we train them to use the editorial workflow to view submissions, conduct peer reviews, and manage the copyediting, layout, and proofreading through the system. We also train them in how to create and assemble an issue.

Several of our journals are based at the University of Pittsburgh, and we can provide in-person training. However, many of our partners are not affiliated with the University of Pittsburgh and are based around the world. For those journals, we provide training via Web-based conferencing tools. The majority of communication outside of the training meetings is through e-mail communication, which allows us to have a record of communication regarding the journal that is not available when discussions are conducted over the telephone.

While the journal is compiling its first issue, we are on hand to answer questions and assist until they are comfortable with the OJS software and the workflow. When the journal is ready to publish, they schedule publication with the ULS at least three business days in advance, with the full issue assembled online and ready for our review at least one business day in advance. The ULS reviews the metadata and article PDF for each issue for quality control. The ULS does not evaluate any of the content from an editorial perspective, but checks that the metadata in the online system matches the information listed on the PDF and also that the DOIs are correct. Once the review has been completed and any required corrections have been made by the journal, the ULS publishes the issue and simultaneously deposits the DOI metadata with CrossRef.

After publication of a journal's first issue, the ULS issues a press release announcing the journal. The journal is then registered with a variety of abstracting and indexing services. The ULS has a standard list of these services with which we register all journals, but we also ask the journal for any discipline-specific services with which we could also include the journal, and we'll apply for those on the journal's behalf as well.

We track usage statistics for each journal's website using Google Analytics. We administer a master account on Google Analytics for all of the journals we publish but share credentials with our publishing partners on an individual basis as needed. We created detailed documentation outlining the specific steps that need to be taken in order to complete this. Journals then have full access at any time to their journal's statistics.

For existing journals, the ULS will offer to work with the editorial staff to host back issues and make the entire run available in one place on the current journal's website.

During the first years of our publishing program, the ULS offered these services free of charge, provided the editors agreed to share the content of the journal with a global audience through open access, without subscription costs. As part of a sustainability plan implemented in 2012, we instituted a schedule of fees for services. This new policy does not cover all of our costs, and the program is still subsidized by the library's operating budget. Incentives are given for open access publications, and discounts apply for journals with editors affiliated with the University of Pittsburgh.

Also in 2012, the ULS acquired the Scholarly Exchange® hosting service, an online journal publishing service offered to the global research community to foster and encourage open access to scholarly research. The Scholarly Exchange® service is also based on OJS software. Offered free for the first year and at a very low cost thereafter, the Scholarly Exchange® service increases opportunities to disseminate research results for scholars in low-resource settings worldwide who may not have the infrastructure or technical expertise in-house to support online publishing ventures. Although this service is very much in line with the ULS' support for open access and our desire to support scholars in disseminating their research findings, it is important to note that the ULS is not the publisher of any journal hosted on the Scholarly Exchange® service.

Copyright for materials published in ULS journals is typically retained by the author under a Creative Commons Attribution license. As part of the submission process, authors are required to sign the ULS' standard Author Copyright Agreement in which they warrant that they own the copyright for the original work submitted and grant to the ULS the nonexclusive right to publish their work in any format. Authors are also required to furnish, at their own expense, written evidence of the permissions or consents for use of any third-party material included within the article submitted. In the event of a copyright infringement claim or other legal challenge to the University of Pittsburgh, the ULS may require the editorial staff to redact or remove the offending material from the journal.

> **By publishing new open access content, libraries can not only help meet the most fundamental needs of the researchers they support, but can simultaneously help transform today's inflationary cost model for serials.**

Because of its commitment to open access to scholarly content, the ULS views its e-publishing activities as a core service. With each passing year and each acquisitions budget cycle, research libraries have more to gain by becoming publishers. By publishing new open access content, libraries can not only help meet the most fundamental needs of the researchers they support, but can simultaneously help transform today's inflationary cost model for serials. The publication model described here can serve as a guide for libraries wishing to implement similar programs.

Reference

Capaldi, E. D., Lombardi, J. V., Abbey, C. W., & Craig, D. D. (Eds.). (2010). *The Top American Research Universities: 2010 Annual Report*. Retrieved June 13, 2013, from http://mup.asu.edu/research2010.pdf.

Appendix

Journal Proposal Form
University Library System, University of Pittsburgh
2011-08-16

1. Title of journal

2. Frequency and schedule of publication

3. Scope, focus, and description of content

4. Target audience

5. Types of content included (essays, research papers, book reviews, etc.)

6. Scholarly review. For each type of content listed in 5) above, describe the intended review process. Address whether the content is peer reviewed, and if so what process is followed to ensure impartiality (single blind, double blind review, etc.). Describe the standards, criteria and process for selecting reviewers.

7. Proposed editorial personnel

   a. Editor(s) in chief
   Identify the individual(s) responsible for academic content and executive management of the publication, including name, title, organizational affiliation, and past experience in scholarly publishing.

   b. Other editors, if any
   Identify the individual(s) involved in day-to-day management of the publication, including conducting reviews, assignment of copyediting, proofreading, layout, communication with authors, etc. For each editor, provide name, title, organizational affiliation, and past experience in scholarly publishing.

   c. Editorial Board (or Advisory Board)
   For each Board member, list name, title, and organizational affiliation.

8. Does a funding source exist for this journal? If so, describe the source of the funds and state how they will be used. Include support from sponsoring institutions or organizations revenues from subscriptions sales or advertising, and any other sources of support. What specific activities does the funding support?

9. Are any author fees charged? If so, provide details. What specific activities do author fees support?

10. Target date for first call for papers with ULS as publisher (Web site go-live date)

11. Target date for publication of first issue with ULS as publisher

ULS Journal Proposal Form

Authors who publish with this journal agree to the following terms:

1. The Author retains copyright in the Work, where the term "Work" shall include all digital objects that may result in subsequent electronic publication or distribution.
2. Upon acceptance of the Work, the author shall grant to the Publisher the right of first publication of the Work.
3. The Author shall grant to the Publisher and its agents the nonexclusive perpetual right and license to publish, archive, and make accessible the Work in whole or in part in all forms of media now or hereafter known under a Creative Commons Attribution 3.0 License or its equivalent, which, for the avoidance of doubt, allows others to copy, distribute, and transmit the Work under the following conditions:
   a. Attribution—other users must attribute the Work in the manner specified by the author as indicated on the journal Web site;

   with the understanding that the above condition can be waived with permission from the Author and that where the Work or any of its elements is in the public domain under applicable law, that status is in no way affected by the license.
4. The Author is able to enter into separate, additional contractual arrangements for the nonexclusive distribution of the journal's published version of the Work (e.g., post it to an institutional repository or publish it in a book), as long as there is provided in the document an acknowledgement of its initial publication in this journal.
5. Authors are permitted and encouraged to post online a pre-publication *manuscript* (but not the Publisher's final formatted PDF version of the Work) in institutional repositories or on their Websites prior to and during the submission process, as it can lead to productive exchanges, as well as earlier and greater citation of published work (see The Effect of Open Access). Any such posting made before acceptance and publication of the Work shall be updated upon publication to include a reference to the Publisher-assigned DOI (Digital Object Identifier) and a link to the online abstract for the final published Work in the Journal.
6. Upon Publisher's request, the Author agrees to furnish promptly to Publisher, at the Author's own expense, written evidence of the permissions, licenses, and consents for use of third-party material included within the Work, except as determined by Publisher to be covered by the principles of Fair Use.
7. The Author represents and warrants that:
   a. the Work is the Author's original work;
   b. the Author has not transferred, and will not transfer, exclusive rights in the Work to any third party;
   c. the Work is not pending review or under consideration by another publisher;
   d. the Work has not previously been published;
   e. the Work contains no misrepresentation or infringement of the Work or property of other authors or third parties; and
   f. the Work contains no libel, invasion of privacy, or other unlawful matter.
8. The Author agrees to indemnify and hold Publisher harmless from Author's breach of the representations and warranties contained in Paragraph 6 above, as well as any claim or proceeding relating to Publisher's use and publication of any content contained in the Work, including third-party content.

ULS Author Copyright Agreement

OJS Design Brief

Part 1: Formatting the Web site's look and feel (CSS layout)

1) Preference of colors

2) Preference of fonts – The journal can pick a font that they would like to use on the Web site. Please be aware that the font you choose will most likely change to one of the seven closest Web-Safe Fonts for the website, but may be used in other parts of the design including the banner and the Word template.

3) Sidebar information to enable/disable

- "Developed By" Block
- Subscription Block
- Donation Block
- Font Size Block
- Help Block
- User Block

- Role-Specific Block
- Language Toggle Block
- Navigation Block
- Information Block
- "Notification" Block
- Web Feed Plugin

4) The Web site design is not fully customizable because the location or properties of certain aspects of the site are tied to core functionality of the OJS software and cannot be altered. The Cascading Style

---

Sheet (CSS) can alter how these elements appear visually, but it cannot necessarily move, rename, or delete these elements, such as those in the top navigation bar or the layout and links in the About pages. The standard OJS functionality allows you to add elements in these places, but full customization of these pages is not possible.

Banner

The banner can consist of images that are provided by the journal (to reflect or match an existing site) OR create a custom banner, which can include the following:

Examples of journal banners

1) Journal's Title and Subtitle with type treatment .

2) Graphic elements, which can include stock images provided by us and/or other images provided by the journal.

3) A journal-provided logo (if available—but it is not required that you have a logo).

   a) The University Library System, University of Pittsburgh will not provide this service.

   b) If you would like to place a logo in the banner but do not have one, the following is suggested for obtaining a professional-looking logo.

   1. Contact a design firm where a team of designers can research what would best represent the journal.

   2. Contact a freelance designer who can research your journal to determine what would best represent the journal.

   3. Search logo-design Web sites to purchase one that may best represent the journal. Some sites will have the option to order a logo especially created for you.

ULS Open Journal Systems Design Brief

90

Submitting Imagery

Files should be submitted as a JPG or PNG files. The image file should be at least 1600px X 1200px and 300dpi for best output for both print and Web design.

For Web images, it may be of smaller dpi, but larger images are preferred to allow for cropping where needed.

Also, it is important to have the appropriate copyright permission for all images submitted.

Please note the following

1. Lower-quality files can also be submitted (if necessary) but are not preferred due to low-quality output when trying to print these image files. As a result, these files may be rejected after review.
2. Other file formats such as TIFF and GIF can be submitted but may be rejected after review.
3. Extremely rich and vibrant colors may have a color shift when converting to CMYK for printing. This is something we will try to avoid and adjust as much as possible when converting your file from RGB (Web) to CMYK (print); however, it is best that the journal is aware of th s possible slight color change.

Example of journal provided images

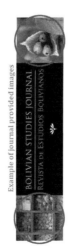

Submitting Logos *We do not provide this service, and having a logo is optional and not required.*

Previously created logos

These logos are best submitted as an EPS file.

Example of journal provided logo

INTERNATIONAL JOURNAL OF
TELEREHABILITATION

Suggestions for creating a new logo

For the best results have your designer use a vector-based program like Adobe Illustrator.

Logos should be in a vector format to allow for good results regarding resizing and avoiding pixelization of the logo. The preferred file type is an EPS or AI file with everything in outlines.

PDF files can also be accepted, but possible font issues may occur if the designer does not have the particular font that was used.

The files described above allow the designer to resize the logo and place it anywhere on the Web site (e.g., a change to the layout of the banner). This format would also allow the designer to enlarge the logo for use in the Word template for articles.

As a precautionary note, however, Illustrator also allows the option of adding rasterized effects, which should be avoided when creating any of the files mentioned above. Files with these raster effects may result in some unexpected outcomes.

Using Adobe Photoshop

Unfortunately, logos created in Photoshop are not recommended. However, if a logo was created in Photoshop, you are required to provide at least two files, one for print and one for web, because it is a raster-based program and it is problematic regarding the 'resizing and pixelization issues mentioned above.

Usually acceptable files from Photoshop include PNG, GIF, JPG, or TIFF.

EPS and PDF files can be created from Photoshop, but these files are generally not completely vector based, which may result in some unexpected outcomes.

If any there are any issues concerning the submission of your logo, you will be contacted as soon as possible to resolve the issue.

ULS Open Journal Systems Design Brief

91

Timeline for Development and changes of banner image and css layout

Part 1: Timeline for Web site design

A graphic design meeting will be scheduled shortly after the initial implementation overview and training.

At the initial graphic design meeting, we will discuss your general preferences for the look and feel of the journal, including all the design elements in section above. This is an opportunity for you to share other sample Web sites, printed publications or any other design ideas that will help us understand the look and feel you wish to achieve.

At the initial design meeting, we will set a target deadline for development of the draft design based on client schedule requirements, the complexity of the design work, and our in-house scheduling capabilities and constraints.

Once the ULS presents to the journal an initial design, the journal will have one month to request design changes, after which the site design process will be closed.

Part 2: Timeline for development of word template

After formatting the Web site's look and feel with the banner and css layout changes, we will request feedback regarding the journal's Word article template design. This design will reflect your Web site as much as possible. This is an opportunity for you to share other sample journal article layouts that you like and how you would like your article layout to look, as well as to help us understand the look and feel you wish to achieve.

We will set a target deadline for development of the template based on client schedule requirements, the complexity of the design work, and our in-house scheduling capabilities and constraints.

After the initial article template design is presented to the journal, the design will be refined according to the journal's specifications. After these changes have been implemented, the designer will provide the journal with the template. You will also be given a template help guide that should aid you in using the template and familiarize you with its features. At this point the journal will have one month to request further design changes, after which the initial template design process will be closed. You will then be given a final template for formatting your journal's articles. Your template help guide will be updated with any newly requested information and/or styles that have been created.

However, as your journal begins to change, the template/help guide can easily be updated to reflect these changes, which will be done by the designer.

ULS Open Journal Systems Design Brief

92

Journal Article Template Design Questionnaire

An important element of the graphic design for a journal is the development of a standard template that defines the appearance, formatting, and layout of every article. For better or for worse, the appearance of an article may greatly affect the reader's perception of the reliability and validity of the content.

Many readers will choose to print individual articles for reading. When printed, the article becomes separated from the online environment. The template must include enough information so that a complete citation to the work can be reconstructed from the printed article and so that the reader can identify and locate the Web site from which the article came. Therefore, we require the following to appear on every page: journal title, journal URL, enumeration and chronology to identify the issue, and DOI.

Since the design of the template should harmonize with the design of the journal Web site, design of the standard Article Template cannot begin until the journal Web site design is complete.

The following must appear on EVERY page of each article.
Please select your preference.

Journal Title	Header	Footer
Journal URL	Header	Footer
Publishing enumeration and chronology Enumeration and chronology that uniquely identify the published issue and match the Issue Title as displayed online (might not use vol #; might include season, month, sections, parts, etc.)	Header	Footer
DOI (Digital Object Identifier)	Header	Footer

The following must appear on at least 1 page of each article.

ISSN	All Headers	All Footers
	End of article only	On first page only
Statement of CC license and Publisher Information/logos	All Headers	All Footers
	End of article only	On first page only

Other decisions to be made by the journal

General Layout Information

	Do you require a page a different size? Yes No	If yes, Rationale/Justification:
Page dimensions will be 8.5" X 11"		
Number of Columns	1	2 3
Separate Title Page (with body of article beginning on second page)	Yes	No
Abstracts	Yes	No
If yes to previous question: Set abstract apart from article other than 'Abstract' Heading?	No	Appear on first page with article starting immediately below
	Yes, by color and/or Borders	Appear on first page alone with article starting on the next page
Reference Formatting	Footnotes	Endnotes
Bibliography / Works Cited / References Section?	Yes	No
Bibliography Appearance	Hanging indent	List (no indentation)
Placement of captions for tables or figures	Above for both	Below for both
	Above for Tables; Below for Figures	Above for Figures; Below for

ULS Journal Article Template Design Questionnaire

Author Information

			Tables	
Location of Author Information in relation to Article Title	Above	Below		
Format for multiple authors	Stacked	Running	If running, separate by a Comma Bullet Dash Other?	
Author's Title	Superscript	Below name	End of article	
Author's Affiliation	Superscript	Below name	End of article	
Author photo	Beside name	Below name	End of article	
Author bio	Superscript	End of article		

Paragraphs, headings and page numbers

Body text alignment	Flush Left	Justified left	
Subtitles	New Line	Set apart with a colon or dash	
Number of Heading Sections	1	2	3 or more?
Heading Section Numbering	Yes	No	
Paragraph Indentation	No indenting	Drop caps for first paragraph	

	Indenting all	Indent only first paragraph under a new heading
Page number placement	Header	Footer
	Side Margin	Centered Footer
Alternating Page Number Location depending on if an even or odd page number	Yes	No
Running Information	Journal Title	Article Title
Check only 2 one for front of page (recto) and one for back of page(verso)		
Running information location	Author/s	Heading Title
	Header	Footer
Include color scheme for Header / Footer / Headings / Borders etc…	No Keep B & W	Yes match website colors
Quotes (Choose as many as you would like)	No Italic	Italic
	Smaller font	Single left side indentation
	Double sided indentation	Extra spacing above and below

ULS Journal Article Template Design Questionnaire

For administrative use only.

ISSN:

Creative Commons license:

(cc) BY Articles in this journal are licensed under a Creative Commons Attribution 3.0 United States License.

(cc) BY New articles in this journal are licensed under a Creative Commons Attribution 3.0 United States License.

(cc) BY-NC-ND This work is licensed under a Creative Commons Attribution-Noncommercial-No Derivative Works 3.0 United States License.

Timeline for development of word template

After formatting the Web site's look and feel with the banner and css layout changes, we will discuss your general preferences for the Word template's design. This design will reflect your Web site as much as possible. This is an opportunity for you to share other sample journal article layouts that you like and how you would like your article layout to look, as well as to help us understand the look and feel you wish to achieve.

We will set a target deadline for development of the template based on client schedule requirements, the complexity of the design work, and our in-house scheduling capabilities and constraints. After the initial article template design is presented, the design will be refined according to the journal's specifications. The journal will have one month to request further design changes, after which the initial template design process will be closed. After these changes have been implemented, the designer will provide the journal with the template.

You will also be given a template help guide that should aid you in using the template and familiarize you with its features. Your template help guide will be updated with any newly requested information and/or styles that have been created. As your journal changes, the template/help guide can easily be updated to reflect these changes, which will be done by the designer.

ULS Journal Article Template Design Questionnaire

ULS Digital Publishing Program

Publishing E-Journals using Open Journals System

Publishing Services

Manuscript tracking software and hardware platform
Web site layout
Publication template design
ISSN registration
Assignation of Digital Object Identifiers (DOIs)
Web site usage statistics
Consultation on editorial workflow and management
Assistance in gaining recognition as a scholarly journal
Press releases and publicity within the library community
Archiving and preservation

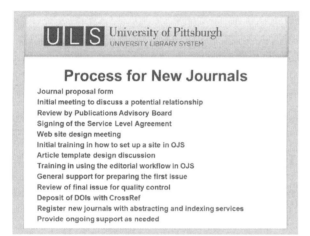

Process for New Journals

Journal proposal form
Initial meeting to discuss a potential relationship
Review by Publications Advisory Board
Signing of the Service Level Agreement
Web site design meeting
Initial training in how to set up a site in OJS
Article template design discussion
Training in using the editorial workflow in OJS
General support for preparing the first issue
Review of final issue for quality control
Deposit of DOIs with CrossRef
Register new journals with abstracting and indexing services
Provide ongoing support as needed

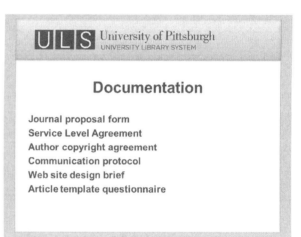

Documentation

Journal proposal form
Service Level Agreement
Author copyright agreement
Communication protocol
Web site design brief
Article template questionnaire

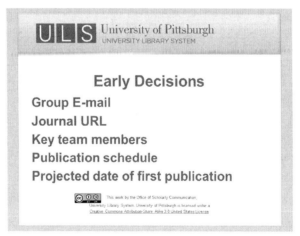

Early Decisions

Group E-mail
Journal URL
Key team members
Publication schedule
Projected date of first publication

ULS Digital Publishing Introductory PowerPoint Presentation

Preserving and Publishing Digital Content Using XML Workflows

Jonathan McGlone

University of Michigan Libraries, Michigan Publishing

3

IN THIS CHAPTER

Theme
Production streamlining

Highlighted Services
Online journal & monographs hosting and production

Software/Platforms Utilized
Drupal, DLXS, Adobe InDesign, Calibre

Resources
Example XML workflows

In digital publishing, encoding documents in XML can produce several advantages for libraries that have invested in hosting and publishing services or plan to in the future. XML workflows enable publishers to output content quickly and easily in several electronic formats (EPUB, HTML, PDF); repurpose content into other channels (catalogs, websites, databases, printers); automate processes; scale their services and publications; and preserve the digital content for the future.

Michigan Publishing (formerly known as MPublishing), the primary publishing unit of the University of Michigan and a part of its University Library, began encoding born-digital documents in SGML—and later XML— to publish journals and monographs in the late 1990s. Over time, Michigan

Publishing has established its own semi-automated XML workflow to achieve these ends in its work with a growing list of publishing partners. Today Michigan Publishing provides web-hosting and conversion services for over 20 active open access and subscription-based academic journals (http://www.publishing.umich.edu/publications/journals), the open access Digital Culture Book Series (http://www.digitalculture.org), and the open access imprint Open Humanities Press (http://openhumanitiespress.org/book-titles.html), among others.

The following chapter will introduce the reader to a few flavors of XML encoding used at Michigan Publishing such as JATS XML, Scribe, and TEI, as well as present a generalized workflow for creating and publishing encoded XML documents for monographs and journal articles that begins with a Word document, outputs an XML encoded document, and presents the article or monograph to readers as HTML and PDF, yet is also available for repurposing into other channels.

Before You Start

Before you start a digital publishing project, determining how the content will be used by readers and the project's preservation requirements are an important first step. Does the content need to be searchable? Will it offer content in multiple formats—PDF, mobi, EPUB2, readable on the Web as HTML? Is there interest in re-purposing specific pieces of the content in other channels such as a library vendor's database? Will you be registering DOIs (Digital Object Identifiers) for the content? Do you need to ensure that your content can be accessed and migrated to new formats five to ten years from now? Twenty years from now?

If your answer is yes to any of these questions, you'll want to strongly consider encoding your documents with a markup language such as XML. If you simply need to present images of the original pages (referred to as page images), then scanning, conducting OCR (Optical Character Recognition), and presenting content on the Web as downloadable PDFs with searchable OCR text may be enough. Because the upfront costs to establishing an XML workflow can be quite considerable and not every digital publishing project requires XML encoded documents, defining the scope and aims of the project as early as possible can help minimize any unneeded efforts, and help to focus your publishing project's production processes (Gross, 2003).

Benefits to Using XML

XML works best with text-based content that has structure. In the academic publishing world, a majority of content published is text based. What's more, traditional journal articles and scholarly monographs use a fairly predictable structure. This is especially true for journal articles.

Since the 1990s, academic publishers have been taking advantage of this predictable structure by implementing XML in production workflows. With XML, publishers can validate content and ensure it is in the correct order; for example, running tests to check that footnotes are at the end of a document or that an abstract appears before the first paragraph. Validation can also ensure there is consistency across multiple XML documents, making sure that headings or footnotes have been encoded the same way. When working with tight deadlines and several projects at once, these types of validation can save a lot of time.

Structure can also be relied upon to automate processes. When converting XML to other formats such as HTML, the structure can be used to programmatically apply character styles to section headings or chapter titles. Or when registering DOIs for journal articles, article metadata can be re-used to automate an XML submission to the DOI registrar, CrossRef.

From a preservation and access perspective there are several benefits to encoding your documents with XML. As an open file format, reading and exchanging your XML data can take place regardless of operating system, platform, or software. Because it is open, chances for the loss of data when sharing your XML content with library vendors or other institutions is greatly reduced. In addition, the open nature of the file format also ensures future access to your XML documents as long as there are programs that can read and write Unicode text.

What's more, because XML aims to keep content separate from the design elements (e.g., line spacings, margins, font types), your content can remain accessible as media and devices evolve and change. For example, if a new tablet reader format emerges, you won't risk the chance of losing any content when migrating to these new formats; you simply need to repurpose your XML to the new format's syntax.

> In order for your XML content to be machine readable and interoperable, you'll want to select a Document Type Definition (DTD) that imposes rules upon how you mark up your content.

Most importantly, encoding documents in XML allows content to be repurposed into other formats using XSL Transformations (XSLT) or other programming languages. Using XSLT, you can move your XML into different XML Document Type Definitions (DTDs), such as InDesign's, for typesetting a PDF, HTML for Web reading, or e-book file formats such as mobi or EPUB. The ability to transform structured data into another format gets at the core of the convenience of an XML workflow in digital publishing.

A Few Flavors of XML Encoding Relevant to Academic Publishing

In order for your XML content to be machine readable and interoperable, you'll want to select a Document Type Definition (DTD) that imposes rules upon how you mark up your content. A DTD is a set of tag names and element attributes that are agreed upon so use and application of tags is the same across documents. While there are many DTDs to select from, the following section reviews those used in Michigan Publishing's journal and monograph workflows.

TEI and DLXS Text Class | http://www.tei-c.org

All of Michigan Publishing's journal content and some of its monographs are available online through a hosted installation of DLXS (Digital Library eXtension Service), digital library collection software developed at the University of Michigan. DLXS provides a storage mechanism for our XML encoded files and indexing and searching tools, as well as a set of customizable XSLT stylesheets to transform content from XML to HTML rendered in readers' web browsers.

Although DLXS has its own Text Class DTD consisting of basic requirements in order for the software to index, search, and transform the XML, we use our own in-house version of TEI to provide higher-level encoding of our documents (DLXS, 2009). In the end, the resulting XML document is TEI wrapped in the Text Class DTD. TEI best suits the needs of Michigan Publishing because of its flexibility and modularity, allowing for customizations related to our digital collection platform.

From the beginning TEI was designed by the humanities research community to be able to support as many kinds of materials as possible, striving to "be applied to any natural language, literary genre, text type without restriction on form or content" (Burnard & Bauman, 2013). TEI was originally conceived to describe print documents in as much detail as possible, representing in electronic form text that already exists in traditional media. Therefore, it is suited well for academic publishing materials, especially dictionaries and running text materials like monographs or journals. In addition to the support of a very active and knowledgeable community of practitioners, the TEI community has developed several conversion tools—to TEI XML and from TEI XML to other formats—that are designed for users to adapt and customize (see http://www.tei-c.org/Tools/Stylesheets/).

Journal Article Tag Suite (JATS) | http://jats.nlm.nih.gov/

The Journal Article Tag Suite (JATS) represents the emergence of a distinct set of XML elements and attributes aimed at academic journals. As a newly created NISO standard, it provides a common XML format for publishers and archives to exchange and preserve journal content. Like the majority of XML DTDS, JATS does not attempt to preserve the journal form or content style (NISO, 2013).

Prior to standardization, JATS was used as the National Library of Medicine DTD. Developed at the National Center for Biotechnology Information (NCBI) and the National Library of Medicine's PubMed Central, it began as a set for archiving life science journals and later expanded as needs grew. It is now used by journals worldwide, especially journal archives at PubMed Central, Portico, and HighWire Press, as well as the Library of Congress and British Library (Beck, 2011).

As Michigan Publishing evolves away from publishing digital content using DLXS and the Text Class/TEI DTD, JATS will become our future journals DTD. As a replacement to DLXS, Michigan Publishing is currently developing web-based tools to allow publishers to easily transform content from Microsoft Word to JATS XML and later deposit and publish this content in HathiTrust (http://www.lib.umich.edu/mpach).

Scribe Markup Language (ScML)

Unlike the other DTDs described above, Scribe Markup Language (ScML) is a proprietary XML format designed for moving documents from a digital to print environment. Specifically developed for the publishing industry, subscribing publishers/institutions have access to the ScML documentation and dictionary along with Scribe's document workflow tools. Scribe's pre-developed set of workflow and conversion tools are extremely useful for publishers looking to begin or transition into an XML workflow. More recently, Scribe has begun developing tools to convert content to e-book formats such as EPUB2.

Because it is designed specifically for publishers, the ScML DTD includes additional elements that indicate elements important to typesetters and the typesetting process, such as first paragraphs, paragraphs after heads, or those that continue onto pages (Scribe, 2013). Using a set of proprietary macros and plugins for Microsoft Word, styles are applied to the Word document manuscript to give the document structure (headings, first paragraph, etc.), which a programmed script interprets to transform the document to the corresponding ScML XML.

Michigan Publishing has adopted ScML and its workflow tools for its print projects under the University of Michigan Press imprint. In addition, adoption of this workflow has allowed Michigan Publishing to develop and offer "rapid typesetting" services for journal publishing partners—producing typeset PDFs for additional fees. Increasingly, with the addition of tools that assist in the conversion to EPUB2 and mobi, ScML will likely become a "pivot" format to produce a version for multiple platforms that also converts to JATS XML or DLXS Text Class/ TEI as a preservation format.

Engineering an XML Workflow

There are two main approaches to XML workflows for digital publishing: XML-In and XML-Out. XML-In workflows involve the creation of the XML files at an early stage in the production process, such as authoring in XML (highly unlikely), having a copy editor prepare a word document for XML conversion, or prior to the design and typesetting process (Bullock, 2012). XML-Out workflows maintain a standard production processes—writing, editing, proofing, and typesetting—and XML is created in a back-conversion process (Strange, 2003, p. 158). Depending on the individual project or your relationship with the content provider, you may use one or the other.

XML-Out

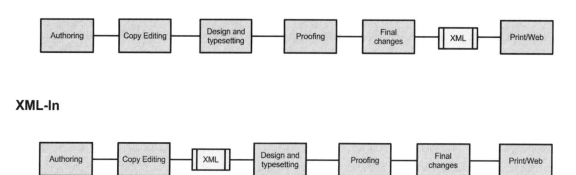

XML-In

Figure 1. XML-In vs. XML-Out.

The sooner content can be converted to XML, the quicker and more efficient your workflow will become. For example, when generated early in the production process, XML can be converted to HTML for online review and proofing by editors and authors before it is typeset. The XML file becomes the source or master file for both your digital and print output. In addition, with an early XML workflow, the typesetting process can be automated using templates in programs like InDesign when importing XML content, a process that is especially useful for journals because of their consistent formatting across volumes and issues.

The digital publishing activities of Michigan Publishing have relied primarily on XML-Out because of our tendency to provide only conversion and hosting services for journals and digital monographs, similar to many libraries providing publishing services. But as demand for typesetting services, EPUB versions, and the need to minimize costs increase, adopting an XML-In workflow where copy editors or conversion assistants structure content in a Microsoft Word document by applying paragraph and character styles while reviewing content is likely to take place.

Basic XML-In Conversion Workflow

In a basic XML-In workflow (Figure 2), content is prepared by the author in familiar authoring tools such as Microsoft Word or Open Office, converted to XML, then transformed to produce PDF, HTML, and EPUB versions of the content.

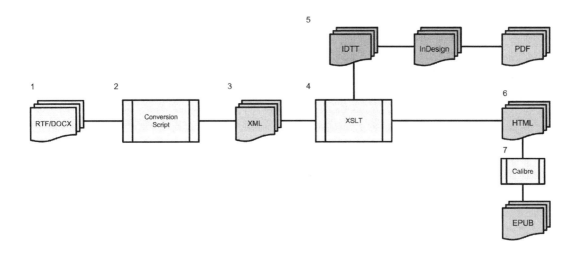

Figure 2. Basic XML-In Workflow. XML is generated after copyediting and just before design and typesetting. The HTML version produced here can be used as the proofing copy.

When receiving the content, customized paragraph and character styles can be applied to the RTF or DOCX file to identify elements such as the author's name, title of the chapter or article, footnotes, paragraphs, blockquotes, and section headings. These styles give a basic structure to the document, which aides a conversion script written in a programming language such as Perl or Python to identify and convert elements to their corresponding XML elements; e.g., paragraphs to <p> tags or blockquotes to <p type="blockquote">. Michigan Publishing uses the proprietary software R2Net (http://www.logictran.net/products/r2net.html) for command line RTF to XML conversion, which offers support for conversion to customized document types, which is essential in conversion to DLXS Text Class DTD. A free and open source alternative for RTF conversion exists in Paul Tremblay's rtf2xml project (http://rtf2xml.sourceforge.net/). In addition, the TEI Consortium has produced a XSL stylesheet to aide in the transformation of DOCX to TEI XML (https://code.google.com/p/oxygen-tei/source/browse/trunk/oxygen-tei/frameworks/tei/xml/tei/stylesheet/docx/from/docxtotei.xsl?r=9).

Once the content is identified in XML, further XSL transformations (XSLT) can be applied to convert the content to other markup languages, such as InDesign Tagged Text (IDTT) for importing into InDesign (see http://help.adobe.com/en_US/indesign/cs/taggedtext/indesign_cs5_taggedtext.pdf), or to any flavor of HTML for display on the Web. When content is in a program such as InDesign, content can be professionally typeset and a print-ready PDF can be generated. Because EPUB is a packaged version of HTML, once your content is in HTML format, converting to EPUB or one of a plethora of other e-book formats using software such as Calibre (http://calibre-ebook.com/) is ideal, as it can help preserve styling and formatting applied to the HTML. Again, the TEI community has developed a set of XSL stylesheets to aid in the transformation of TEI XML to other formats such as HTML, HTML5, EPUB, and EPUB3.

103

Journals (XML-Out Workflow)

Traditionally, Michigan Publishing's journals workflow has worked as a standard XML-Out workflow, primarily determined by our relationships with publishing partners. For example, journal editors conduct their peer review, copy editing, and in most cases, typesetting, independently. Once content has been finalized, it is submitted to Michigan Publishing based on pre-defined specifications for submitting content in the form of a checklist to ensure all figures, tables, images, and manuscripts are present and correctly named.

When providing hosting and conversion services, you need to decide how flexible you will be in what formats you will accept. If you have a loose policy on deliverable formats, be prepared to receive all different types of formats and content from partners. In the past, not wanting to preclude publishing based on a partner's established authoring and editing workflow, Michigan Publishing has allowed publishing partners to deliver manuscripts in the form of Word documents; Rich Text Files; PDFs; InDesign, Quark, and TIFF files; and bound volumes and paper documents, thus forcing the development of several different and diverging conversion workflows. As we are now operating at a larger scale, our preferred delivery formats for content bound for the Web are Microsoft Word documents or PDFs.

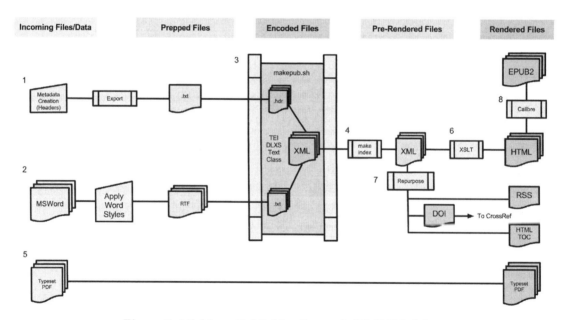

Figure 3. Michigan Publishing Journals XML Workflow.

Figure 3 demonstrates a typical journal workflow, where Word documents and a typeset PDF are delivered to Michigan Publishing to offer HTML, PDF and EPUB2 files available to readers. In Step One, metadata for each article is entered into a customized Drupal database, recording information such as the author(s), title, keywords, volume, issue, DOI (which will be registered upon publication), and other relevant article and issue information. Database metadata is exported to an XML encoded text file that serves as the header of article, later to be joined with content. Metadata is purposely stored separately from the content of each article to easily manage and apply global changes to journal information and to reduce the number of keystrokes by using calculated database fields.

Separately, a Word document is converted to an RTF file where it is given structure by applying custom Word styles to the elements of the article, as described in the previous section. Using a script developed at Michigan Publishing, the RTF file is converted to an XML encoded file, which is joined with a corresponding header and validated. Often, the conversion from RTF to XML is not a perfect process, requiring manual corrections before proceeding. Having a validation process in place ensures content is marked up uniformly and can be indexed and transformed to HTML correctly. After passing validation, it is indexed in the DLXS system. When a reader requests a specific article, a complex system of XSL stylesheet templates transforms the XML on the fly into HTML in the reader's browser. Using Calibre e-book management software, HTML content is converted to EPUB2 files, which are presented to readers for download in addition to or in place of a typeset PDF. In Step Seven, XML's custom Perl scripts are used to repurpose XML to generate a HTML table of contents for the current issue and RSS feeds, and automate the registration of DOIs with CrossRef. In addition to this type of repurposing, having our content in XML allows us to also submit content to bibliographic and full-text databases interested in indexing specific journals.

Monographs (Scribe Well-Formed Document Workflow, XML-In)

Michigan Publishing has published open access monographs on the web since 2001 using a variety of XML workflows, from back conversion of scanned PDFs to a similar process described above in Figure 3. Currently it is experimenting with a fully integrated XML-In workflow that utilizes Scribe's Well-Formed Document Workflow to aid typesetting, allow for in-house conversion to various e-book formats, and to present open access versions of texts to readers on the Web in HTML.

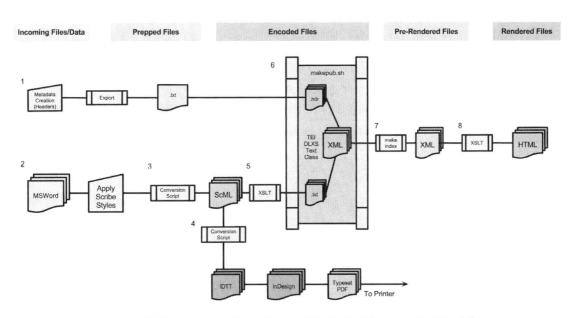

Figure 4. Michigan Publishing Desired XML-In Monographs Workflow.

Similarly to the workflow described in Figure 3, in Figure 4 basic metadata is keyed into a central database, which is later exported as marked-up TEI XML, merged with the body of the content, and used for the online version of the monograph. After receiving the draft manuscript in Microsoft Word DOCX format, copyeditors give structure to the document using Scribe-specific Word styles. This process is very similar to the process described in Figure 3, with the exception that the styles transform to ScML XML. After the copyediting process is completed and final, the DOCX is transformed to ScML and validated. Once in ScML, Scribe's conversion script generates an InDesign Tagged Text file for importing to InDesign, where images are inserted, the content is typeset, and the document is prepared for export to PDF and other formats for small-run printing or print on demand services. Although not utilized at this point, Scribe also provides tools to flow the typeset content from InDesign back to ScML for conversion to EPUB and other e-book formats. For web delivery, ScML is transformed to DLXS Text Class using XSL stylesheets, and run through the same process journals receive. It should be noted that with monograph publishing and production, the XML workflow should be flexible because monographs often have unique features and aspects that won't fit smoothly into your XML DTD or workflow.

Manual Intervention and Quality Control

While most of this process is automated, manual intervention and clean-up is always necessary during the conversion process. Often with RTF or DOCX to XML conversions for both journals and monographs, applied styles in Word do not get translated to the proper XML elements. This is where validation and error reporting post conversion can come in handy—if errors occur in the transformation, they will be identified and can be manually corrected before proceeding. It should also be stressed that a round of quality control or review of HTML is always necessary when converting content to ensure that XML elements are being transformed and rendered in the web browser correctly.

> **It should also be stressed that a round of quality control or review of HTML is always necessary when converting content to ensure that XML elements are being transformed and rendered in the web browser correctly.**

The Future of XML Workflows

XML is well suited for publishing traditional scholarly content in multiple formats, repurposing into multiple streams, and preserving content for the long term. While these needs will continue to exist, new and emerging forms of scholarly communication will require new and different workflows. From another perspective, existing XML workflows should not constrain authors who want to experiment in new forms of publishing that might not fit into traditional production models.

For example, does it make sense to migrate content such as blog posts from HTML to XML when re-publishing them in electronic form? If a publisher is opting to take on diverse projects where content layout and format varies from manuscript to manuscript, does it make sense to impose a strict XML workflow on these projects (Daly, 2013)? What about projects that use HTML5 for video and user interaction? Beginning these projects with XML may not be a worthwhile effort because it can't represent video and coded interactivity. If EPUB3 allows for both JavaScript and HTML5 and does not utilize XHTML, what is the point of using XML at all? In short, as scholarly web publishing begins to rely on various types of content, interaction, and multimedia, XML and XML-based workflows may not always be the most efficient answer for non-traditional scholarly publishing.

References

Beck, J. (Summer 2011). NISO Z39.96 the Journal Article Tag Suite (JATS): What happened to the NLM DTDs?. *The Journal of Electronic Publishing*, 14(1). Retrieved from http://dx.doi.org/10.3998/3336451.0014.106

Bullock, A. (2012). *Book production*. London: Routledge.

Burnard, L., and Bauman, S. (Eds.). (2013). *TEI: P5 guidelines* (2.3.0 ed.). Charlottesville, Virginia: Text Encoding Initiative Consortium. Retrieved from http://www.tei-c.org/release/doc/tei-p5-doc/en/Guidelines.pdf

Daly, L. (2013, February 1). The unXMLing of digital books. *Safari books online: Publishing & technology*. Retrieved from http://techblog.safaribooksonline.com/2013/02/01/the-unxmling-of-digital-books/

DLXS (2009). Working With Text Class Markup. Retrieved from http://webservices.itcs.umich.edu/mediawiki/dlxs15/index.php/Working_with_Text_Class_Markup

Gross, M. (2003). Data capture & conversion. In W. E. Kasdorf (Ed.), *Columbia guide to digital publishing* (pp. 179–218). New York: Columbia University Press.

Kay, M. (2008). XSLT 2.0 and XPath 2.0 programmer's reference. National Information Standards Organization (2012, August 22). *NISO publishes Journal Article Tag Suite (JATS) Standard: Provides common XML format for exchanging journal content*. Retrieved from http://www.niso.org/news/pr/view?item_key=d92a2bc93b43db6831e68914e134c731d83cbdd1

Scribe. (2013). Scribe Well-Formed Document Workflow. Retrieved from http://scribenet.com/about/
    well-formed-document-workflow

Strange, J. (2003). Organizing, editing, & linking content. In W. E. Kasdorf (Ed.), *Columbia guide to
    digital publishing* (pp. 155–178). New York: Columbia University Press.

Emerging Opportunities in Library Services: Planning for the Future of Scholarly Publishing

Mark P. Newton, Eva T. Cunningham, & Julie N. Morris

Columbia University Libraries/Information Services

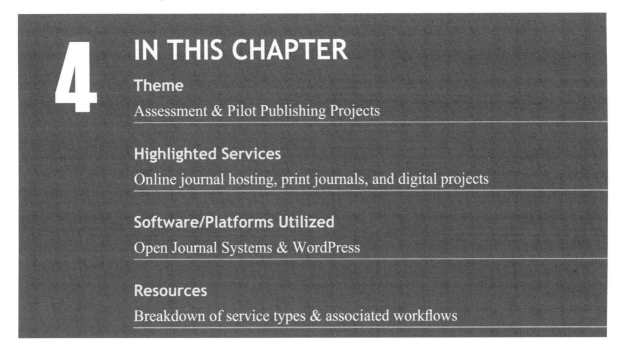

4

IN THIS CHAPTER

Theme

Assessment & Pilot Publishing Projects

Highlighted Services

Online journal hosting, print journals, and digital projects

Software/Platforms Utilized

Open Journal Systems & WordPress

Resources

Breakdown of service types & associated workflows

In 2007, the Columbia University Libraries/Information Services (CUL/IS) established the Center for Digital Research and Scholarship (CDRS) to explore and provision new research support services for the university in all areas of scholarly communication, including online scholarly publishing[1] (Renfro and Neal, 2012). One of six organizations comprising the Digital Programs and Technology Services group within CUL/IS, CDRS assists faculty, students, staff, and university affiliates with their scholarly communication and digital research needs through a suite of services: publishing support, digital research repository, conference websites and

[1]   Columbia University Libraries/Information Services Strategic Plan 2010–2013: http://library.columbia.edu/content/dam/libraryweb/general/documents/strategic_plan_2010-13.pdf.

video recording, research data management, and more.[2] Nine of its 17 full-time employees belong to a production team comprising developers, designers, and project managers from diverse academic and professional backgrounds, only one of whom holds a master's degree in library science.[3]

CDRS seeks publishing partnerships with a variety of on-campus groups and individuals (Perry, Borchert, Deliyannides, Kosavic, & Kennison, 2011) and embraces partnerships with allied organizations such as scholarly presses and societies as well (Kennison, Panourgia, & Tartar, 2010). A proponent of eliminating barriers to the progress of research, CDRS advocates for open access (OA) publishing models. This is exemplified by *Tremor and Other Hyperkinetic Movements*, the peer-reviewed, faculty-run OA journal now indexed in PubMed, which CDRS publishes. To help offset the OA journal publication costs, *Tremor* authors pay an article-processing fee, although waivers and alternative methods of funding are available[4] (Perry et al., 2011). In practice, CDRS' approach to publishing support is business model–neutral, however, and OA is not a requirement for partnership.[5]

> # A strategy for keeping this service sustainable and scalable has been the adoption of a tiered structure based on design and customization needs to control flow.

The journals program at CDRS has been successful, providing publishing support to 16 journals using the Open Journal Systems or WordPress platforms and interactive tools such as blogs and wikis in subject areas ranging from sciences to the humanities. A strategy for keeping this service sustainable and scalable has been the adoption of a tiered structure based on design and customization needs to control flow. Projects can take anywhere from one week for a barebones installation to over 17 weeks for the Premier service (Perry et al., 2011).

Drawing on digital project management best practices, a typical project goes through several phases. Following a requirements-gathering and analysis phase, a Master Service Agreement and project plan are drawn up. Production work consisting of information architecture, design, and development ensues, followed by quality assurance testing prior to launch. Accessibility and usability principles are adhered to throughout the lifecycle of each project. CDRS provides extensive technical and administrative support throughout its publishing services: applying for International Standard Serial Numbers (ISSNs), procuring domains, hosting, reporting Web analytics, maintaining and updating websites, content archiving, and providing training.[6]

---

2   Center for Digital Research and Scholarship. http://cdrs.columbia.edu/.

3   Ibid.

4   *Tremor and Other Hyperkinetic Movements*: http://www.tremorjournal.org/index.php/tremor/about/submissions#authorFees (accessed 6 April 2013).

5   Ibid.

6   Center for Digital Research and Scholarship. http://cdrs.columbia.edu/.

Service Evolution

The scholarly publishing program at CDRS, informed by the broader discussion around publishing in libraries with and without the partnership of a scholarly press, therefore began with an initial development and rollout of publishing services and campus partnership projects. Throughout the short history of the program, however, partners have presented projects to the Center staff with requirements and contexts that fall outside of the expectations of its explicit offerings. As a service of the libraries to the Columbia campus community, CDRS' approach to such project proposals is to be adaptive and modify specifications through amendments to the Master Service Agreements, so long as the resultant project still falls with the CDRS mission statement and scope.[7] This open approach to project partnerships has enabled the staff of the Center to identify some emergent Web publishing project types through the application of some broad categories to be explored in this chapter: support for projects with significant or near-total external development contributions; projects with pronounced Web-first orientations; and projects that supplement existing publications.

Emergent Service Type 1: Hosting With Help

Description: A hosting service for publishing projects with varying technical requirements. Service is provisioned ad hoc, as parameters are determined through initial partner meeting rounds.
Value to Partners: Institutional support and badging. Platform and succession stability. Access to vendor services.
Value to CDRS & Importance to Library-Based Publishing: Increased support for a new class of publishing partners. The convergence of ease of tools and prevalence of technical aptitude calls for services that accommodate sophistication of users and a variety of project types.

There exists a tension among providers of scholarly publishing service in libraries: are providers of a hosting service to campus publications providing publishing services?[8] The appetite for a hosting service remains healthy among CDRS' publishing partners, and the most basic levels of the tiered journal service offering are frequent gateways to deeper publishing commitments and complex digital projects.

There has been a marked uptick in recent months, however, in project proposals that lead with a CDRS-hosting solution beyond the "setup and self-administer" paradigm. Whether the manifestation of a more technically adept disposition toward online publishing, the result of large online help communities, or the proliferation of viable open source publishing platforms, both new and returning publishing partners have entered requests for hosting arrangements that support active publication development on the partner side.

---

[7]   http://cdrs.columbia.edu/cdrsmain/about/.

[8]   See Charles Watkinson's write-up of this discussion at the 2011 Library Publishing Services: Strategies for Success workshop series: http://www.webcitation.org/6FkgAfkJn.

Some examples:

- A political science journal, the editor of which would like to build a custom content management system (CMS) on Rails for closer integration with the CDRS-managed Academic Commons digital repository and to streamline the process of the journal production for his fellow editors. In the proposed workflow, CDRS would become a partner in the maintenance and ongoing development of the journal once the student developer (now a sophomore) graduates and leaves the journal staff.

- *Columbia Business Law Review*: The CBLR editors were afforded a development sandbox to prepare some changes to the journal site that didn't otherwise fit into the CDRS production schedule on an acceptable timetable. Changes to the application code were later quality checked and merged back with the main code repository.

- *Baraza Online*: The publication staff constructed an online publication on Joomla using an external developer to begin the work of community building and to demonstrate proof of concept to acquire institutional support. The project has now become a partner-managed Joomla-to-WordPress migration with hosting and infrastructure support mediated by CDRS.

Institutional context is significant; lack of access to adequate computing resources drives entrepreneurial power-users to seek unconventional opportunities. The problem is especially pronounced at Columbia, where access to LAMP infrastructure[9] is brokered by cost-recovery central IT gatekeepers, barring the majority of savvy users from self-installing common applications, let alone those that run on popular alternative frameworks such as Ruby on Rails.

Emergent Service Type 2: Native Digital Publication

Description: Scholarly publications developed in ways that exploit the online digital format rather than replicate print processes and workflows.
Value to Partners: Combination of Web development, social media, and open access scholarly publishing expertise. Flexible publishing models and full hosting support. Consultation and regular meetings to enhance the project as needs and library publishing landscape shift.
Value to CDRS & Importance to Library-Based Publishing: One-off projects become case studies for testing the limits of available Web publishing platforms, and research for the evolving needs of scholars. CDRS and partners together explore a native digital approach to scholarly publishing that is enhanced by the online format.

This second service type demonstrates CDRS' increasingly prevalent role in support of new, digitally native publications. In this role CDRS is both publisher and Web development team; both advisor on best practices for open access scholarly publishing and guide for utilizing the tools the online medium offers to enhance the content's readability, reuse/share-ability, and reach. These scholars come to the Center with the desire to publish original online scholarly content that is readily available for public consumption, with the need for a system that conforms

---

9   Linux, Apache, MySQL, and PHP.

to both their content and their editorial process, and with a good amount of knowledge of the Web's inherent ability to propagate ideas rapidly among a global community of users.

One example of such a group is a team of scholars in the fields of cultural studies and education, who approached CDRS with initial plans for a new Web-based journal known as *Cultural Formations (Cf.)*. For the *Cf.* team, whose first issue is introduced with the editorial statement, "Education is no longer concentrated in its institutions (was it ever?), but now circulates via popular culture and the media. Tracing its course, we find ourselves, and in our institutions, we see its inverted image..."[10], the act of pushing the boundaries of academic learning, thought, and publication is in itself part of the journal's central message.

A principal need of the *Cf.* editors in coming to CDRS was to find a platform that would enable them to take a collaborative approach to editing submissions to the journal, and then to publish them in an open access online journal. Having explored what was offered by the Public Knowledge Project's (PKP) Online Journal Systems (OJS) software, the editors knew they needed some added flexibility in the editorial workflow beyond what is offered through OJS alone.[11] After trying on several initial solutions, including a combination OJS/WikiScholars[12] site, as well as an Alfresco[13] account for editorial collaboration combined with a WordPress site for journal publication, CDRS and the *Cf.* editors together landed on the system that would work to publish the first issue. The decided-upon CMS was WordPress: a custom CDRS theme based on Carrington Blueprint [14], with the EditFlow[15] plugin installed to provide a flexible editorial workflow.

---

[10]   From http://culturalformations.org/.

[11]   OJS Workflow Chart: http://pkp.sfu.ca/files/OJSinanHour.pdf, p. 12.

[12]   http://www.wikischolars.columbia.edu/.

[13]   Alfresco is a collaborative content management platform used by Columbia University Libraries/Information Services; see http://www.alfresco.com/.

[14]   Carrington Blueprint (http://gastongarcia.com/carringtonbp/category/carrington-blueprint/) is a Carrington Text WordPress Theme (http://carringtontheme.com/) with the Blueprint CSS (http://www.blueprintcss.org/)framework applied. CDRS created a custom theme from this flexible base to meet the design aspirations and content formatting choices of the journal.

[15]   The EditFlow plugin (http://editflow.org/) allows editors to accept submissions, engage in a collaborative peer-review process, communicate with authors through e-mail or in-page comments, and publish the accepted papers to the website, all within the WordPress dashboard.

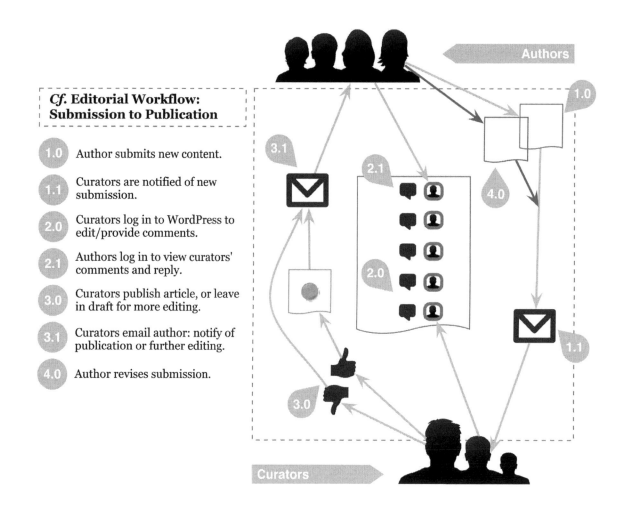

Figure 1: Custom Editing Workflow Diagram Arrived at for Cf., Enabled Through Customization Options Within the Editflow Wordpress Plugin.

CDRS will continue to work with Cf. on a second phase of the project, in pursuit of the following goals:

- Modify the website design and architecture with a focus on responsiveness to enhance readability of content across mobile platforms.

- Structure the content metadata with custom taxonomies to enhance searching.

- Provide tools for descriptive content modeling to improve the representation of various content types within article text (e.g., images, captions, block quotes).

Publishing partners such as the Cf. editors represent the emergence of a demand for a flexible, Web-first model for scholarly publishing in libraries. The CDRS staff accordingly expands its approach to and way of thinking about publication of scholarly materials to be innovators in exploring tools for Web publishing that take advantage of the online medium to enhance the story and bend to meet the needs of new publishing models.

Emergent Service Type 3: Companion Site to Print Publication

Description: CDRS develops, hosts, and maintains a website which acts as a complementary online presence for an existing publication.
Value to Partners: Journal managers maintain existing connections and agreements with established publishers while increasing online presence, especially when such visibility is limited by subscription access. The CDRS partnership enables publication of content that may fall outside of the scope, mandate, and publishing schedule of print formats.
Value to CDRS & Importance to Library-Based Publishing: Ability to accommodate partners in a transitional stage between print and online publication. Opportunity to share ideas in promotion of open access to scholarly research, while providing a mechanism for experimentation with different subscription-based models. Opens the door for partnership with established, institutionally affiliated publications.

A large proportion of CDRS' existing and new publishing partners represent existing print-based publications looking to expand their reach to online audiences. In many cases these are undergraduate- or graduate-level student journals and law reviews that rely on subscription fees to cover publication costs, and typically manage the journal's peer-review process through e-mail or through in-person meetings. While they occasionally express frustration with their editorial workflow, as well as some desire to provide greater access to their journal's content, they are not ready to upend their editorial workflow or to move away from a subscription-based model of financial support. They come to CDRS instead with the intention of building or improving their Web presence: placing some new or teaser content online and establishing a connection to online readership.

> **By strengthening connections with established scholarly publications, CDRS is better positioned to identify areas of support that may be needed as more journals respond to the larger shifts in scholarly communication.**

By strengthening connections with established scholarly publications, CDRS is better positioned to identify areas of support that may be needed as more journals respond to the larger shifts in scholarly communication: 1) print to online media as a central format for publication; and 2) paid to free access to scholarly content.

Some examples:

- The editors of *Social Text* and *Comparative Studies of South Asia, Africa and the Middle East* (CSSAAME), both published through Duke University Press, are working with CDRS to prepare companion sites for their journals that comply with the expectations of their publishing agreements (namely that 90% of the published content needs to remain behind the subscription paywall managed by the publisher).

- *CSSAAME* editors seek to provide a space for short-form articles and discussion pieces as well as multimedia galleries related to the original content that would not translate effectively in the print format.

- *Social Text* has partnered with CDRS to create a sidebar to the main journal, called Is This What Democracy Looks Like?,[16] loaded with timely free-to-access, Creative Commons–licensed essays related to the Occupy Wall Street movement.

- *Current Musicology* journal, in publication since 1965 and with much of its backlist material accessible to the journal editors only in print form,[17] has approached CDRS for assistance in making a transition to both an online submissions and workflow system and open access to journal issue contents. CDRS has initiated efforts in digitization of backlist print journal archives. Further discussion around the provision of editorial workflow management software and new issues publication, as well as consultation around options for flexible open access models in conjunction with support for any impact on subscription revenue, have been a part of the partner support package.

Through partnership with journals in transition between print and online publication models, CDRS has identified a space for library-based publishing services as a bridge between long-standing historical models that no longer suffice and future aspirations for the success and longitude of the publication.

Conclusion, Questions, and Next Steps

The aforementioned emergent service types break some of the expectations built into the current service offerings and will need to be formalized if they are to become more than ad hoc reactions to shifting descriptions of publishing support needs. As noted at the outset, CDRS is situated among a tight cadre of library-based digital service centers at Columbia. Immediate next steps to examine the supportability of these emergent service types therefore include collaboration and discussion among CDRS' internal peers, and this work is already underway.

- The approach at CDRS has been to make every effort to accommodate new partner relationships, especially where providing scholarly publishing support services out of the libraries is challenged beyond its current definitions. Not only do the Master Service Agreement templates need to be updated and amended to accommodate

---

[16]   http://what-democracy-looks-like.com/

[17]   http://www.music.columbia.edu/~curmus/

new opportunities, but a fresh slate of service support questions arise, and answers are yet in short supply:

- How can the technical support be supplied when a partner-developed project breaks after the original developers are no longer with Columbia?

- What kind of upgrade path exists for partner-developed projects?

- How can we best ensure a model of security with the libraries' IT group for a new class of users with direct server access during development?

- What measures should CDRS have in place to encourage responsible code check-in, deployment, and maintenance practices for partners who share development responsibilities?

In responding to these challenges, the goal will be to initiate new service agreement templates and new messaging to the campus community (both directly and through the network of librarians at Columbia). Some of the support requests CDRS receives fall outside the boundaries of available project resources or supported infrastructure or both. Not all service types identified here will mature, but the exercise of categorizing and assessing them provides the Center with the means to anticipate, grow, and advocate for change in effective ways. On the whole, consumers of library-based publishing services are becoming more technologically adept and increasingly accepting of the library as a capable partner in the production of scholarship. Publishing programs in libraries may likewise grow in capacity with their partners, graduating ad hoc solutions into the service suite over time.

References

Kennison, R., Panourgiá, N., & Tartar, H. (2010). Dangerous citizens online: A case study of an author-press-library partnership. *Serials: The Journal for the Serials Community*, 23(2), 145–149. doi:10.1629/231456

Maughan Perry, A., Borchert, C. A., Deliyannides, T. S., Kosavic, A., & Kennison, R. (2011). Libraries as journal publishers. *Serials Review*, 37(3), 196–204. doi:10.1016/j.serrev.2011.06.006

Renfro, P., & Neal, J. G. (2012). The integration of libraries and academic computing at Columbia: New opportunities for internal and external collaboration. *Journal of Library Administration*, 52(2), 162–171. http://dx.doi.org/10.1080/01930826.2012.655594

Publishing Books & E-books

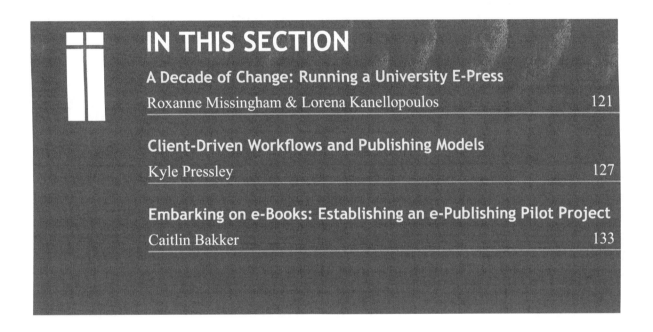

A Decade of Change: Running a University E-Press

Roxanne Missingham & Lorena Kanellopoulos

ANU E Press, The Australian National University

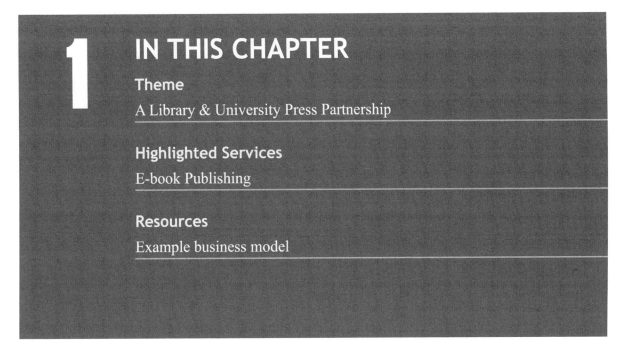

1 **IN THIS CHAPTER**

Theme
A Library & University Press Partnership

Highlighted Services
E-book Publishing

Resources
Example business model

In 2003, The Australian National University established the ANU E Press, an innovative publishing solution that was managed by the library. The vision was of a world-class academic publisher taking advantage of new emerging information and communication technologies, which was a major development for the university. It was a response to pressures within the existing model of scholarly communication. In particular, the establishment of the press derived from a recognition of the urgent need to find an effective mechanism for disseminating ANU scholarship that was of high quality but lacked a ready commercial market; a determination to lower or eliminate barriers to access inherent in traditional academic publishing; an acceptance that within the university the operational overheads of the conventional academic press were no longer affordable; and a realisation that emergent electronic press technologies offered a feasible alternative to the conventional academic press in terms of cost and available infrastructure (Kanellopoulos, 2007).

Works are made available through two brands—ANU E Press (http://epress.anu.edu.au), a fully peer-reviewed program, and ANU eView (http://eview.anu.edu.au), which delivers less scholarly publications that are peer reviewed internally at the university. Both imprints publish books and journals electronically and in print. The online version (referred to as e-books) are published freely online, with printed copies available for purchase through a print-on-demand service.

The university's history in publishing is similar to that of many U.S. universities. The ANU Press, a traditional print publishing operation, existed until 1984. It ceased operation because of financial viability issues.

Discussions on forming an electronically based national university press began in 2001. In 2002, Mr. Colin Steele, University Librarian, and Professor James Fox approached Vice Chancellor Professor Ian Chubb to urge the establishment of an ANU E Press. This led to an initial draft of a scoping document by Colin Steele in August 2002, which was developed over the course of the year. It became a formal proposal supported both by Professor Robin Stanton (Pro Vice Chancellor) and Professor Malcolm Gillies (Deputy Vice Chancellor, Education). The proposal was accepted by Professor Chubb and he agreed to provide funding for $1.2 million for three years under the condition that the Division of Information provide funding to support the press as a long-term program.

In the decade following, achievements have included approximately 5 million downloads, 60 titles a year, a well-established set of editorial boards and peer-review processes, changes in the technical platform, and the maturity to be a B-ranked publishing house (SENSE, 2012, http://www.sense.nl/qualityassessment). Significant change has occurred in the acceptance of open access publishing and open access policy reflecting a maturity in scholarly publishing.

This establishment phase was based on a high degree of advocacy and collaboration between the research community, the library, and leadership in a time of turbulent change in scholarly communication. A major factor in the current success of the press is the continued close collaboration with academics.

Reflections on Contributions to Scholarly Communication

After almost a decade of publishing, the ANU E Press has now reached a level of maturity which is recognized across Australian universities. Two of the Group of 8 (leading research-intensive Australian universities) have developed e-presses modelled on ANU E Press, the University of Adelaide (http://www.adelaide.edu.au/press/) and Monash University Publishing (http://publishing.monash.edu).

The business model has been refined, with a publishing subsidy grant scheme (http://anulib.anu.edu.au/about/library-committees/publications-subsidies-committee/) introduced.

Subsidies are determined by the Publication Subsidy Committee and two rounds are offered throughout the year. Priorities for funding in 2012 were based on the following principles:

- Author/s are publishing with the ANU E Press.

- Priority is given to emerging scholars.

- Non-ANU E Press publishers must be recognized as quality scholarly publishers.

The subsidy can cover items such as copyediting, indexing, and copyright clearance costs of images for authors of ANU publications.

Business Model

Books and journals are published with:

- free access online in a range of formats, including PDF, HTML (view online), ePub and mobi: catering for iPad, Kindle, Apple products, and PC users;

- printed (softcover) copies available for approximately $25. The production of printed copies is contracted out.

ANU E Press bears the costs of the:

- graphic design of the cover,

- publication of the work in the different formats,

- support of the editorial boards and advisory committee,

- running of the website, including the production, website, shopping cart facility, and administration, which includes reporting,

- marketing, promotion, and distribution,

- and dealing with all orders for print copies.

Authors find separate funding for:

- copyediting,

- indexing,

- any image or copyright material costs,

- and other promotional costs such as book launches.

A major factor in the success of the press has been the editorial committees. There are 22 committees covering all subject disciplines. They are very active soliciting proposals and encouraging early-career researchers.

Processes are focused on the authors. The members of the editorial boards work very proactively with academics to encourage the development of publication proposals. Within each faculty and research discipline, board members raise the profile of the press as a publishing option through meetings, seminars, and communication with individual researchers. If feedback is required to encourage a proposal to be better developed, it is undertaken by the author.

When the board approves a publication, ANU E Press staff work very closely with authors. The publishing agreement is very short and clearly written in plain English, and documents including templates are provided with strong support to assist in publication.

Publishing is a streamlined process, with clear instructions on what is required provided to authors. This includes information about the book and how the files are to be provided to the press. The press asks that all files be copyedited and styled (using the E Press template) before production commences. By streamlining these processes, the press is able to provide a turnaround time of between two to four months, as opposed to one to two years as with traditional publishers. Streamlined publishing ensures that the E Press can produce over 60 books a year at a low cost.

ANU E Press has developed a number of cooperative agreements with other organisations to publish a wide range of scholarly materials. The Centre for Aboriginal Economic Policy Research (CAEPR), the Australia and New Zealand School of Government (ANZSOG), Aboriginal History Inc., and Social Sciences Academic Press (China) publish their works through ANU E Press.

Access to titles is convenient and easy. Readers come through Amazon CreateSpace, Google Books, Google Scholar, JSTOR, and the Directory of Open Access Books as well as standard search engines. Additional access can be found through the university's catalogue, the Australian National Bibliographic database, and the National Library of Australia's Trove service. Opening up access by providing bibliographic records to libraries has increased scholars' ease of finding titles.

Authors and readers report that the high quality, peer-reviewed process is one of the most important characteristics of the press. The press is recognised under the government's Higher Education Research Data Collection (HERDC) scheme, which aggregates research income and research publications data submitted by universities each year (Australia Department of Industry, Innovation, Climate Change, Science, Research and Tertiary Education, 2012).

New Challenges

Changes continue in scholarly communication. Open access is undoubtedly the game changer of the decade. The peak body for Australian universities has called for greater commitment to open access:

> Universities Australia believes that there is enormous public benefit in increasing access to the outcomes of all research, especially research that has been publicly funded. There are a number of logistical, practical and commercial issues that need to be addressed to achieve this goal and Universities Australia, with the support of government, is committed to making Australia's high-quality research output freely accessible to all (Universities Australia, 2013, p. 44).

Both major government funding agencies, the Australian Research Council (Australian Research Council, 2013) and National Health and Medical Research Council (National Health and Medical Research Council, 2012), now have open access mandates requiring open access publication of research outputs from funded research to be deposited into institutional repositories. These policies shape revitalised engagement with researchers to increase access to research. The ANU E Press is rising to meet this challenge.

New technologies are also at the core of e-book production. In addition to responding to new readers by producing books in formats that can be read on Kindles and iPads, multimedia has been incorporated into works, such as audio-visual material included in *Sounds in Translation: Intersections of Music, Technology and Society*. It includes a variety of video and audio files that are essential to an understanding of the book's exploration of the idea of the "soundscape" and investigation of acoustic environments. Another example is the publication *Precedence: Social Differentiation in the Austronesian World*, which is accompanied by an hour-long documentary, *Contestations: Dynamics of Precedence in an Eastern Indonesian Domain*, that serves as a companion piece to the text.

And Next...

Scholarly publishing and the ANU E Press are facing a new set of challenges. While the ANU was an early e-book publisher, the industry has now matured, leading to a completely new set of issues. Maintaining a focus on scholarship and research means that only limited insights can be gained from looking to commercial publishing.

The emergence of popular e-book readers such as Kindle and iPads has led to greater use of e-books and has led to a huge increase in the number of e-books published throughout the world. It has created an environment where there is much greater competition for visibility. ANU E Press uses social media such as Twitter and Facebook. Not only are there followers on these social media tools, but tweets are available from the E Press homepage, significantly increasing awareness of new titles. Undoubtedly social media products and new access tools such as Flipboard and Zite will change in the coming years. Our focus is on solutions that adapt and deliver content to these new services.

> Exploring the need for other published resources to support education developments...will create e-publications with richer and more complex content.

All ANU E Presstitles are searchable through search engines, ranking highly with Google Book Search and Google Scholar. With over 100 institutions linking directly to ANU E Press titles, the global access to these e-books is considerable. Growing services to academic libraries to support easy access is also a focus, with Books at JSTOR our newest venture. Data/text mining will be an area for exploration in the coming years, as this has the potential to reach more readers and provide deep access to content.

125

Reviewing issues in 2013 has identified opportunities to expand into new areas of publishing, particularly e-textbooks, by using new technology in areas such as language skills. This will require the development of new skills in the publishing area and a new relationship with teaching staff to understand how online learning can be supported by the press. Exploring the need for other published resources to support education developments, such as massive open online courses (MOOCs), will create e-publications with richer and more complex content.

New forms of publishing are arising: for example, we see a rise of scholarly short monographs providing more immediate communication of ideas. And more forms will come. Our journey as an e-press continues to provide opportunities to reconceptualize the book in the modern scholarly environment.

References

Australian Research Council. (2013). *Open access—The sharing of research insights for mutual benefit*. Canberra: ARC. Retrieved from http://www.arc.gov.au/media/feature_articles/march13_open_access.htm

Australia. Department of Industry, Innovation, Climate Change, Science, Research and Tertiary Education. (2012). *Higher Education Research Data Collection (HERDC)*. Canberra: The Dept. Retrieved from http://www.innovation.gov.au/RESEARCH/RESEARCHBLOCKGRANTS/Pages/HigherEducationResearchDataCollection.aspx

Group of Eight Australia. (2013). Website. Retrieved from http://www.go8.edu.au/

Kanellopoulos, L. (2007). The ANU's Electronic Publisher: ANU E Press. Paper presented to Australian Partnerships for Sustainable repositories conference *The Adaptable Repository* Thursday, 3 May. Retrieved from https://digitalcollections.anu.edu.au/handle/1885/46830

National Health and Medical Research Council. (2012). *Dissemination of Research Findings*. Canberra: NHMRC. Retrieved from http://www.nhmrc.gov.au/grants/policy/dissemination-research-findings

SENSE Research School for Socio-Economic and Natural Sciences of the Environment. (2012). *WASS-SENSE book publishers ranking list 2011*. Amsterdam, SENSE. Retrieved from http://www.sense.nl/qualityassessment

Universities Australia. (2013). *A Smarter Australia: An agenda for Australian higher education 2013–2016*. Canberra: Universities Australia. Retrieved from http://universitiesaustralia.s3.amazonaws.com/wp-content/uploads/2013/02/Universities-Australia-A-Smarter-Australia.pdf

Client-Driven Workflows and Publishing Models

Kyle Pressley[1]

Michigan State University Libraries

2 IN THIS CHAPTER

Theme
Managing a Print-on-Demand Service

Highlighted Services
Book block setup and production on the Espresso Book Machine

Resources
Sample file submission guides & cost analysis elements

The Espresso Book Machine at the Michigan State University Libraries is a unique and evolving self-publishing service. With a business model that requires energetic and creative clients, we've been able to initiate a well-used and well-liked service in the Greater Lansing area. In just two years, the self-publishing service has blossomed to include a community-wide client base, a diverse range of services, and an accessible price-point that a wide range of clients can utilize. Our clients range from MSU faculty, students, and staff to community members in East Lansing and abroad. Our varying services draw people in the door and provide an easy avenue to return for future projects.

---

[1]   Kyle Pressley, as of June 2013, works as the Social Media Specialist at Mercy Health

What Is the Espresso Book Machine?

In Fall 2011, the MSU libraries purchased an Espresso Book Machine (EBM) using a grant furnished by the MSU provost's office. Geared toward promoting and utilizing new technologies in teaching and learning, the EBM fit perfectly into the campus' strategic plan and by extension into the libraries' mission. The grant funded the purchase of the machine and the monthly service costs for three years. This funding mechanism heavily influences how we serve our clients, price our products and services, and, as explored in Ruth Ann Jones' chapter "An Experiment in Progress: The MSU Student Comic Art Anthology," selecting and publishing our own books.

Our service differs from traditional publishing services because of its small mechanical production footprint, its true on-demand nature, and most importantly its client-driven nature. Production of the physical volumes is completed in a small footprint: printing and binding both happen in a 24-ft^2 area. The machine prints a full-color cover and a black-and-white interior, binds the two together, and trims it all in less than 10 minutes. Clients, regardless of demographic, drive their own project from concept to completion. This workflow differs greatly from traditional publishing houses because the client manages all creative processes leading up to the production of the physical volume. To guide and assist people through this process, we offer specialized services and multiple levels of involvement.

What Do We Offer?

Because the Espresso Book Machine is designed for authors who often have little to no design or production knowledge, we've chosen to offer services that assist in both. The EBM requires two files: one PDF (Portable Document Format) for the cover and one PDF for the interior of the book. The software that manages our clients' production files has a few technical requirements for these PDFs. We've settled on a comprehensive offering of services through research of other EBM locations' services, discussions about what the MSU libraries *should* or *should not* offer, and trial-and-error with customers.

The first step in the process is to contact the Espresso Book Machine coordinator and set up an appointment. During this initial contact (done via e-mail or phone call), some basic details of the project are discussed. We get a sense of their project's needs, where they are in the process (writing, editing, etc.), and what their desired timeline is. During the initial meeting, the client chooses between two setup packages: basic (a low-cost option for those clients that are completely ready to print: they've already designed the cover and the interior and it is formatted for print) or premium (a higher-cost option for those who require some coaching through the process and would like to see a proof copy before sending the project to the press). Clients who come with documents that are print-ready have already read and followed the Submission Guidelines, available at http://img.lib.msu.edu/about/ebm/SubmissionsGuidelines. pdf.

Those clients who have either outside designers or are fairly technically proficient themselves tend to choose the basic package. At a low cost, the package only covers the time needed for the EBM coordinator to look over the production files to ensure they're printable and to send the project to the press. The cost is a flat fee, based on the EBM coordinator's salary and the assumption that less than five minutes will be needed to assess the files.

We've found that most people choose the premium package option. This package allows for the EBM coordinator to work with the client and give basic guidance on how to format the interior of the book following the EBM specifications. Though we've made available a comprehensive guide to designing and formatting for the service, we've found many people are more comfortable and better served through hands-on guidance. This package allows for a 30-minute meeting where any number of formatting/design questions can be answered, basic formatting can be accomplished on the spot, and the door for future questions is opened. The package also covers the cost of a proof copy (a single print of the project that is reviewed and accepted by the author before sending the project to the press) and the time required to load the files into our print catalog.

This initial meeting is crucial in setting expectations for the client. Though they drive the process and manage the project, we still work with them to understand the expected production timeline. We've found it to be essential to set checkpoints with the client: finished interior files to us by week two, meet again in week 3, discuss cover options and settle on design by week 2, etc. Often, the client has a clear idea of how long they will need to finish a given step, but sometimes they need a slight suggestion or nudge to accomplish the task. We check in with the client periodically to make sure they're moving along with the agreed timeline and offer any assistance we can.

We've found it to be essential to set checkpoints with the client...

The next step in the process is to discuss additional services required. Many authors find designing the cover to be a difficult task to accomplish. Some have limited design experience and most lack the proper software to execute the formatting. For this reason, we've hired a graphic design student to design covers. Billed at an hourly rate, we work with the client to understand the content of their book, their design preferences, and provide several meetings and drafts to achieve a professional and polished product. This has proven to be successful in both client satisfaction and in expediting production times (the design student is trained in designing specifically for the machine).

In addition to cover design we offer various options when it comes to print production. The production is entirely staff-managed: the EBM coordinator supervises student work to manage production and schedules jobs to go to print. The client can opt for a standard book, or for an additional fee we offer a variety of paper stocks (e.g., white is standard, cream is extra) and color interior printing (for photos or color texts on the book's interior). These two options were added after many clients expressed interest in utilizing the options.

This point is also when we discuss book pricing. Pricing client books has proven to be a challenge due to the nature of our funding, the demand from our clients, and the cost of supplies and maintenance. After discussion and research on other institutions, we decided to price books on a per-page fee. How did we decide that fee? Xerox, the company that sold us the Espresso Book Machine, provided us with a Microsoft Excel calculator to price each book. We can calculate the cost of each book by taking into account the page length of the book, machine maintenance costs, the EBM coordinator's salary, projected sales per year, and fees assessed by On Demand Books. Through varying the page length field in the calculator, we were able to set a retail cost for each page length possible on the machine.

> **We can calculate the cost of each book by taking into account the page length of the book, machine maintenance costs, the EBM coordinator's salary, projected sales per year, and fees assessed by On Demand Books.**

The tool provided by Xerox is excellent in calculating printing costs, but it does not aid in setting the costs for setup packages. We use a balance of market research, percentages of salaries of those involved, and (most importantly) conversations with our client base to decide what to offer and how much to price the package.

Consumables	Labor	Fees
Paper per 5000 sheets	EBM Coordinator Salary	ExpressNet fee per book
Cover stock per sheet	Production time	Lease/amortization
Cover ink per cover		Monthly maintenance contract
Glue		Royalties/shipping feees

Elements of the Cost Calculator

Our clients have been very pleased with our price points. We've adjusted them a few times to account for the increase in the cost of supplies and to cover some of the maintenance costs, though return clients are always accepting of the increase and understand why we're doing it. We've aligned the increases with the change of semester dates and have only increased costs gradually over time.

Who Uses the Service?

Though the service is housed in the MSU libraries, we're not limited to academic/university-affiliated users. By making the services and products available community- (and world-) wide, we've seen an interesting and diverse set of clients. Patrons not necessarily affiliated with the university but with deep MSU/East Lansing roots are our highest-volume clients. They order more, have more projects, and require more time with formatting and development of content. Students and faculty also make up a large portion of our business. Printing dissertations, course packs, anthologies, and other academic-related works is the reason we started the service.

Conclusion

Client-driven models are rare in the publishing world. But for those who wish to retain complete control over their content and want a true print-on-demand solution, self-publishing is the most cost-effective and creatively open process and author can choose. We aim to assist as much or as little as the client wants and mold our services to each individual project, leading to a highly successful and well-received program. Our clients, both on and off campus, take advantage of a service that truly works for them.

Embarking on e-Books: Establishing an e-Publishing Pilot Project

Caitlin Bakker

University of Northern British Columbia

In October 2011, Wilfrid Laurier University launched its institutional repository, Scholars Commons @ Laurier, which aims to promote and preserve works of scholarly, cultural, and historical value associated with the university. WLU Press is home to the long-running Life Writing Series, which features memoirs, letters, and other biographical and autobiographical accounts. Four manuscripts intended for this series were not published when initially submitted in 1998 and had been stored in the archives since that time. In early 2012, Laurier Library began investigating the possibility of using the institutional repository to make these works available.

Upon review, it was found that three of the four manuscripts had since been published elsewhere. *O! Call Back Yesterday* by Ellen Joyce Trott, however, had not. Fortuitously, the Trott manuscript was the only one for which there was a signed publishing agreement on file. In April 2012, Mrs. Trott signed an additional agreement for the electronic publishing and agreed to make the work accessible under a Creative Commons Non-Commercial Attribution license. The author was given the opportunity to revise the work. In October 2012, production on the e-version began.

The workflows established and the tools chosen are determined by the existing skills and expertise available at a specific institution. At Laurier, we were fortunate to be able to incorporate diverse skill sets from a broad range of individuals and departments. The archivists are the resident experts in the digitization and preservation of materials and metadata creation. The university press has the necessary publication experience, specifically in crafting author agreements, providing substantive editing, and creating marketing strategies and features like cover images. This breadth of knowledge is a luxury, but the cultivation of a well-rounded team enhances productivity and improves output. If formal partnerships are not possible, an informal advisory committee could serve the same purpose.

A small team entirely devoted to the task of formatting, conversion, editing, and validation would be ideal. Depending on staff availability, the library may wish to call on student assistants for some of the more routine tasks. While this process is not particularly laborious, it requires concentration and attention to detail. It should not be considered as an additional task to be completed at various times throughout the day, as this will most likely result in a less than optimal product.

The Anatomy of an ePub

While the focus of this paper will be on the practical tools, strategies, and workflows to create ePubs, understanding the ePub as a document format is a necessary starting point. ePub is an open e-book format developed by the International Digital Publishing Forum and is the most widely supported vendor independent file format (Garrish & Gylling, 2013).

An ePub is essentially a zip file that contains a number of other files in various formats, including a special mimetype file, a navigation file, and a META-INF directory. The mimetype file acts like a label, indicating to e-readers that the zipped file contains an ePub, while the META-INF directory holds an XML file that points to bibliographic and structural metadata. The OPS directory holds the content documents—the table of contents (.ncx or .nav), the XHTML files, and the CSS stylesheet, as well as any images that may be included.

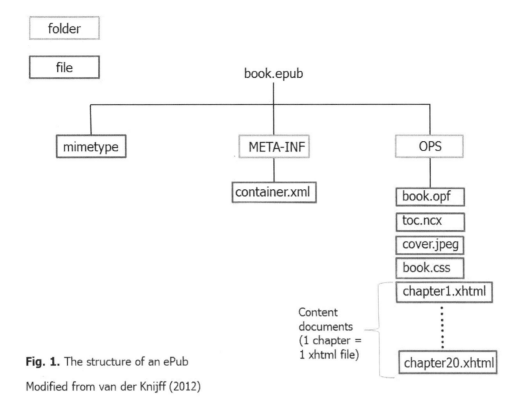

Fig. 1. The structure of an ePub

Modified from van der Knijff (2012)

For our purposes, we are going to focus on the XHTML content documents—the transformed versions of the content—and the means of automatically generating the other files in the most straightforward way possible. "Since an ePub file is essentially XHTML content in a special wrapper, all that is required is that we properly 'wrap' our XHTML content" (Maxwell et al., 2010). While unzipping an ePub can seem like opening Pandora's box, fortunately for libraries, tools exist to create these wrappers.

Conversion

The workflows developed depend on the tools used. In all cases, it will be necessary to work with the files both before and after conversion. The distinction is in where the bulk of time is spent. Using a tool like Book Glutton focuses on correctly formed HTML at the outset while Calibre, the tool ultimately chosen by Laurier, requires tweaking the code after the fact. Although it is possible to automate a great deal of the ePub creation process, this should not be taken to mean that a significant investment of time is unnecessary. The conversion can be automated, but the process of editing and perfecting the item cannot.

> **Using a tool like Book Glutton focuses on correctly formed HTML at the outset while Calibre...requires tweaking the code after the fact.**

Book Glutton (http://www.bookglutton.com/api/convert.html)

Book Glutton involves more upfront effort in crafting HTML materials. Two strategies were explored with this option: the use of Book Glutton's downloadable template and saving items as HTML documents in Microsoft Word. The latter requires the effective and consistent use of styles and other advanced features. The process for creating effective HTML documents in Microsoft Word is somewhat complex and those wishing to pursue this option would be wise to consult a resource such as *EPUB Straight to the Point* by Elizabeth Castro.

The downloadable template is a straightforward option which may appeal to those with less experience in working with HTML. It contains detailed instructions on how to correctly paste and format content, and ensures that all necessary files are included in the conversion process. While Book Glutton is unable to offer batch conversions, it is an online tool, meaning that users do not need to be concerned with installation. This, combined with the template, arguably makes it the most user-friendly option.

Calibre (http://calibre-ebook.com/download)

Calibre offers a batch conversion function, which makes it an attractive tool with regards to scalabilty. However, as the majority of time will be spent in the revision and editing of the ePub, the ability to convert in batch does not overcome all issues of creating multiple ePubs.

There are a limited number of import and conversion options. Although it is possible to import Word documents, for example, the format is not supported for conversion. However, conversion does work fairly well with both text and HTML formats. Calibre has some difficulty determining headings and where files should be split. As such, it is not uncommon to see multiple chapters combined into a single file, or for the chapter title to be listed at the end of the previous chapter.

The Tweak Book function allows the user to "Explode Book" in order to have access to the XHTML, stylesheets, and other related files. While this can similarly be accomplished by saving the ePub to the desktop and unzipping it, Calibre allows the user to consolidate these actions. The files do need to be revised using an ePub editor, but this can be done from the Exploded Book window and changes can be saved directly. After making changes, the user selects "Rebuild Book" and the ePub is immediately altered. This is a more efficient strategy than saving, unzipping, and zipping, and it also eliminates the possibility of having multiple copies in various stages of editing and development.

Editing and Revision

Regardless of which tool and subsequent workflow are selected, it will be necessary to revise and edit the newly converted ePub. In order to do so, an editing tool must be chosen. A review of all available text editors far exceeds the scope of this paper, as they range from the most familiar and simple, such as Notepad, to more complicated proprietary software, such as the Oxygen XML Editor. Unlike the decision in conversion software, the choice of text editor has less impact on workflow and is more indicative of personal preference. It is also possible for different members of the team to work on the same project using different text editors.

In an ideal proofreading and revision scenario, the item would pass through one proofreader, be revised and approved by that individual, and move on to at least one other individual who would re-read the item, make note of any necessary revisions or corrections, and return it to the earlier stages of the process. While it may not be possible to devote two individuals to the proofreading process, it should be noted that the second of these two individuals would have a less significant time commitment than the first. At Laurier, it was necessary to combine these roles into a single position due to staffing constraints. This led to the process being repeated one additional time to ensure accuracy.

Sigil (https://code.google.com/p/sigil/)

Sigil is possibly the most widely known and used ePub editor. It offers an intuitive, user-friendly interface and requires very little technical knowledge. This is a highly adaptable tool that can be used by those individuals with little technical knowledge or experience. However, it also offers more advanced options for content creators more familiar with the ePub creation process.

Sigil features three columns: the book browser, the main text area, and the table of contents. There are two views available within the main text area: the Code View and the Book View, the former giving access to the HTML while the latter mimics the final ePub. This is a particularly useful feature as it allows an individual to seamlessly move between the code and a close approximation of the finished product and eliminates the need to download additional software or use multiple tools to create the same effect.

Notepad ++ (http://notepad-plus-plus.org/)

Unlike Windows' built-in text editor, Notepad++ allows for multiple open tabs, zooming, and find and replace, among other features. Although Windows' basic Notepad can be used to edit ePubs, as all text editors can be used to edit HTML and CSS files, Notepad ++ provides a more user-friendly interface specifically designed for source code editing. Those familiar with text editors such as Vim will find Notepad++ more aesthetically similar to these tools than its namesake.

Notepad++ is a remarkably robust tool, but the familiarity of the text editor lessens resistance to adoption. It should, however, be noted that in order to emulate the comprehensiveness of a tool like Sigil, Notepad++ should be used in conjunction with another software—for example, Calibre or Adobe Digital Editions (http://www.adobe.com/ca/products/digital-editions/download.html)—in order to review both the ePub and the code. Using multiple monitors to view both items simultaneously is a useful means of identifying issues and increasing efficiency in the revision process.

Validation

Despite careful proofreading and revision of the ePub, validation is still a very necessary component of the workflow. It is also the point at which the workflow may appear to become more iterative, as it will likely be necessary to return to the formatting, conversion, or editing stages depending on the number and nature of errors and the workflows selected. Unfortunately, unlike the conversion or editing tools, it is not possible to select a single validation option but instead is necessary to use a variety of tools. At minimum, EpubCheck (https://code.google.com/p/epubcheck/), FlightCrew (https://code.google.com/p/flightcrew/), and the Kindle Previewer from Amazon (http://www.amazon.com/gp/feature.html/?docId=1000765261) should be used to ensure compatibility with most e-readers.

> # Using multiple validators allows for the most thorough examination of the ePub.

Using multiple validators allows for the most thorough examination of the ePub. The different validators will report different errors, and the different tools will offer different levels of specificity in error reporting. As a result, consolidation can prove challenging. The simplest way to keep track of results is through using spreadsheets or tables. This gives an opportunity to make note of the error, its location (this is very important as different devices will display errors in different locations and without the benefit of page numbers as guidance), and the format or device.

File	Position	Error Message	Validator	Meaning/Solution	Location in Text
book.epub/chapter001.html	30,67	calibre_toc_17': fragment identifier is not defined in 'chapter015.html'	epubcheck	reference in table of contents not properly linked to chapter heading in Chapter 15	Table of Contents listing for Chapter 15
book.epub/chapter005.html	11	attribute value expected	FlightCrew	missing attribute value for <p class="">	<p class="">Among a large part of the British population...
book.epub/chapter005.html	11,7	Open quote is expected for attribute "{1}" associated with an element type "class"	epubcheck	missing attribute value for <p class="">	<p class="">Among a large part of the British population...
book.epub/chapter005.html	0000399	Closed unclosed tag: <div class="calibre2" id="calibre_pb_10">	Kindle previewer	unclosed <div> tag?	
book.epub/chapter006.html	0000019	Tag rejected due to improper usage: </img>	Kindle previewer	incorrect use of <img> tag	img 2 (Trott family portrait)
book.epub/chapter006.html	0000024	Tag rejected due to improper usage: </img>	Kindle previewer	incorrect use of <img> tag	img 4 (Evelyn in 1930)
book.epub/chapter006.html	0000029	Tag rejected due to improper usage: </img>	Kindle previewer	incorrect use of <img> tag	img 5 (Ernest in 1933)
book.epub/chapter015.html#calibre_toc_17		Hyperlink not resolved	Kindle previewer	reference in table of contents not properly linked to chapter heading in Chapter 15	Chapter heading of Chapter 15
book.epub/OEBPS/style.css	n/a	This resource is present in the OPF <manifest>, but it's not reachable	FlightCrew		
book.epub/OEBPS/toc.ncx	2	Unsupported protocol in URL	FlightCrew		
book.epub/OEBPS/toc.ncx	20,45	assertion failed: identical playOrder values for navPoint/navTarget/pageTarget that do not refer to same target	epubcheck	duplicate numbers in toc.ncx file	<navPoint id="navPoint-2" playOrder="4">
book.epub/OEBPS/toc.ncx	26,45	assertion failed: playOrder sequence has gaps	epubcheck	missing item in toc.ncx file (navPoint playOrder="3")	
book.epub/OEBPS/toc.ncx	32,45	assertion failed: identical playOrder values for navPoint/navTarget/pageTarget that do not refer to same target	epubcheck	duplicate numbers in toc.ncx file	<navPoint id="navPoint-4" playOrder="4">

Fig 2.

Sample spreadsheet tracking validation errors

In the pilot project, it may also be advisable, when possible, to take more time to reexamine the original text or XHTML files and determine what decisions can be made earlier in the process to streamline the workflow and maximize efficiency at a later point. This is essentially the beginning stages of formatting in-house best practices. It is also an opportunity for the team to familiarize themselves with the validation tools and devices available, and in turn to make note of any idiosyncrasies or points of interest that they may find in using these tools.

Workflows

In the *O! Call Back Yesterday* project, Calibre and Notepad++ were selected as the tools of choice. As a result of this decision, more work was done following the conversion to ePub format rather than before the conversion.

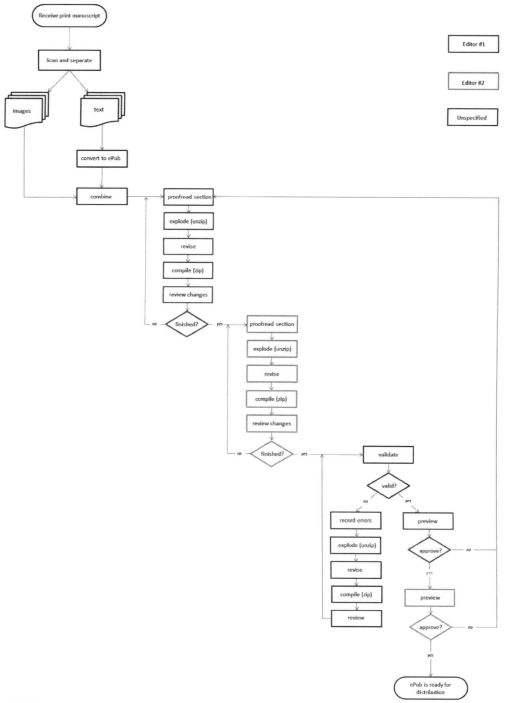

Fig. 3
Basic workflow for ePub production

As the manuscript existed only in paper format, it was necessary to scan the item to create the digital counterpart. The original photographs were also unavailable, so it was necessary to use the photocopied images in the manuscript. Fortunately, the archives were able to capture and enhance these photographs. While the scanning of the document can be done by the library or the archives, it may be preferable to have the latter do so if possible, as they would likely have access to superior machines and OCR software.

The print manuscript was essentially split into two components—the text and the images. Calibre was used to convert the text portion into ePub format. At this time, images were moved into a folder within the ePub, as seen in Figure 1, and HTML was used to insert the pictures and their captions into the document. After ensuring that the ePub was readable, it was proofread for conversion errors such as issues with headings, page breaks, accented characters, and so forth. Proofreading the document should also take aesthetic elements into account, as changes to the CSS are easily made at this time.

At Laurier, the press and library used a shared position which devoted 0.5 FTE to the project. While this met needs for the *O! Call Back Yesterday* project, it may be preferable to have the editing and revision done by two separate individuals. This would allow for a diversity of skills and could accommodate other priorities for staff. The item as a whole is edited at least twice. However, it is important to note that revision is an iterative process in that the item should be saved, recompiled, and opened multiple times. This ensures that the solution implemented for a specific problem is the correct one, and that, if a major error is made, it can be caught sooner rather than later. Recompiling the ePub a minimum of once a chapter is highly recommended.

Once the ePub has been approved by both editors, it moves on to validation. There was some debate as to whether validation should be incorporated into the revision process as part of the iteration. However, it was felt that adding that additional step in the earlier phases would complicate the revision process and would be a less efficient workflow, as the proofreading often corrected validation errors without that step. Validation and subsequent revision will likely be recursive. As was the case with revision in the editing phase, revision due to validation errors should also be done in stages. If one change leads to further validation errors, this becomes very difficult to isolate if all changes are made in a single cycle of revision.

After the item has passed through validation, it is wise to have both editors preview the item to ensure that the item is ready for distribution. Although further revision is unlikely to be necessary at this time, it is an excellent opportunity to view the finished product in its entirety.

While there are many distribution platforms from which to choose, Laurier opted to make the work available through its institutional repository. Libraries that do not have an institutional repository or find that their IR is not a suitable distribution platform should begin to investigate alternatives at the outset of the project. Although we did not have this added complexity in the *O! Call Back Yesterday* project, use of a variety of platforms will call for a review of requirements, particularly with regard to formatting and metadata.

Conclusion

The process of ePub creation is an iterative one of trial and error, more cyclical than linear at many points. Completed in December 2012, the *O! Call Back Yesterday* project gave Laurier an opportunity to expand services and further develop the skills and competencies of staff from multiple departments. It also posed a unique set of challenges. Although not possible in this case, the most successful strategy is one that considers the ePub as an endpoint from the earliest stages of content creation, including the requirements, limitations, and nuances of the item and its production. While issues of scalability and the library's role in the publishing process remain, this initial collaborative venture raised awareness of emerging technologies while strengthening relations and drawing on the unique expertise of the archives, the press, and the library.

References

Castro, E. (2011). *EPUB straight to the point: Creating ebooks for the Apple ipad and other ereaders.* Berkeley, CA: Peachpit Press.

Garrish, M., & Gylling, M. (2013). *EPUB 3 best practices.* Farnham, UK: O'Reilly.

Maxwell, J. W., MacDonald, M., Nicholson, T., Halpape, J., Taggart, S., & Binder, H. (2010). XML production workflows? Start with the web. *Journal of Electronic Publishing, 13*(1). doi: http://dx.doi.org/10.3998/3336451.0013.106

van der Knijff, J. (2012). EPUB for archival preservation. Report for the National Library of the Netherlands. Retrieved from http://www.openplanetsfoundation.org/system/files/epubForArchivalPreservation20072012ExternalDistribution.pdf.

The author would like to thank Julia Hendry and Cindy Preece of Wilfrid Laurier University Archives & Special Collections, Dr. Brian Henderson and all of the staff at WLU Press, Carol Stephenson at OCUL, and, most importantly, Mrs. Trott, for giving us the opportunity to share her story.

Library as
Journal Publisher:
Organizational Aspects of
Journal Publishing

Journals Are People, Too: The Human Factor in Sustainable Journal Publishing Partnerships

Rebecca A. Welzenbach

Michigan Publishing, University of Michigan Library

1 **IN THIS CHAPTER**

Theme

Sustainability in Journal Publishing

Highlighted Service

Print and online journal hosting & production

Resources

Example partnership proposal form

The University of Michigan Library has been publishing journals on the Web since the late 1990s. To date, Michigan Publishing has partnered with 32 journals and serial conference proceedings (MPublishing Journals, 2012). We have been quite catholic in our approach to new projects: our journals' disciplines vary from music to chemistry, philosophy to feminist studies. Journals are not required to have any connection with the University of Michigan (although we prioritize supporting faculty where possible), nor have they been required to adhere to any single model of distribution: most are open access, some delay publishing material online up to one year after publishing a print issue, and two use a traditional subscription-based model. Typically, journal editors manage submissions, review, and editing (including copyediting), delivering the final content to Michigan Publishing for publication on our platform.

Of our 32 partners, six have permanently ceased publication and three are on indefinite hiatus. As of May 2013, 10 had published new content in 2013, activity which ranges from producing new articles each week to delivering four volumes of backlogged content at once after a long silence. Thirteen had not yet published new content in 2013, which might indicate that they are right on schedule to publish their spring issue soon, that they have forgotten to send us the files for their most recent issue, or that they have ceased to publish altogether. The term "serial," suggesting regularity, consistency, and predictability, does not quite capture the wide range of activity we observe among our journal partners each year.

As coordinator of Michigan Publishing's journals program (a new position as of November 2012), it is my job to chart the future course of our journal publishing program. Michigan Publishing's aim is to "create innovative, sustainable structures for the broad dissemination and enduring preservation of the scholarly conversation," in service of a larger goal: "to ensure that the benefits of scholarship accrue to everyone" (MPublishing About Us, 2012). We want to make excellent scholarship available to as wide an audience as possible, and to preserve and distribute work that might otherwise remain unseen.

...when it comes to journals, excellence and ideals are not enough.

However, when it comes to journals, excellence and ideals are not enough. Sustainable journal publishing depends on long-term relationships: when we form a partnership, we agree to work with the editors for the life of the journal, and commit to helping them make that life as long and productive as possible. Trends, technologies, and practices will come and go over time. It is the human factor—the motivations, priorities, goals, expectations, and engagement of each editor that determines whether a journal will thrive in partnership with us. I want to clarify that here I am not talking about the success of the journal according to traditional measures of impact, citations, or circulation. Rather, I am referring to the success of the relationship between the library and the publication: Is the partnership fruitful? Sustainable? Do both parties benefit?

The answers are not always so clear. Our partnership agreements outline what each party has agreed to do, but do not address *why* we are doing it, or whether our "whys" are the same, complementary, or at odds. Our journal partnerships are typically born when a person or small group approaches us *for one reason or another*, and we decide to take on the project, *for one reason or another*. Hitting on the right combination of reasons is the key to developing a partnership that will thrive. The wrong combination can lead to projects that drain resources on both sides, without meeting the expectations of either.

Motivating Factors for Journals

Michigan Publishing provides similar services to most of our journal partners, so it is easy to forget that they initially came to us with different needs and goals. Even where our services are the same, their reactions, expectations, and level of engagement will all be shaped by these initial driving factors, some of which I describe below. These examples, of course, are not exhaustive, but portray some common circumstances in our shop.

Tech Support

It is not uncommon for the editor of an existing print journal to seek a partnership with Michigan Publishing in order to establish an electronic version of their publication. Our ready-built infrastructure, support for conversion of content to XML, and commitment to long-term preservation are appealing to individual editors and small scholarly societies lacking the funds, technical expertise, or institutional home base to put their journal online. Because the print journal is already up and running, this can be a great way to get a publication off the ground quickly. However, the long-term success of the partnership depends on the extent to which the journal is willing to reconfigure its existing practices to support collaboration with Michigan Publishing.

For example, when journals continue to publish in print on their own, delivering the final files to Michigan Publishing is often the last step in their process, sometimes even after the issue has been published and distributed. If there is an embargo between print and online publication, the issue might not be expected to go online until months later. In these cases, editorial staff sometimes forget to send the files, or even to document this step so that new staff know to do this. We have on occasion contacted a journal to inquire about recent issues, only to discover that the editorial board had turned over, and the new staff did not know about our partnership.

On the other hand, if the editors of the journal are motivated to move to an online-first model, there is a good opportunity for mutual benefit. Because Michigan Publishing is the primary home for the publication, the editors cannot forget to stay in touch. When issues already exist, we can add the journal to our platform in short order. The editors' labor and costs are reduced because they no longer need to support typesetting, printing, or subscriptions/circulation. Michigan Publishing benefits from adding a known publication to its portfolio. In this scenario, the motivations of the journal align with the practical requirements of the partnership, so working together comes naturally.

Backup Plan

In three cases, Michigan Publishing has partnered with journals that are already publishing on their own external websites. These editors are often drawn to the long-term preservation provided by the library. More than one editor has alluded to anxiety about what will happen to their journal when they retire: journals are frequently the pet projects of extremely dedicated individuals who worry about handing off the work or losing hosting/programming support at their home institution if they leave. Michigan Publishing can provide a neutral, stable home for this content—one less thing for the editor to worry about as he or she plans for the future of the journal. These partnerships are most satisfactory when the editor is willing to make Michigan Publishing the primary home for the journal's content. This way, we can avoid duplicating content, falling out of sync if an article changes, and confusing users (including third-party indexing sites) about where the canonical home for the content is. However, we often find that there are obstacles to doing this. In two cases, our partner was simply invested in the look, feel, and functionality of their own website, and unwilling to switch to our platform. In a third case, the partner wants to make Michigan Publishing its primary home, but fully integrating the journal's idiosyncratic infrastructure for managing submissions and publishing manuscripts with our own system has turned out to be the work of years.

When content lives in two places, editors tend to think of their own website as "the journal," and Michigan Publishing's version as "the archive." Whether or not we consider this a successful partnership depends a great deal on how we define success: we have ensured long-term preservation of and access to this content, and met the needs of the editor. As a *library* publisher, perhaps we have done well. On the other hand, editors sometimes forget to send new issues on to us, meaning we must chase them down or risk our version of the publication becoming outdated. As well, Michigan Publishing becomes rather invisible as a participant in the journal's publication. For example, one of our journals is listed in the Directory of Open Access Journals (http://www.doaj.org/) only under its external host. Our archive is not mentioned. In this case, Michigan Publishing does not get much return on investment, in terms of visibility or reputation, for hosting and preserving this content. As a library *publisher*, it is difficult to make the case that this is a successful partnership.

Breaking New Ground

Some of our most energetic, symbiotic partnerships occur when editors develop a new journal with Michigan Publishing as the original publisher. In these cases, the journal's workflows and practices can be established from the start to integrate with Michigan Publishing's and the new journal benefits from its affiliation with our brand. Usually, we share an interest in open access and in exploring new models of editing and review. These editors are also typically quite involved: They tend to be the most fastidious about previewing content before it goes online, because Michigan Publishing is the site of first publication. They are also the most likely to request improvements to our interface and site functionality, because they envision their journal looking and behaving a certain way. These requests often lead to valuable developments that can be applied across the board, benefiting all of our journals.

Establishing new publications together with editors is exciting, meaningful work. However, it is a heavily front-loaded, labor-intensive process. It can take several years from initial discussions to the publication of the first issue, and without an ongoing publication schedule providing regular opportunities to communicate, it is easy to fall out of touch. Some journals fade away before they ever publish a first issue. Others fall off the radar for years, resurfacing suddenly, ready to go, at a moment when we may not have the capacity to leap into action. It is disheartening to invest a great deal of time into a publication that struggles to get off the ground. While it is certainly important to expect change and remain flexible, it is also important to nurture this nascent partnership by keeping in regular contact with the editors so that changes of direction come to light sooner rather than later.

Conclusion

As Michigan Publishing becomes more strategic and proactive about acquiring new journals, I aim to build on the example of our most fruitful partnerships. We have developed several strategies for better understanding our partners' motivations and needs early on in our planning process. Perhaps most importantly, we have developed a proposal form (Appendix) that asks editors to describe the working relationship they envision with Michigan Publishing (among other things). There is no single right answer to this question, but asking it establishes the expectation that our partnership will require mutual engagement and collaboration, and gives us a glimpse of the partners' point of view.

> Asking [editors to describe the working relationship] establishes the expectation that our partnership will require mutual engagement and collaboration...

Here's the rub: in order to evaluate the fit of a partners' needs and priorities, we must first be able to clearly identify our own. This is the real challenge that lies before us and, I wager, any library publishing operation. It is easy enough to tell when a partnership is not going well—communication lags, issues fall out of date, the partner does not seem to understand us. But unless we can state clearly what we want out of a publishing partnership, we will not be able to tell whether we have achieved it, or predict whether a future project is likely to. Broad goals to do with affordable, open, responsive preservation and dissemination of the scholarly record keep our eyes on the prize, but for the day-to-day work of sustaining journals and their

> Here's the rub: in order to evaluate the fit of a partners' needs and priorities, we must first be able to clearly identify our own.

champions, we need to get more specific. There must be something we want. After all, library publishers are people too.

References

Michigan Publishing. (2012). MPublishing Journals [web page]. Retrieved from http://www.publishing.umich.edu/publications/journals/

Michigan Publishing. (2012). MPublishing About Us [web page]. Retrieved from http://www.publishing.umich.edu/about/

Appendix

Example of Michigan Publishing journal partnership proposal form:

Michigan Publishing works with scholars to design affordable and sustainable publishing solutions for material of interest to scholars in many fields, extends the University of Michigan Library's commitment to the production and distribution of scholarship, and experiments with new possibilities for library-based publishing.

If you are interested in becoming a publishing partner, supplying details about your project will help us determine whether it is a good fit for the services we offer. It will also help us identify which tools and resources might suit your needs most effectively.

Please send A) two letters of reference and B) your completed application to mpublishing@umich.edu. Letters of reference should be written by individual(s) who can speak to the role your publication will play in its field, and administrator(s) able to provide information about levels of institutional commitment and support.

Institutional Information

Please supply your name, email, phone, departmental affiliation, website URL, and name (or working title) of your proposed project. Tell us about any supporting institutional framework, organizations, or societies affiliated with your project. What is the mission or charge of each group for which your publication will be an organ?

Project Goals & Audience

Please describe your project's ultimate purpose. Be as specific as you can in providing context for this project, including the field in which it will be positioned, and the contribution it aims to make to that field. This will help us to assess how the project corresponds to Michigan Publishing's mission, and understand the types of resources (editorial, design, programming, etc.) you will need to achieve your goals.

Please describe your projected (or existing) readership. Is your publication aimed at a general readership, a scholarly readership, or somewhere in between? Are there existing publications for your readership? Where else are your contributors publishing their work? What distinguishes your publication from existing journals in this field?

Content

Please tell us about the current status of your project (e.g. under development, content solicited but not yet written, content finished and in need of distribution channels, etc.). What is your anticipated timeline for the initial launch of your publication, as well as the timeline for future issues (if applicable)?

What kind of formats will your project include? Please describe analog and digital formats that will be included (word processing files, XML/HTML, PDFs, digital images, books or documents to be scanned, multimedia, etc.).

Regarding the appearance and functionality of your publication, please describe what you hope your project will look like and how your readers will engage with it—online and/or in print (if applicable). If there are existing online or print publications that you have looked to for inspiration, please list them, along with specifics about why they appeal to you.

If your project will include both print and online components, please be sure to describe the particulars of each as applicable (frequency of publication, trim size, design requirements, etc.) as well as the role each format plays in meeting your project's overall goals as described above.

Editorial & Peer Review

Please describe your editorial workflow and the composition of your editorial board (names, titles, affiliations, etc.). If published content will undergo peer review, please describe the criteria for selecting reviewers as well as the guidelines for reviewing submissions.

Financing & Support

Do you plan to make your publication available for free (as an Open Access resource) or for a fee? Please provide a few sentences explaining the rationale behind your choice. Please describe any revenue streams, financial resources, or institutional support that will be used to subsidize your publication, including available labor and expertise at your disposal.

Wayne State University Press and Libraries: A Case Study of a Library and University Press Journal Publishing Partnership

Joshua Neds-Fox, Lauren Crocker, & Alicia Vonderharr

Wayne State University

2 IN THIS CHAPTER

Theme
Workflow & organization between a library & press publishing partnership

Software/Platforms Utilized
Digital Commons by bepress

Highlighted Service
Print and online journal hosting & production

Resources
Example library and press collaborative workflow and discussion of responsibilities & skill-set for each party

The Wayne State University Press Journals program comprises 11 scholarly print serials. When the press sought to deliver its journals electronically, in-house, for the first time, it established a mutually beneficial collaboration with the Wayne State University Libraries to host, format, manage, and preserve its content online. A strong university press/library partnership is possible because the goals of the two institutions are complementary: both exist to support the research, teaching, and service mission of the university. By collaborating, the press extends the reach of its scholarly journal publications by making them available, in-house, digitally. The libraries expand their intra-institutional services and collections available to their constituents, and advance their scholarly communications agenda. Both increase the value of investments in infrastructure. This case study explores the relationship between the two units, describing what one successful press/library partnership looks like.

History of the Partnership

Wayne State University Press publishes only one journal in the natural sciences, *Human Biology*. It is especially important for journals in this field to maintain a strong online presence. The libraries had subscribed to bepress's Digital Commons (a hosted institutional repository software with a range of modules, including a full journal publishing platform) in 2005, but as of 2010 it remained underutilized, and the libraries were interested in expanding its use. In support of that goal, a position was created in the libraries specifically tasked with developing the institutional repository. Coincidentally, the press was searching for a tool to support the online publication of *Human Biology* while the libraries were hiring the institutional repository specialist. Upon learning of the mutual goal, the two started the discussion about bringing *Human Biology* into DigitalCommons@WayneState (http://digitalcommons.wayne.edu, our implementation of the Digital Commons software, also DC@WSU). This ultimately involved the press re-creating the journal's online home as a site inside DigitalCommons@WayneState, and preparing the necessary policies and pages. The press sent the journal's current content, both digital and print, to the libraries, who processed and loaded it into the newly created site.

Although the press and libraries' budgets are separate, the existence of a complete editorial and hosting resource for journals inside the Wayne State ecosystem, with costs justified for the libraries by its alternate function as an institutional repository, presented such an opportunity for synergy between the units that it seemed irresponsible not to pursue it. With the success of *Human Biology*'s implementation, the press quickly sought to offer all of its journals on the Digital Commons platform, and the two entered into partnership with a memorandum of understanding regarding shared services.

Organization of Workflow

The press oversees the production of their journals, including copyediting, typesetting, design, printing, and distribution. Because the dissemination of digital files occurs at the end of the production process, the initial press workflow is unchanged by the partnership. Upon receipt of the final files from the compositor, the press distributes final PDF files to all online partners, including the libraries (files are transferred via SFTP over an internal network).

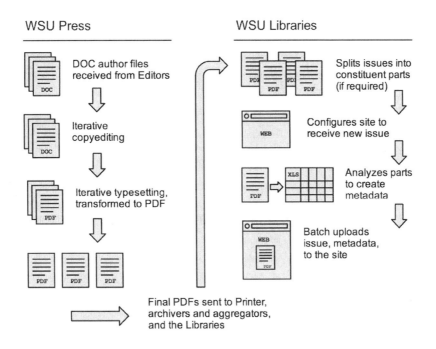

Figure 1. New issue workflow from Press to Libraries.

The libraries mount new issues upon receipt of files from the press, and have been responsible for the digitization of print back issues and the ingest of back files to DigitalCommons@ WayneState. These tasks generally involve document analysis and metadata creation for each issue, and may also include OCR for back issues or files delivered as image-based PDFs. The libraries also handle the bulk of training for journal editors and other parties administering EditKit (the journal submission and publishing backend to the Digital Commons Journal module).

The press and libraries share responsibility for configuration and administration of the backend of DC@WSU. This is done informally, with each unit delegating duties between themselves as issues arise. For example, it is equally likely that press or libraries staff will respond to editors when they encounter a problem with the configuration of their particular journal or editorial process, and often both units will handle aspects of an individual case. Communication is generally handled via e-mail, although the staff usually meet together two to three times a month, with other face-to-face meetings taking place as needed for specific tasks.

One of the elements helping make the partnership work is a shared journals intern, jointly interviewed and hired by the WSU Press Journals department and the libraries' Digital Publishing team, and splitting time between the two. The internship is unpaid, but the split workload gives the position a broad exposure to both traditional publisher workflows and digital library workflows. This window into the separate cultures and concerns of both units is of benefit to the internship. The intern participates in metadata creation and batch ingest of material to the journals' websites. On the press side, the intern assists in the production of journal issues and producing marketing materials for Wayne State University Press journals.

Making the subscription journal available digitally on a traditionally open-access platform requires a per-article payment layer. Wayne State University Press uses Authorize.Net, a payment gateway service provider, to accept credit card payments ($5/$10 per article) through DC@WSU. Users receive immediate access upon payment without having to visit a third-party site to complete transactions. This per-article payment layer has been valuable to the press in providing instant access to scholars and students who do not have digital access via their institutions or personal subscriptions. *Human Biology*, situated in a field that values online open access, takes advantage of Digital Commons's core module to offer a pre-print series in advance of publication. These are cross-linked both from the landing page of the journal and at the article level once the definitive issue is posted.

Skills and Lessons Learned

The partnership has been surprisingly instructive. One of the chief benefits has been the sharing of skill sets exclusive to either the publishing or library worlds. These have ranged broadly beyond the mere administration of the DC@WSU system. As outlined in the workflows above, the libraries have taken the lead in teaching press staff and scholarly journal editors how to use DC@WSU to meet their various needs. The press in turn has shared their understanding of the intricacies of their 11 scholarly journals, including the differences among editorial staffs and cultures, format, content, and the myriad "exceptions to the rule" that comprise each individual journal.

The press has expanded its understanding of metadata and XML schemas. When the press decided to start supplying their own XML citation data for a science journal in the PubMed database, the libraries assisted with technical help conforming to PubMed's schema (PubMed Journal Article DTD Version 2.6, http://www.ncbi.nlm.nih.gov/books/NBK3828/). This included XML basics, like how to determine required vs. optional elements and attributes and how to correctly nest tags—skills the libraries find to be second nature by now but which the press is just acquiring. The press has also greatly improved the customer service offered to journal subscribers, benefitting from the libraries' experience providing off-campus access to vendor materials. Digital Commons can provide access via IP or domain recognition, or through individual user accounts. Armed with the knowledge of how the Wayne State University Libraries provide off-campus authentication to their students and faculty (through a proxy service), the press has been able to suggest alternatives to customers who wish to provide this for their students.

The libraries have been afforded a crash-course in PDFs and publication standards. Making backlist issues available online has required digitizing print volumes, subjecting the output to optical character recognition (OCR), and generating readable PDFs. Digitization required that the libraries acquire and implement a high-end book scanner (ATIZ BookDrive Pro), and OCR required an investment in enterprise-grade software (ABBYY Enterprise Edition). Even so, the PDFs that libraries are accustomed to interacting with in the archive/preservation world do not always follow the same specifications that are required in the print publishing world. Where libraries are often comfortable with machine OCR and Dublin Core metadata, publishers require "Web-ready" PDFs, meaning internally cross-linked, >99% accurate OCR, and optimized for smaller file sizes (when submitting material to aggregators like Project Muse, WSU Press conforms to the NISO JATS standard).

> **Where libraries are often comfortable with machine OCR and Dublin Core metadata, publishers require "Web-ready" PDFs, meaning internally cross-linked, >99% accurate OCR, and optimized for smaller file sizes.**

Along the same lines, the press has learned much about the working world of librarianship. The libraries have set up meet-and-greet sessions with the press and libraries staff in order to teach the press more about library acquisitions and the continuing needs of academic libraries during the shift from print to digital. The libraries were very forthcoming with their personal recommendations about specific online partners and the benefits they bring, and the press learned how link resolvers work to connect individual journals to their corresponding location with an external aggregator. This insight has allowed the press to make educated decisions regarding the aggregators through which to disseminate their journals, deciding to actively pursue a partnership with JSTOR and to keep new journals restricted to Project Muse and JSTOR. This has positively benefited the press's library subscribers and users, including the WSU libraries.

The libraries gained valuable insight into the nature of a scholarly journal, through collaboration with the press and its processes, but often simply through the logistical contortions necessary to bring individual issues online. What constitutes a journal? Is it a collection of articles, perhaps divided into various types (feature, book review, editorial)? Is it whole, to be offered as a single document, like a monograph (and analogous to its print counterpart)? What about journals with thematic (as opposed to structural) divisions, which aren't as easily captured in the Digital Commons platform? Figure 2 shows example elements from three different WSU Press journals. *Merrill-Palmer Quarterly* is a traditional journal in the social sciences, and its articles can be represented as discrete elements. Individual issues of *Framework*, a humanities journal, are often curated, and internal structures with no analogue in Digital Commons, like "dossiers," can complicate the presentation of individual articles; often in this case, many articles are concatenated into one document. *Fairy Tale Review* is a literary review, and the varied length and format of its contents makes offering individual works problematic; each issue is presented as a whole.

157

Figure 2. Comparison of three WSU Press journals with different content models. Some journals lend themselves to an atomized structure (each article a discrete element). Others require aggregating some or all discrete elements together in a dossier- or issue-based structure.

Knowing when to atomize the content in a journal and when to treat a journal issue like a monograph has paid dividends for the libraries, e.g., when considering how to model content for journals and journal-like digital objects being preserved in other library systems outside DC@WSU. The libraries have already developed content models for journal-like objects (in this case, digitized issues of a weekly newspaper) based on experience with the press: an article or section is part of an issue (an article is optionally part of a section), an issue is part of a volume, and a volume is part of a periodical. This model allows the libraries to ingest journals and journal elements into a digital object repository (Fedora Commons) for future front-end development. In fact, the difficulty in modeling journal issues to fit the Digital Commons repository software informed the libraries' decision to begin developing a Fedora Commons repository, where digital objects might be more variously and robustly modeled.

The libraries have also been able to assess what a sustainable journal production process might look like for open access journals published in-house. The press has been invaluable in sharing its experience and perspective on managing editorial staff, and the libraries have developed a familiarity with copyediting and scholarly editorial processes by working with the pre-print and pre-press versions of the documents, and by the many snap decisions that must be made regarding arrangement and formatting of articles online. The libraries' sense of the workload provides a baseline for planning and policy regarding future journal projects outside the press partnership.

Positive Press/Library Relationship

The positive relationship that has developed between the libraries and the press has proved essential in running a successful operation. It makes possible the loose, almost informal division of labor, and there's a sense of a free exchange of information. The libraries gain a good understanding of current trends in publishing, while the press keeps up-to-date on developments involving open access journals and fair use, among other topics. Together, the press and libraries are able to have meaningful discussions on important topics, often uncovering coinciding interests and ideals.

This collaboration has afforded a number of other expected and unexpected benefits. The partners enjoy a unique advancement of parallel goals: the press expands its publishing capacity without incurring extra costs, and offers native electronic formats, per-article access, and an electronic backlist; the libraries expand their digital publishing activities, collaborate intra-institutionally, and establish digital workflows (e.g., OCR) that support a range of library activities. Because the partnership is unforced, the partners avoid the dysfunction that can arise when units are combined by administrative fiat, and are free to expand their activities in any mutually agreeable direction.

As an example, the press and libraries, upon the demonstration of the successful journals collaboration, have expanded the scope of their partnership. The units are exploring the digitization of print backlist monographs, which would provide the press with accurate OCR and metadata to send to conversion vendors and the libraries with e-book titles to offer the Wayne State community. More informally and perhaps more valuable in the long term, the relationship has opened up avenues of communication that weren't previously available: conversations between the two about a variety of issues (how do interpretations of recent judicial copyright decisions differ between the libraries and press, for instance) have resulted in a broader range of understanding for both parties, and uncovered areas (e.g., perspectives on fair use) where the two share unexpected common ground.

Conclusion

As academic libraries continue to cross over into the publishing world, and university budgets adjust to future economic realities, partnerships like that between the Wayne State University press and libraries will look more and more attractive to both academic presses and libraries. As outlined here, such partnerships strengthen the university as a whole and the units specifically, provide for expanded service by both partners, and pay dividends in skill-sharing and new perspectives. Wayne State University Press and Libraries look forward to continued fruitful collaboration as both gain a better picture of exactly what a university press and an academic library can aspire to be.

Publishing *Inti*: A Suite of Services Case Study

Mark J. Caprio & Christiane Marie Landry

Providence College

3 IN THIS CHAPTER

Theme

Establishment of a publishing services department

Highlighted Service

Journal publishing & archives

Software/Platforms Utilized

Digital Commons by bepress & Adobe InDesign

Resources

Example organizational charts and production templates

Supporting the teaching, learning, and research (TLR) continuum is an organizing principle for engagement between Providence College's Phillips Memorial Library (PML) and its community—a lens through which all PML departments realize their mission. The Digital Publishing Services (DPS) Department (initially called "Digital Services Department") at the PML was established in 2007 to investigate new collaborations and publishing models for supporting local faculty and student scholarship and creative works. The mission of DPS is demonstrated through its collaboration with the faculty editor of the journal *Inti: La revista de literatura hispánica*.[1]

Digital Publishing Services: A History

Phase I: Tactical

The PML at Providence College (PC) is part of a consortium of higher education and special libraries (i.e., Higher Education Library and Information Network/HELIN Consortium). Early in 2005, the HELIN Central Office, supported by the HELIN Board of Directors, submitted a grant application to the Davis Educational Foundation to support implementation of a consortium-wide institutional repository (IR). With grant funds, a distinct repository would be created for each participating HELIN institutional library. Each library's IR would implement unique institutional domain names and branding. Additionally, an "umbrella site" with a HELIN brand would be created encompassing all content included in each IR for cross-searching, and metadata with links to IR content pages would be harvested from each repository and ingested into the consortium-wide single catalog.

In August 2005, a new library director arrived at PC's PML, and at the end of 2005, HELIN was awarded the aforementioned grant. The library director recognized the potential value of IRs and had previous experience with them, but his previous experience had been with an open source solution that required extensive local support resources. The HELIN grant application had cited bepress (Digital Commons) as its technical infrastructure partner (including ongoing support for IR development), and the library director was enthusiastic to explore this software as a service solution (SaaS).

In early 2006, the library director, recognizing the need for dedicated support to IR development and supporting services, reengineered an existing, open faculty-librarian position accommodating Digital Commons-PC[2] needs. The open cataloging position was restructured as the Cataloging and Digital Projects Librarian (CDPL). Fifty percent of this position's energies would provide oversight of cataloging services, and fifty percent would manage IR development, working closely with Special and Archival Collections to identify and digitize materials for publication through Digital Commons. The debut (project presentations and discussion) to formally announce Digital Commons to the PC community was scheduled for February 14, 2007.

At the time of the opening, there were still no formal facilities (workspace/lab) or dedicated staff to support the new work beyond fifty percent of the CDPL's time. The library director, along with the CDPL, developed plans for pertinent equipment, facilities (space), and additional staff. Furniture and technology requests were submitted through existing college funding channels to outfit a vacant space within the library (i.e., desks, chairs, Macintosh computers, scanners, optical character recognition [OCR] software, and Adobe's Creative Suite). Two non-exempt, open positions (one full-time, one half-time), from Archives and Interlibrary Loan (ILL) respectively, were restructured and moved to a newly created Digital Services Department, both reporting to the CDPL. With the new department in place, the library director and CDPL increased their engagement with the campus community, identifying college- or faculty-owned (copyright-secured) collections that would gain benefit and bring benefit to the research audience through digitization and publication.

Phase II: Agile-Strategic

The Digital Services Department continued to evolve, growing in directions informed by advances in technology, changes in scholarly communication, and institutional needs. Early in 2009, the CDPL left for another position. The library director once again reviewed the position relative to library strategic thinking/planning and decided to shift the position's focus to more strongly develop a library digital services program (e.g., the position's title descriptors were flipped, becoming Digital Services and Cataloging). The position was filled in January 2010, and shortly thereafter an additional full-time staff position was added to the Digital Services Department from an obsolesced library function. The Digital Services and Cataloging Librarian position was again refocused and renamed in 2011 as the Head of Digital Publishing Services. This new title reflected the library's commitment to establish a set of publishing services and to accommodate further expansion of services and staff within the department (the department title also changed to Digital Publishing Services).

Since 2011, the department has increased its staff (6.5 FTE), redefined and promoted existing staff, and increased collaboration across the college with students and faculty, significantly increasing digital publication output and development of open educational resources. In 2011, Digital Publishing Services Coordinator and Digital Media Specialist positions were created in response to increased requests for services and the need for increased outreach to the community. The department no longer simply provides support services, but rather increasingly behaves as an equal collaborative partner in the creation, management, preservation, and delivery of TLR resources.

> **Digital Publishing Services staff assist and collaborate in...publication options, copyright advisement, scanning/digitization, media creation, graphic design, text processing and encoding, metadata consultation, and publishing platform R&D.**

As of this writing, Digital Publishing Services[3] (DPS) staff assist and collaborate in a wide variety of knowledge creation activities, providing expertise in areas such as publication options (Web and print), copyright advisement, scanning/digitization, media creation, graphic design, text processing (OCR) and encoding (TEI), metadata consultation, and publishing platform R&D. The DPS Lab[4] is equipped with high-end 27-inch iMacs and PCs, which include a suite of media creation software, and a selection of scanners, digital cameras, and audio recorders for capturing analog as digital surrogates.

Engaging Inti

In 2007, *Inti*'s faculty editor supported Digital Publishing Services' proposal to digitize and OCR (optical character recognition) early issues, providing greater journal visibility through Digital Commons, **INTI Archivo**.[5] This early project phase focused on digitizing issues using a method of reformatting optically recognized text. Initial workflows evolved over time through trial and error, primarily involving scanning bound print issues on a flatbed scanner (using SilverFast Ai scanning software) and performing OCR using ABBYY FineReader. DPS staff then manipulated optically recognized text in a text editor to imitate the corresponding print issue's layout, exporting it as a PDF. In 2011 (again using ABBYY), DPS transitioned from reformatting optically recognized text to recognized text-under-image digital surrogates. This method provided both full text searchability and views of page image originals. Text-under-image digital surrogates restored a more authentic journal-viewing user experience and created a quicker and more efficient method for processing issues.

> # Text-under-image digital surrogates restored a more authentic journal-viewing user experience and created a quicker and more efficient method for processing issues.

In 2011, Digital Publishing Services assumed responsibility for preparing future issues of *Inti* as digital print-on-demand. *Inti*'s faculty editor had a pre-existing external partnership for some of the publication workflow, so at the outset, inherited workflows and technologies had to be identified, evaluated, and either retained or updated (the workflow chart is available as Appendix A). DPS made an immediate decision to move from Adobe PageMaker to Adobe InDesign as the principal desktop publishing tool. Facilitation and coordination of the digital print-on-demand process was assigned to the Digital Publishing Services Specialist (DPSS). Because DPS had limited experience with InDesign, staff went through in-house and Web-based (Lynda.com) training. Following training, the first publication period was marked by due experimentation.

Mimicking the layout provided by print issues and the obsolete PageMaker files, the DPSS created a flexible, but consistent InDesign master page template (the template is available as Appendix B). After preparing the template, text and born-digital or digitized images were ingested. This step, rooted in trial-and-error, allowed for further workflow refinement—principal concerns being consistency of the text and the formatting, font rendering, and time spent. Current iterations of the ingestion process rely on e-mail submission of Microsoft Word (.doc, .docx) or text-recognized Adobe Acrobat (.PDF) files, which are then formatted in Word to closely match *Inti* specifications. "Pre-staging" the text in this manner allows for effective use of the Place function within InDesign, which creates a new object based on an external file and retains its formatting. All that remains after ingestion is a consistency check and the application of unique page headings. Some exceptions, such as linked graphics, extend the length of time spent. In total, ingestion and formatting times typically range between two to three months, depending on staff obligations, faculty editor modifications, and the relative size of the particular *Inti* issue.

Inti issues contain many contributions, so tracking is a crucial part of the entire workflow and is managed from start to finish through a Microsoft Excel worksheet, structured to reflect necessary steps and issue progression. Any change in article order is immediately updated and reflected in the tracking document to create an accurate index for reference. Thus, tracking management takes on the same level of importance as any other step in the publication process (the tracking template is available as Appendix C).

Once a "final" draft is completed, a third-party proofreader, typically a colleague of the faculty editor, reviews the draft. DPS involvement at this stage consists primarily of providing the proofreader with the draft and the original submissions, and serving as an intermediary between the proofreader and the faculty editor. At first, this transmission of documents was done through paper copies due to a proofreader's technical comfort. Currently, all documents required for proofreading are uploaded to a shared Dropbox.com folder. Any edits resulting from proofreading are tracked and implemented subsequent to faculty editor review. At this stage, the faculty editor makes any final reflections and the publication moves to pre-flight status.

The DPSS then coordinates the pre-flight process on two levels: the first within InDesign, conducted during the ingestion period; and the second based on outsourced digital print-on-demand contractor (McNaughton & Gunn[6]) specifications. The immediate point of concern is establishing a quote for the material. This quote is requested by the DPSS after calculating the total materials required as reflected in the total number of pages and mix of paper stock (if images are included). *Inti*'s faculty editor is provided with the quote and either amends the request or approves it. Once approved, the text is exported as a PDF alongside an InDesign-generated package containing any linked images, fonts, document metadata, and, lastly, the Adobe Illustrator-designed cover. This package is then uploaded to the printer's production server via FTP. A pre-print copy, requested and reviewed by the faculty editor, ensures that the final printed copy is as desired. If no further changes are needed, the lot is printed and delivered to the faculty editor, and Digital Publishing Services' role in the digital print-on-demand process is complete.

Since beginning digital print-on-demand publication support for *Inti* issue 71–72, DPS has assisted in publishing a second issue with a third in process—completion and distribution dates are set for the middle of 2013. The current publication model (leveraging technology, local expertise, and faculty editor/DPS proximity) has resulted in a fruitful collaboration between the faculty editor and DPS. DPS support has streamlined the publication workflow and freed up the faculty editor's time to pursue new content opportunities and collaborations.

Inti PLUS

Late in 2011, DPS and *Inti*'s faculty editor entered discussions for creating a website (***Inti*** **Web**[7]) for promoting forthcoming print issues of *Inti*. Since its launch, ***Inti*** **Web** has evolved into an ever-fuller complement to the printed issue, expanding on it and incorporating digital media formats not possible in print. Planning is underway to introduce a **Spotlights** section for providing information on current and past *Inti* contributors, many of whom have won prestigious awards and Medals of Honor in Literature and Arts; and to introduce a section called **Voces Transfronterizas (Transborder Voices)**, which will include forms of "writing" and expression only possible through digital media. Undergraduate students within the college's Foreign Languages Department will be selected by the faculty editor to work with DPS staff on developing these sections. The students will engage in guided research, providing scholarly contributions to this scholarly enterprise.

Supporting Ongoing Change

Digital Publishing Services' collaboration with *Inti*'s faculty editor continues to evolve as *Inti* evolves within the current disruptive scholarly communication landscape. The department is providing support for both *Inti*'s traditional and new communication channels through distributed roles and responsibilities—a suite of services through concurrent overlapping workflows, which require ongoing coordination and adjustment (the Suite of Services Workflow/ DPS organization chart is available as Appendix D). DPS continues to remain true to its original mission to investigate new collaborations and publishing models for its community by staying attuned to evolving national and international practices and local needs (i.e., looking for global patterns, while respecting local idiosyncrasies) and incorporating continuous departmental self-assessment and training.

Appendix A

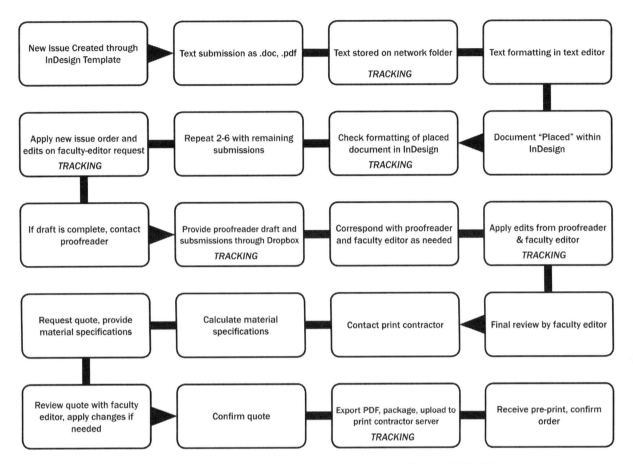

Digital Publishing Services' Inti Digital Print on Demand Workflow

Appendix B

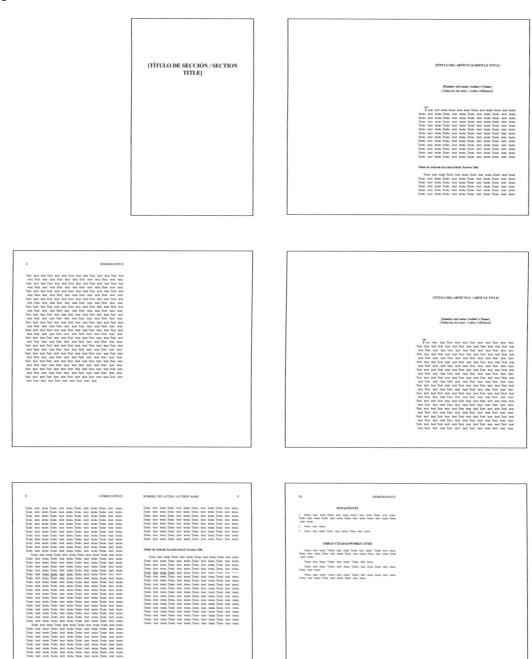

Sample of Inti Template, Created in InDesign

Appendix C

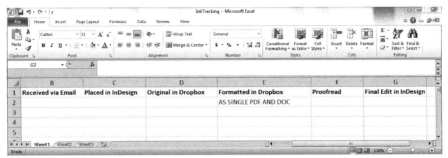

Tracking Template in Microsoft Excel

Appendix D

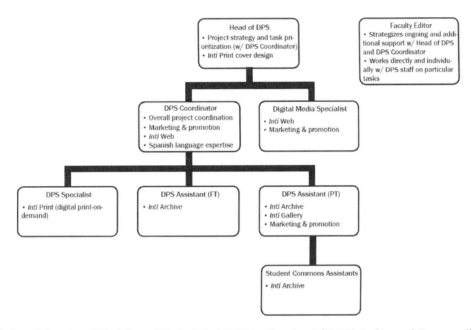

Inti Suite of Services Workflow: Digital Publishing Services' (DPS) Roles and Responsibilities

Endnotes

[1] *Inti* is a paper subscription-based, peer-reviewed journal first published in 1974, dedicated to publishing the results of academic research in all areas of Latin American and Spanish Peninsular letters.

[2] http://digitalcommons.providence.edu

[3] http://www.providence.edu/library/dps/

[4] http://www.providence.edu/library/dps/Pages/Resources.aspx

[5] http://digitalcommons.providence.edu/inti/

[6] http://www.bookprinters.com/

[7] http://library.providence.edu/dps/publications/inti/

Content and Collaboration I: A Case Study of Bringing an Institutional Repository and a University Press Together

Michael Spooner & Andrew Wesolek

University Press of Colorado, Utah State University

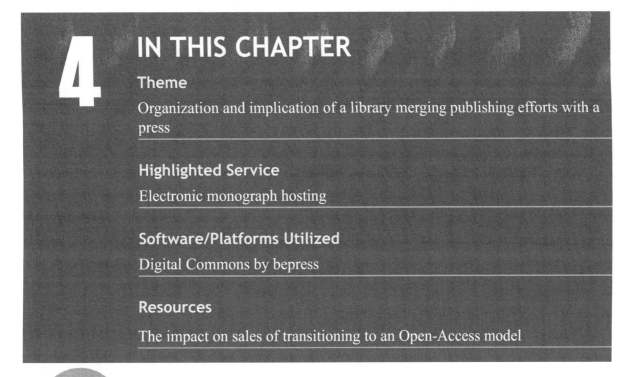

4

IN THIS CHAPTER

Theme

Organization and implication of a library merging publishing efforts with a press

Highlighted Service

Electronic monograph hosting

Software/Platforms Utilized

Digital Commons by bepress

Resources

The impact on sales of transitioning to an Open-Access model

Profile of a Merger: In 2009, the dean of libraries and the director of the university press at Utah State University proposed a departmental merger to their central administration. They argued that through restructuring reporting lines so that the press became a department of the library at least three important benefits could be achieved. First, the central administration was at the time hoping to cut costs by consolidating operations in various parts of the university; merging the staff reporting lines of the university press into the library offered an opportunity for consolidation. Secondly, integrating the press into the library promised it some relief from the structural vulnerability it had suffered historically as a department among "other instructional activities" reporting directly to the provost. And for the university library, to move the press into a structural collaboration would bring an established publisher of e-books into the library, representing a steady source of book-length content for the digital institutional repository that the library was consciously building. In short order, and spurred by the impacts of the Great Recession on higher education, the merger was approved.

Goals, Resources, and Complications

The Utah State University library was an early adopter of the Digital Commons software published by bepress (originally Berkeley Electronic Press), and by 2008 it had committed long-term resources to developing an institutional repository. As part of its IR acquisitions strategy, the library invited the university press to submit copies of its published monographs to the IR for scanning and deposit. USU Press had been publishing electronic editions of its books routinely since the late 1990s, and had recently completed a project of scanning its earlier books. These electronic editions were targeted for the library market (very few personal e-readers were available in the 1990s), and were distributed through vendors such as ebrary, ebooks.com/EBL, netLibrary, and Questia. The format of those texts, of course, was often modified for delivery through the vendors' proprietary platforms—always in flux. But the underlying files from the late 1990s forward were sturdy PDFs. (These had been "distilled," in the early days, from postscript files, and later, as Adobe software developed, had been exported from typography directly to PDF as a routine part of the preprint production process.) Originally based on a handshake and good intentions, depositing these backlist e-books could become systematic with the reconfiguration of the university press as a division of the library.

The collaboration, however, faced a conundrum that pitted free and open circulation (one of the highest values of library culture) against the pragmatic reality of how university presses are funded—mostly through sales of what they publish. In the course of moving the press into the library, the university administration rescinded 40 percent of the press's budget, yet did not adjust the library budget to balance that reduction. Sales revenue had been balancing the costs of book production and contributing to salaries for many years, but the central administration had funded a separate budget line since 1972 to support the primary salaries at the press. This is the typical arrangement for university press funding, and this is the budget that was reduced by USU administrators to help address cuts in state funding. Thus, simple arithmetic required that revenue from book sales be protected (or even increased) for support of the press and the new collaboration.

While the budget is always a concern at USU Libraries, generating self-support is normally *not* a concern. Moreover, the institutional repository is not conceived as a profit center. So a conundrum faced the USU libraries and press: the goal of enhancing the open-access IR with texts published by the press depended on protecting the sales revenue that financed creation of those texts. Accordingly, the library and press established a process of acquisition that would incrementally increase USU Press publications in the IR by focusing immediately on backlist titles (the older books) and gradually adding newer books.

In a normal year, a publisher's frontlist—books in their first 12 months of life—substantially over-represent themselves in a publisher's revenue and thus are critical to support of new books to be published in the following year. The backlist is also critical, but because it is a much larger group of books and each book contributes less and less individually to revenue over time, to move the backlist gradually into an open-access collection is a process with lower financial risk to the press. Accordingly, the USU library and press established an embargo period after the publication of a new book, during which time it would contribute its predictable best months of sales to support the press. After that period, the book would be deposited in the IR collection. Through this process, the collection of USU Press e-books began gradually growing within the IR.

> # The goal is to honor the traditional academic values of rigorous peer review and intellectual excellence, while particularly sponsoring work with a commitment to digital scholarship and expression.

An additional acquisition for the IR was a series of born-digital publications published by USU Press under the imprint Computers and Composition Digital Press (CCDP). This series was established through collaborative efforts at a number of institutions, including University of Illinois, Ohio State, Miami University, and Illinois Institute of Technology. Committed to publishing innovative, multimodal digital projects, CCDP specializes in digital projects that cannot be printed on paper (they may include video, audio, database, and other elements not well suited for publication in print formats), but that have the same "intellectual heft" as a book. The goal is to honor the traditional academic values of rigorous peer review and intellectual excellence, while particularly sponsoring work with a commitment to digital scholarship and expression. In the context of traditional resistance among humanities faculty to granting tenure credit for digital publication (as was the case when the series was established), CCDP represents an important kind of scholarly activism—an effort to circulate the best work of digital media scholars in the field of English composition studies in a timely fashion and on the global scale made possible by digital distribution. These goals dovetail perfectly with the mission and ethos of the USU repository.

As the USU libraries integrated the USU press, library IT resources were found to establish a secure server to host the CCDP series. As an open access digital-only series, there was no revenue potential in these publications; thus, after initial expenses of IT development, of establishing referee, editorial, and production standards, and modest ongoing overhead expenses of monitoring the referee process, all work on CCDP volumes was handled by authors and volunteers from faculty at collaborating institutions. Accordingly, each CCDP volume is carefully reviewed by peer specialists in the field, with particular emphasis on the volume's unique, original, and significant contribution to scholarship in literacy or digital literacy studies. This much is typical of university press publishing, and is especially important to authors whose career advancement depends on publication through a certified referee process. In addition, and of special interest to this series, is how well and to what extent a proposed volume exploits the potential of digital media to convey its content. Work that could easily be presented in print formats is discouraged, and priority is given to work that studies and depends in significant ways on video, audio, database, Web-based, or other digital content. The series editors negotiate a revision (or rejection) with the author, based on the referees' and the editors' own specific recommendations. With endorsements from the peer review process and from the editors, USU Press staff present the work to the USU Press faculty editorial board for approval, and then to the University Press of Colorado board of trustees for formal authorization of a contract for publication. The series, innovative in its own field, among repositories, and at university presses, now includes seven volumes—two of them award winners.

Early Metrics and Various Impacts

Response to the availability of USU Press books in the IR has affirmed both the value of the collaboration and the financial prudence of the strategy adopted. Usage reports generated by Digital Commons software show that full-text downloads from the accumulating content provided by USU Press since approximately the middle of 2010 now exceed 100,000. For a small library/press collaboration and experiment with an open access collection, we consider this a positive indicator of circulation and impact. At the same time, we feel it is important to monitor the reciprocity between this open access collection and the stream of retail publications that maintain it. There is obviously the potential for free downloads to overwhelm book sales and hence to collapse the financial support that is critical to the long-term existence of this part of the IR collection itself.

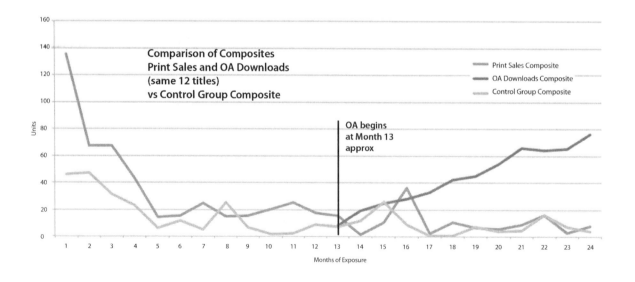

In late 2012, the authors of this article charted the individual download performance of several representative USU books in the IR collection and compared it to hard copy unit sales for the previous two years of those same books. What we conclude from this study is two-fold.

> ...we find no evidence that the open access presence of these books in the IR contributed to a decline in sales of the books measured.

First of all, we find no evidence that the open access presence of these books in the IR contributed to a decline in sales of the books measured. We attribute this lack of negative impact to our choice to embargo the books during their frontlist period. As implied above, the majority of sales for the typical scholarly monograph occur within its first year in the market; sales often drop dramatically through the second and third year, and then they plateau at a low level for the rest of the life of the book—this is the "long tail" that statisticians and marketing researchers discuss (e.g., Anderson, 2006). Our choice to begin the open access tenure of a book at the beginning of the book's long tail was a strategy that we hypothesized would protect most of the book's predictable revenue stream, yet still leave an impactful life for its later open-access circulation. Our study of these representative books seems to support our hypothesis.

The second major conclusion we draw from the study is that we see no evidence to support the prediction by some (and what seems a popular folk belief among librarians), that open access visibility will create increased demand and sales for the original book. (See especially Suber's early thoughts on this—e.g., http://bit.ly/oa-overview.) In our study, although downloads through the IR were significant, ongoing, and international, no measurable increase occurred in book sales during the open access period we measured.

> Our choice to begin the open access tenure of a book at the beginning of the book's long tail was a strategy that we hypothesized would protect most of the book's predictable revenue stream, yet still leave an impactful life for its later open-access circulation.

As for the digital series, the CCDP, where revenue is not critical, we are also achieving our goals. Metrics on hits for these volumes indicate a broad international audience, and the acceptance of digital publication for academic promotion credit seems to be well established at this point. In 2012, one of these volumes received a prestigious disciplinary book award, and in 2013, CCDP volumes garnered three more book awards. Of course, the series here is only one contributor to a broad academic/cultural movement toward acceptance of refereed non-print publications, but for work like this to gain "book" awards—such traditional and conventional endorsements—from learned societies in the less than five years since the series was established, we feel indicates a watershed moment in the history of digital humanities publication.

The Once and Future Collaboration

The most recent chapter (one wouldn't want to say the final chapter) in the case of the USU Libraries and USU Press collaboration brings a complication. By 2011, although the worst effects of the Great Recession were past, the USU central administration, in another cost-cutting move, elected to rescind the remaining budget that supported salaries at the university press— and again they chose not to balance this cut with an equivalent addition to the library budget. Thus, although the library could continue to provide office space and overhead, it did not have the budget to take on additional salaries. This is a complex narrative that has been described in another forum (Spooner, 2012), but, to our purposes here, we can report that the university press at USU was not ultimately shuttered as planned. Instead, the library and press found a new collaborator in the University Press of Colorado (UPC). In a multi-part agreement, UPC acquired copyrights to all USU Press content; remaining USU Press staff were terminated at USU and became employees of UPC; and all USU Press revenue was redirected to UPC. USU Press exists at this writing as an imprint of UPC, and publishes for the same disciplines in which it has long been established. UPC leadership has confirmed the relationship with USU Libraries and continues depositing USU Press titles into the USU repository.

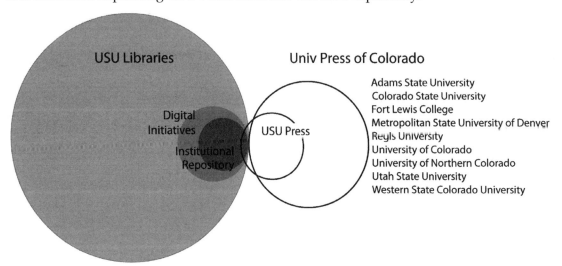

As a consortium, UPC is not a division of one university but is collectively supported by nine separate institutions, now including USU. Thus, in a real sense, what began at USU as a relationship between one modest library and one small press at one land-grant university now represents a collaboration endorsed by a collective of institutions with a joint interest in seeing it succeed and evolve.

References

Anderson, C. (2006). *The long tail: Why the future of business is selling less of more.* New York, NY: Hyperion.

Spooner, M. (2012, June). "Fundraising (and alternatives) in a tough economy: The case of Utah State University Press." Paper presented at the meeting of the Association of American University Presses, Chicago.

Suber, P. (2004–2013). Open access overview. Retrieved from http://bit.ly/oa-overview

Open Access Journal Incubator at University of Lethbridge Library

Sandra Cowan

University of Lethbridge

5 IN THIS CHAPTER

Theme
Developing library-based publishing systems through an incubator program

Highlighted Service
Open Access journal management & hosting

Software/Platforms Utilized
Digital Commons by bepress, Open Journal Systems, & Drupal

Resources
Shared workflow checklists of technical considerations & discoverability

The University of Lethbridge Library entered into collaboration with English faculty member and digital humanities scholar Dr. Daniel Paul O'Donnell and the School of Graduate Studies in order to establish a journal incubator to publish open access journals. As part of the library's broader initiative to become a campus collegium for the management of scholarly research lifecycles, the library's Research Support Services group has been working with Dr. O'Donnell over several months in order to identify ways in which the library can be involved with the journal incubator. The Research Support Services group consists of librarians Sandra Cowan, Rhys Stevens, Marinus Swanepoel, Maxine Tedesco, and Associate University Librarian Wendy Merkley. As a small university library, this is an opportunity to integrate stakeholders and resources across campus in order to successfully implement a library-based publishing model.

The journal incubator came to the library with a stable of three peer-reviewed open access journals: *Digital Medievalist, Digital Studies/Le champ numérique,* and *The Canadian Journal of Netherlandic Studies.* Library administration agreed to provide an office in the library for journal incubator operations. Office space is shared by the graduate student editors of the three journals. The School of Graduate Studies supports students in this work because it recognizes the value of the journal incubator in providing transferable and marketable skills to the students, and so it provides funding through special research assistantships of $7,000 per year in addition to the graduate students' standard graduate teaching assistantships. Currently, the journal incubator is sustained by this funding for graduate student staffing, along with in-kind contributions on the part of Dr. O'Donnell, faculty board members and editors, and the library. The group is beginning to pursue grant funding in order to develop, document, and share standard processes for open access journal publication as well as—more ambitiously—broader scholarly research lifecycles.

The journals have already been in publication for several years, and one of them has recently transitioned from print to digital. Each journal has a different format, and different software and processes are used in their production. The idea was to bring them together to streamline and standardize processes. The journal incubator project has several goals, which include to:

- Streamline production and business models.

- Reduce duplication of resources and effort in journal production on campus.

- Establish a process or "package" that can be offered to scholars interested in starting up new open access journals.

- Increase the research profile of the university by attracting and producing quality scholarly journals, and by acquiring external funding to facilitate the project.

- Increase the impact of the journals being published.

- Provide graduate students with an opportunity to develop professional skills and experience in publishing and editing.

- Leverage the expertise of librarians in order to enhance the scholarly publishing process.

- Enhance the library's role in scholarly research and publication.

Journal incubator operations have been housed in the library for about a year, but it took some time to define the role of librarians in the project, because editing, production, and communications were being handled by the graduate student editors. After some discussion of the journal incubator processes, lacunae were identified. It became clear that there were several areas in which librarians had expertise to offer, such as:

- Metadata standardization
- Discoverability: indexing, cataloguing, aggregators, search engine optimization, and social media
- Researching and recommending standards in publishing format and software
- Impact and bibliometrics
- Archiving standards, procedures, and space
- Intellectual property standards and recommendations

Metadata Standardization

There are a few different opportunities for metadata creation and standardization, primarily in website encoding and in cataloguing for inclusion in the library catalogue, from which the records will be uploaded into OCLC's WorldCat. Journal- and article-level metadata should be optimized for discoverability by search engines, and to ensure the option of indexing in key databases. For example, the Directory of Open Access Journals (DOAJ) requires metadata to be in XML. Different indexes may have different standards and requirements, so it is important to target the most important ones for each journal.

Discoverability

Metadata is necessary for discoverability; if the design and metadata are good, the journal's content should start showing up in search engines such as Google Scholar within a few weeks as Google's crawlers locate it. Databases and aggregators require application for inclusion, and most of the major ones require the journal to have published a certain number of years and/or articles and to measure up to other criteria before being considered for inclusion. The library can catalogue the journals and include them in our local catalogue, which will periodically be uploaded into OCLC's WorldCat for international exposure. The library can also help publicize the journal incubator through our social media venues, currently including Facebook and Twitter.

Publishing Format and Software Standards

Librarians are well positioned to research different publishing systems available, such as Open Journal Systems (OJS), bepress Digital Commons, or a homegrown system, and make recommendations for selecting one as the standard for the journal incubator, which is currently producing each journal on a different and idiosyncratic system. Likewise, librarians are able to research output formats, whether HTML, XML, PDF or EPUB, and make recommendations about which ones are better for long-term sustainability, accessibility, indexing, and discoverability.

Impact and Bibliometrics

Impact factors are important in the reputation and professional recognition of both the journals and the contributors. Typically quantified by citation statistics which are calculated to inform impact factors (for journals), and h-index (for authors), these are important data in the scholarly world. Getting into Google Scholar, and—once the journal has established a track record of publication longevity and quality—applying to be included in databases such as JSTOR and Web of Science are critical to the measurement of citation impact.

Archiving Standards, Procedures, and Space

The library has expertise in digital collections and archiving, and we are looking into ways that we can share both the expertise and resources with the journal incubator. We are investigating the potential use of LOCKSS and Archive-it for archiving the journals, and we are learning about how to create permanent Web locations and access points—whether through a persistent URL or a digital object identifier (DOI)—in order to manage permanent access to the journals. Once a journal is indexed by the DOAJ, it will be included in the DOAJ e-Depot archives, an archiving project that the DOAJ is piloting with the National Library of the Netherlands for the long-term digital preservation of scholarly journals. Finally, we have recognized the need for more stable backup procedures and locations for the journals, and are discussing options such as a dedicated backup server and developing easier and more consistent backup processes in order to address this.

Intellectual Property

Researching and recommending standard licensing agreements to balance open access and intellectual property rights between the journals and the contributors, as well as between the journals and different databases, through Creative Commons or other licensing is an important task. Librarians can work with the University Copyright Officer to make recommendations.

Although we are a much smaller university with fewer resources, we have looked to the University of Michigan Library's MPublishing program as an inspiration for our journal incubator project. Ultimately, we hope to include all aspects of the scholarly research lifecycle: from institutional and data repositories, to text encoding, to aggregator inclusion and intellectual property rights recommendations.

Each of the librarians involved has taken on one or more of the above areas with the goal of researching and recommending best practices in each area. By researching, recommending, and implementing best practices in many of the above areas, the library can make a substantial contribution to the journal incubator apart from simply housing its operations in-house. The collaboration is an opportunity to professionalize the journal incubator, and to expand the publication process to support further nascent scholarly journals. There is an additional benefit in increasing the professional skills and knowledge of the librarians involved in the project, while better positioning the library in the context of scholarly communication, open access, and the scholarly research lifecycle.

The obstacles that we have encountered up to this point have much to do with the usual librarianly problem of having many diverse tasks to accomplish, and not quite enough people or time to work on everything that we would like to accomplish. None of the librarians have yet been able to devote significant amounts of time to the journal incubator research, given the myriad of other duties we are engaged in, and so we are moving forward slowly—but surely.

Something as simple as a preliminary workflow checklist has already helped the journal incubator by placing journal publication within a larger context that considers factors such as archiving and discoverability (see Appendix 1). Another simple solution was to include all of the existing journals in our library catalogue, which we quickly realized was missing two out of the three. We have begun investigation of a regional LOCKSS network as a possible archive for the journals, and we have begun to learn more about the criteria that indexes and aggregators use for journal inclusion, with the goal of getting all three journals into DOAJ first.

The group recently completed a grant application that may provide us with funding to develop a series of academic community colloquia and workshops around scholarly communications lifecycles, of which the journal incubator and the research issues that we have identified around it would be a significant part. From there, we intend to apply for more sustainable funding that would allow us to expand the journal incubator and to devote more librarian time to the endeavor. We are also considering hiring a library science graduate student intern for short periods of time to assist with the project. In the meantime, the incubator continues production of peer-reviewed, open access journals; the graduate student editors continue to learn valuable skills in editing, communications, project management, and document encoding; and the library continues to support the journal incubator as a library-based publishing initiative, as the librarians involved carve out time to contribute the project.

References

Canadian Journal of Netherlandic Studies. (2011). Retrieved from http://www.caans-acaen.ca/Journal/current.html

Digital Medievalist. (2013). Retrieved from http://www.digitalmedievalist.org/index.html

Digital Studies/Le champ numérique. (2012). Retrieved from http://www.digitalstudies.org/ojs/index.php/digital_studies/index

Directory of Open Access Journals. (2011). *The Online Guide to Open Access Journals Publishing.* Retrieved from http://www.doaj.org/bpguide

O'Donnell, D. P. (2012). The Lethbridge journal incubator: Leveraging the educational potential of the scholarly communication process. Retrieved from http://www.uleth.ca/lib/incubator/proposal. html

University of Michigan MPublishing. (2012). Retrieved from http://www.publishing.umich.edu/

Appendix 1: ULeth Open Access Journal Incubator Workflow Considerations

Technical Considerations:

1. Decide on software/format

   - Options include Open Journal Systems (OJS), bepress Digital Commons, Drupal, homegrown system, XML, HTML, PDF, etc.

   - Consider search engine optimization (SEO) and accessibility issues

   - Consider workflow and version control

2. Ensure server space(s)

3. Establish domain name

Journal Review and Publication:

1. Request an ISSN for journal

2. Staffing:

   - Editorial board

   - Editorial staff (grad students)

   - Peer reviewers

3. Solicit articles

4. Review and publication process

5. Creative Commons licensing

6. Distribution

Discoverability and Impact:

1. Journal and article standardized metadata

2. Search engine optimization (SEO) (eg. keywords, metadata)

3. Ensure SEO specifications to be included in Google Scholar (provides citation data)

4. Catalogue and include in local library catalogue and WorldCat upload

5. Apply for inclusion in Directory of Open Access Journals (DOAJ)

6. Apply for inclusion in Ulrichsweb Global Serials Directory

7. Apply for inclusion/indexing in major databases relevant to journal's discipline, such as:
   - JSTOR, EBSCO
   - ISI Thomson Web of Science (provides citation data and impact factors)
   - European Reference Index for the Humanities (ERIH) (Humanities)
   - Scopus (Sciences)

Digital Preservation:

1. Ensure back-up routines
2. Encourage authors to deposit articles in institutional repository
3. Investigate use of Archive-it for archiving
4. Investigate use of LOCKSS system for archiving
5. DOAJ e-Depot archives (pilot project)

Digital Publishing at Feinberg Library: The Institutional Repository as Outreach Initiative

Joshua F. Beatty

SUNY Plattsburgh

6 IN THIS CHAPTER

Theme

The role of outreach in publishing through an institutional repository

Highlighted Service

Publishing and hosting through an IR

Software/Platforms Utilized

Digital Commons by bepress

Resources

Discussion of publication processes and example publications

Feinberg Library is a medium-sized academic library at SUNY Plattsburgh, one of New York's teaching-oriented public comprehensive colleges. In 2012 Feinberg librarians launched "Digital Commons @ SUNY Plattsburgh," (http://digitalcommons.plattsburgh. edu) an institutional repository and publishing system hosted on Berkeley Electronic Press's (bepress) Digital Commons platform.

Outreach Philosophy

From the beginning our Digital Commons has been conceived of as an outreach initiative rather than a systems-side initiative. This initially came about as a practical decision, as the library needed to fill a reference and instruction position and added research of an institutional repository (IR) to the job duties. But the decision was fortuitous, as the view of the IR as a tool primarily for outreach grew into a central tenet of our vision.

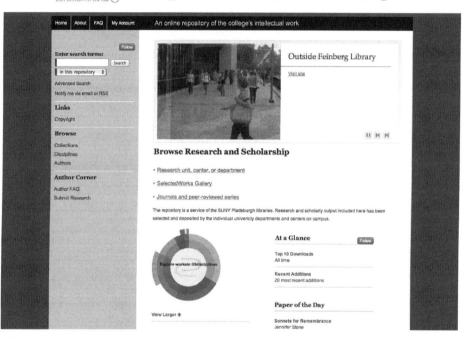

This philosophy has led us to deemphasize the traditional role of the institutional repository as an archive of previously published work. One of our primary concerns has always been to avoid "roach motel" syndrome, in which data enters the digital archive and never comes out (Salo, 2008, p. 98). We wanted to ensure that whatever documents we had in the repository mattered to faculty or students currently at the college. This meant forgoing sources often used to rapidly populate a repository. For example, we decided that we would not start our Digital Commons by digitizing old masters' theses.

Instead of archiving previously published work, we have instead focused on publishing original student and faculty materials. Thus, we wanted to allow Plattsburgh faculty and students to showcase their work in ways that simply were not possible on any other college-run service, such as personal or class websites. The goal is to put in materials that people from both inside and outside the college community will want to see. And the best way to do that was to work with individual faculty and their students to identify the work that excited them, and that they wanted to make available.

Publishing Process

Thus, we have made it a key tenet of our repository to encourage faculty and students to take part in the publishing process. We do not want to just publish materials for students or faculty, but to work with them to build something new and to best showcase their work within the particular space of the repository.

As a result, we have relied on word of mouth to find materials for the repository. All librarians at Feinberg serve as liaisons to several departments. Those librarian-teaching faculty contacts have been key in identifying professors who want to be engaged in publishing material with us. Though we are publishing undergraduate and graduate student work as well, we are not directly contacting them; the first meetings are always with a faculty member mentoring students.

In theory, the repository manager and the faculty member have clearly delineated roles. The repository manager has responsibility for setting up the series, training the faculty member, and troubleshooting any issues. Faculty are expected to upload documents, add metadata, and make any necessary edits. In practice, the repository manager shoulders some of those duties. They step in more often to assist faculty who are less comfortable with technology. And if administering a series means simply uploading two text documents a year, it is just as easy for the manager to quickly add the materials. But for more complex series requiring more frequent maintenance, we insist that the faculty member take at least an equal share in administrative duties.

The repository manager meets in person with the interested faculty member. Here we listen to the patron and find out what material he or she wants to publish, and if he or she has a pre-existing idea for how the material should appear in the repository. Digital Commons has a number of different "gallery" types appropriate to different collections of work. We often open up a three-way conversation among the repository manager, the faculty member, and bepress's (outstanding) support staff to discuss the best way to publish the material.

The repository manager and library staff might upload some of the materials themselves, but we do not want this to be fully our responsibility. Instead, we add the faculty member as an administrator of their materials. We sit down with the professor for a one- to two-hour session to show them the ins and outs of the Digital Commons interface. During this session we walk the patron through the publishing process, showing the faculty member how to upload materials and how to enter metadata for the collection.

The repository manager, to be sure, will still have to troubleshoot issues. The point is not to push the faculty member or student to shoulder all administrative responsibilities, but to actively engage them in the process of digital publishing. By understanding the particular platform on which they publish, they will be better able to communicate their needs back to the repository manager. The instruction session, we have found, serves much the same purpose as a reference interview. Through the process, the librarian comes to better understand the patron's specific needs and can, when necessary, suggest solutions that neither would have considered otherwise.

Digital Commons, we have found, is particularly well suited for a repository in which responsibility for administration of individual collections is shared by librarians and teaching faculty. It is based on the EduKit publishing platform. Neither the librarian nor faculty member needs programming knowledge. The interface is Web based and fairly simple. After an initial instruction session, even faculty with limited computer skills have been able to manage their own materials. And they can very quickly see the results online. Digital Commons is particularly strong at search engine optimization. When we post work, we find that it shoots to the top of Google searches within days. Authors are invariably delighted when they Google themselves and see their repository publication near the top of the results.

Examples

Student Work: Expeditionary Studies

Because our repository intends to emphasize student work as well as faculty work, we want to work with enthusiastic faculty to help put their students' best work online. Perhaps our most successful initiative so far has been a partnership with Plattsburgh's Department of Expeditionary Studies (http://www.plattsburgh.edu/academics/exp/). During their senior years, students majoring in Expeditionary Studies first plan for and then travel on an adventure expedition. Their plans are the length of a typical senior thesis and include an itinerary, a list of supplies, and a detailed description of their emergency preparations. After the plan is approved by a department committee, the students then follow through on the plan. In recent years, students have kayaked around the Isle of Skye and through the rivers of the Mekong Delta, climbed Devil's Tower in Wyoming, and skied the backcountry of the Sierra Nevadas.

In December 2012, working with the department chair Larry Soroka, we began putting the expedition proposals online in our Digital Commons (http://digitalcommons.plattsburgh.edu/expeditionproposals/). The response was immediate. Students were happy to have a place to show off their proposals to the world. It became easier for juniors beginning to plan for 2013–2014 to get a sense of the task before them. And interested people from beyond the college wrote the students to ask for more information about their trips.

As the proposals were so well-received, the department has asked us for help in making further materials available. After returning, each student makes a presentation about their expedition. The form of the presentation varies by student. It might be a PowerPoint or a slideshow; it might include video or audio footage. Working with the faculty and the students, we plan to begin adding these presentation materials to the Digital Commons. Our goal here will not be to archive everything, but to use the particular form granted by our publishing platform to tell the student's story through a selective group of materials. In other words, it will be curated content.

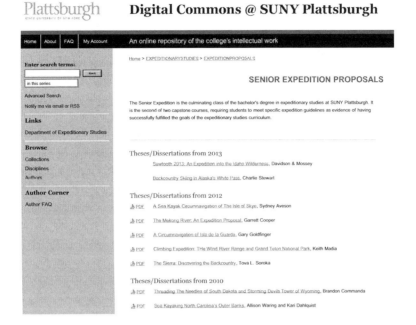

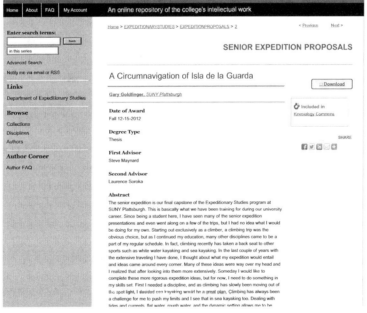

Faculty Partnerships

We are also using our Digital Commons to identify and publish work that, while worthy, cannot be published via traditional methods. The scholarly publishing crisis is real; the humanities, in particular, are in a difficult spot. Many university presses are closing and those still open now release fewer books, even as there is more and more pressure for faculty to publish. Thus, we want to partner with faculty to publish work that would otherwise not see the light of day.

If the market for monographs is limited, the market for edited primary sources is even more so. In the fall of 2012, the library's liaison to the English department alerted the repository manager that a modern languages professor, Isabel Arredondo, had been unable to find a publisher for such a book. Arredondo had published a Spanish-language edition of a book of interviews with Mexican women filmmakers, but she was unable to find a press interested in producing an English edition. Arredondo wanted to make these interviews available to the public and to be able to cite them in an upcoming monograph. We have used Digital Commons to make the English-language manuscript (http://digitalcommons.plattsburgh.edu/modernlanguages/1/) available—Arredondo, of course, retains the copyright.

Arredondo's monograph will be published later this year. The publisher of that book is delighted to have the primary sources available online. We are adding information about the monograph to the Digital Commons page for the interviews manuscript. That page is already very visible in search results; Arredondo hopes that by associating it with the upcoming monograph she can raise the profile of both.

Peer-Reviewed Journals

One of the most powerful features of the Digital Commons platform is the ability to publish peer-reviewed journals online, and to conduct the entire submission, review, and revision process through Digital Commons. The author submits a .doc or .pdf file directly to Digital Commons. An editor receives the submission and passes it on to peer reviewers, who in turn read the manuscript and send back comments to the editor and then to the author. All communication among author, editor, and reviewers, then, is through the Digital Commons interface, and Digital Commons keeps track of where the article is in the publishing workflow.

We have encouraged existing journals and magazines to shift their digital publishing to our Digital Commons. And we have worked with our Center for Teaching Excellence to produce a new, born-digital journal. At the end April 2013 the CTE announced *The Common Good: A SUNY Plattsburgh Journal on Teaching and Learning* (http://digitalcommons.plattsburgh.edu/commongood). The journal is intended to feature cross-disciplinary writing in the new field of "scholarship on teaching and learning" and includes work by both faculty and students.

Setbacks

Our model of emphasizing outreach and shared responsibility has been quite successful as we come up on the one-year anniversary of opening our Digital Commons. But not all has gone smoothly.

The advisor of a student literary magazine asked us to help the students publish a digital version on our Digital Commons. The repository manager and the library's Web design expert worked with two student editors of the magazine to design a site for the digital journal. The editors trained on the platform and practiced on a demo site. But, just before the final site was to go live, the others students on the magazine staff protested that the site did not properly reflect their individuality. The advisor bowed to pressure and abandoned Digital Commons.

In retrospect, the student advisor had not been fully engaged with the planning process, nor had she taken the training workshop. She had left execution to the two bright and dedicated student editors. But when the other students raised concerns, the student editors did not have the power to overrule them, and the advisor did not have the understanding of the platform to explain the benefits.

The Digital Commons site for the student literary magazine still exists; if the next year's students want to use it we will happily work with them. But our failure to make sure that the faculty advisor as well as the student editors was fully engaged with the publishing process led to disappointment for us, a lost opportunity for the students to publish on a professional platform, and a great deal of wasted effort by the student editors.

Conclusion

Our first year using our Digital Commons as an outreach initiative has, overall, been a success. But the success of each individual publishing project has depended on the rapport formed between the repository manager and the faculty sponsor of the work. When the faculty member has been fully engaged with the publishing process, their projects have attracted interest and led to further possibilities. When the professor has taken a hands-off approach, the projects have stagnated. It is thus the librarian's responsibility, under an outreach model, to listen to what is said and not said, to take the partner's hopes and fears into account, and to continually find creative solutions to problems expected and unexpected—the same, then, as in any other good conversation with our patrons.

References

Salo, D. (2008). Innkeeper at the Roach Motel. *Library Trends, 57*(2), 98–123.

Library as Journal Publisher: The Faculty-Led, Library-Supported Journal

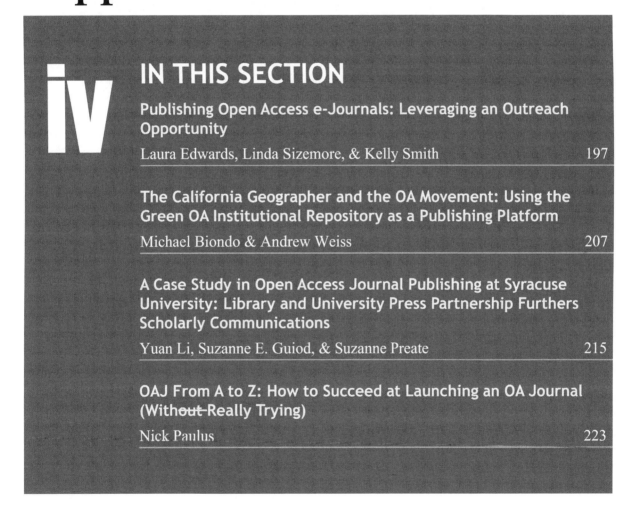

Publishing Open Access e-Journals: Leveraging an Outreach Opportunity

Laura Edwards, Linda Sizemore, & Kelly Smith

Eastern Kentucky University Libraries

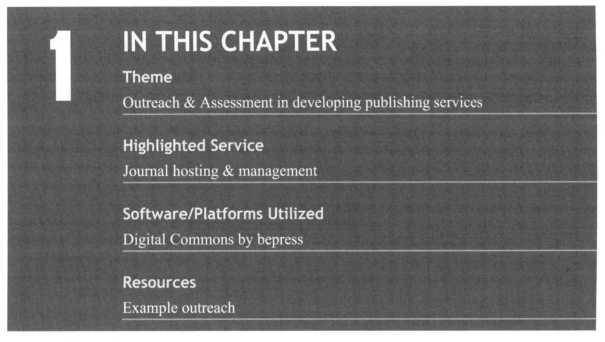

1

IN THIS CHAPTER

Theme

Outreach & Assessment in developing publishing services

Highlighted Service

Journal hosting & management

Software/Platforms Utilized

Digital Commons by bepress

Resources

Example outreach

"A library, to modify the famous metaphor of Socrates, should be the delivery room for the birth of ideas, a place where history comes to life."
~ Norman Cousins[1]

Eastern Kentucky University (EKU) Libraries began exploring the institutional repository (IR) landscape in 2009 with the intention of publishing electronic theses and dissertations (ETDs), journals, special collections, images, videos, sound files, or anything else that would fit a need for us. The hosted systems we examined were effective as either platforms for displaying special collections or platforms for managing publishing processes. However, we didn't find a system that did both of those things well. The existing open source platforms were capable of ingesting and effectively displaying a wider range of file types (including images files), but these systems required technical staffing levels that we could not support. After assessing the different systems, the ability of our staff to support them, and the needs of our institution, we realized we would have to narrow our publishing scope and identify fewer goals for the hosted repository, and let those goals inform which platform to choose.[2]

Discussion

Informed by the SPARC research report *Library Publishing Services: Strategies for Success Research Report* (Mullins) finding that publishing services were a growth area for academic libraries, EKU librarians determined that journal hosting would provide the most valuable service for our campus community. Specifically, we identified a potential for increased faculty engagement, having been approached by several faculty members expressing interest in editing journals to host locally. This would provide our scholars with an opportunity to publish unique content and contribute high-quality peer-reviewed journals in niche areas of strength at EKU (such as Fire Science and Regional Engagement). Additionally, we identified local journal publishing as a way to disrupt the unsustainable journal publishing model and to contribute to the open access (OA) movement in the scholarly communication system.[3] We concluded that the future of academic libraries involved more than just serving as a "middleman" to the provision of content but rather as a participant in the production of scholarship.

> **EKU librarians determined that journal hosting would provide the most valuable service for our campus community.**

EKU Libraries did not have enough programmers on staff to support an open source solution, so bepress' Digital Commons was chosen. Built on a journal publishing platform, Digital Commons' ability to serve as a management tool for journal hosting was its primary benefit. Additionally, it could serve as a container for other potential collections of our repository: electronic theses, faculty scholarship, curated data, and limited archives materials.

After choosing the platform, we began the process of determining what needed to be communicated to potential journal publishers. There were three categories of editors: those who had expressed an interest in editing journals based at EKU, those who were editors for print journals based at EKU, and those who were editors for journals not based at EKU. The following goals for communicating with these editors or potential editors were identified:

- Educate faculty about OA and the unsustainability of current scholarly communication models

- Inform faculty of the journal publishing tools in bepress

- Market the library as a host for the processes of production and distribution of information as opposed to simply a warehouse of published information

- Market librarians as partners in the scholarly communication process

- Market the repository as a tool for highlighting the scholarship of our institution and region, in line with the regional stewardship goals of EKU

- Convey the potential of the repository to allow EKU to make a unique contribution to OA digital scholarship

- Provide a forum for librarians and novice and experienced editors to share editorial knowledge, experience, ideas, and questions

Professional Learning Community

To achieve these goals, Dean of Libraries Carrie Cooper asked Edwards and Sizemore to design and lead a professional learning community (PLC). At EKU, PLCs are typically semester-long, active collaborative learning experiences with regularly structured scholarly activities leading to an end product such as a report or presentation.[4] A PLC can be ingrained in the infrastructure of an organization as a way of working together which results in continuous school improvement (Hord, 1997). EKU's professional learning communities are modeled on Peter Senge's description in *The Fifth Discipline Fieldbook* (1990, p. 5), as spaces "where people continually expand their capacities to create the results they truly desire, where new and expansive patterns of thinking are nurtured, where collective aspiration is set free, and where people are continually learning how to learn together."

EKU's Teaching and Learning Center (TLC) has been using the approach of PLCs for several years as a means to address issues and challenges confronting EKU faculty and students.[5] In the fall of 2010, Dean Cooper approached the TLC about hosting a PLC on "Becoming a Successful Journal Editor." The TLC agreed to host it and to help subsidize refreshments for each session. In addition to providing financial support, they worked with Edwards and Sizemore to find ways to tie the PLC to the campus-wide Scholarship Week event scheduled later that year. Once details of the partnership with the Center were finalized, we focused on recruiting participants for the PLC.

Recruitment

Dean Cooper reached out to faculty members who had already approached her to express interest in either starting a new journal or transferring an existing journal to the Encompass platform, and she simply invited them to participate in the PLC. The TLC also suggested additional faculty members, based on their conversations with faculty members who had discussed journal editing with them. Because the number of faculty members pre-identified already met the recommended number of participants for a PLC (8–12), we decided not to issue a campus-wide call for participants and instead focused on writing formal letters of invitation (see Appendix A) to the identified faculty members (as recommended by the TLC). The 12 faculty participants included Edwards and Sizemore, plus a mix of seasoned journal editors and faculty interested in becoming journal editors.

Curriculum

Instead of being didactic, the curriculum for the PLC was structured around active learning techniques where the leaders facilitated conversations. The goals of the PLC were to encourage discussion, exchange knowledge/information among participants, and expose participants to the newly acquired Digital Commons publishing platform, branded "Encompass" (http://encompass.eku.edu/).

Sizemore and Edwards selected a broad theme for each session that served as a launching pad for the discussion. They gave the participants opportunities to tailor the PLC to their interests, first by sending tentative session ideas to the participants for their review and feedback and later by spontaneously changing the theme of a session in order to address questions that were raised in a previous discussion. After feedback was received, a final schedule was developed and distributed to the participants (see Appendix B). The sessions were held in the spring of 2011.

For the sessions that did not feature guest speakers, the facilitators began with open-ended questions to prompt discussion (e.g., as an editor-in-chief who is also a faculty member with teaching and service responsibilities, how do you manage workflow with limited staff for a journal?). Additionally, participants came prepared with their own questions related to the topic at hand.

The sessions featuring guest speakers proved especially successful, as PLC participants appreciated engaging with experts in an intimate setting and exploring each topic in-depth:

1. The Journal Editor panel featured two editors of well-respected journals: Dr. Vic Kappeler, an editorial board member for *Criminal Justice Review*, a peer-reviewed scholarly journal focused on criminal justice issues in the United States, and George Brosi, the editor of *Appalachian Heritage*, a literary quarterly featuring creative writing and art of the Southern Appalachian region. The facilitators sent a brief list of questions about the process of editing and/or managing a journal to the guest editors in advance of the PLC so they would know what to expect (see Appendix C).

2. The Scholarly Communications session with Lee Van Orsdel, Dean of Libraries at Grand Valley State University and scholarly publishing expert and OA advocate, was integrated into the series of events planned for EKU's Scholarship Week. After presenting a campus-

wide lecture on the current state of scholarly publishing and the emergence of OA due to its importance in addressing the crisis in journal pricing (bit.ly/10132Ai), Van Orsdel met privately with PLC participants to discuss OA in more detail.

3. Lastly, Russell Helms, managing editor for *Jelly Bucket* and *Aurora*, two creative writing journals produced at EKU, shared tips on maximizing journal quality, and the "dirty business of running a journal." In addition to suggesting ways to attract quality submissions, he discussed the importance of paying attention to the design elements of a journal (logo, text design, use of color, etc.), as the visual elements of a journal are usually the first things a reader notices and thus will influence his or her opinion about the quality of the journal.

Outcomes

EKU Libraries considered the Journal Editor PLC a success because it inspired thoughtful conversation, opened new lines of communications with faculty, and led to the development of several locally hosted journals. Journals emanating from PLC group members include:

- *Kentucky Journal of Excellence in Teaching* (http://encompass.eku.edu/kjectl/)

- *PRISM: Journal of Regional Engagement* (http://encompass.eku.edu/prism/)

- *Journal of Military Experience* (http://encompass.eku.edu/jme/)

- *ninepatch: A Creative Journal of Women & Gender Studies* (http://encompass.eku.edu/ninepatch/)

- A forthcoming peer-reviewed journal: *JARFS: Journal of Applied Research in Fire Sciences*

> **[The program was] a success because it inspired thoughtful conversation, opened new lines of communications with faculty...**

Participants who arrived feeling uncertain about where to start with journal editing left with insights into the practical responsibilities of editing and hosting a journal: time commitments, workflow design, article submission processes, copyediting, obtaining an ISSN, designing a logo, organizing the website, etc.

The PLC brought more awareness of the differences between publishing in print and publishing online and exposed some faculty to the concept of high-quality peer-reviewed OA online journals. Furthermore, it expanded the discussion about OA journals on campus and illuminated the debate between the humanities and sciences on the feasibility and importance of OA publishing. There were good "devil's advocates" in the group that enlivened the discussions of OA, particularly around the issue of creative works.

There were a few challenges. In the participant feedback forms only one participant felt that he did not learn new information. Scheduling was problematic: Several of the participants were not able to attend regularly due to time conflicts. Additionally, this was quite a large time commitment for librarians Edwards and Sizemore who planned and facilitated the PLC, and was challenging to fit the work in with regular job responsibilities.

After launching Encompass in 2011, it quickly became a popular destination for researchers. In its first year, the 2,453 items deposited in Encompass were downloaded 75,226 times (an average of 30.6 downloads per item). In 2013, the *Journal of Military Experience* was profiled in the *New York Times* (Simon, 2013). As of the writing of this report, the repository's sixth journal, *The Journal of Retracing Africa* (http://encompass.eku.edu/jora/), has started accepting submissions.

References

AllthingsPLC. (n.d.). *About PLCs: History of PLCs.* Retrieved from http://www.allthingsplc. info/about/evolution.php

Burns, C., Lana, A., & Budd, J. (2013). Institutional repositories: Exploration of costs and value. *D-Lib Magazine, 19(1/2).* doi:10.1045/january2013-burns

Eastern Kentucky University. (2011). *Professional learning communities.* Retrieved from http:// www.tlc.eku.edu/professional-learning-communities

Hord, S. M. (1997). *Professional learning communities: Communities of continuous inquiry and improvement.* Retrieved from http://www.sedl.org/pubs/change34/

McGuigan, G. S. & Russell, R. D. (2008). The business of academic publishing: A strategic analysis of the academic journal publishing industry and its impact on the future of scholarly publishing. *Electronic Journal of Academic and Special Librarianship, 9(3).* Retrieved from http://southernlibrarianship.icaap.org/content/v09n03/mcguigan_g01. html

Ovadia, S. (2011). Open-access electronic textbooks: An overview. *Behavioral & Social Sciences Librarian, 30(1).* Retrieved from http://www.tandfonline.com/doi/abs/10.1080/13614533. 2010.509542

Paiz, J., Angeli, E., Wagner, J., Lawrick, E., Moore, K., Anderson, M., Soderlund, L., Brizee, A., & Keck, R. (2013, March 1). *APA formatting and style guide.* Retrieved from http://owl. english.purdue.edu/owl/resource/560/01/

Shilling, L., & Fuller, L. (1997). *Dictionary of quotations in communications.* Greenwood. Retrieved from http://bit.ly/11eSYI6

Simon, C. C. (2013, Feb 03). Warrior voices. *New York Times*. Retrieved from http://www.nytimes.com/2013/02/03/education/edlife/veterans-learn-to-write-and-heal.html?smid=pl-share

Mullins, J. L., Murray-Rust, C., Ogburn, J., Crow, R., Ivins, O., Mower, A., … Watkinson, C. (2011). *Library publishing services: Strategies for success research report version 1.0.* Retrieved from http://docs.lib.purdue.edu/lib_research/136/

Waltham, M. (2010). The future of scholarly journal publishing among social science and humanities associations. *Journal of Scholarly Publishing, 41(3).* Retrieved from http://utpjournals.metapress.com/content/W30108T03P1140T2

Endnotes

[1] Shilling, p. 135.

[2] See Burns for a research study examining the costs and values of IRs, especially as they relate to the types of services offered and the size of the institution.

[3] Several studies have explored this. For example, see McGuigan, Waltham, and Ovadia.

[4] See http://www.tlc.eku.edu/professional-learning-communities and http://www.allthingsplc.info/about/evolution.php

[5] See http://www.tlc.eku.edu/faqs

Appendix A

EASTERN KENTUCKY UNIVERSITY
Serving Kentuckians Since 1906

EKU
TEACHING & LEARNING
CENTER

201 Keen Johnson
521 Lancaster Avenue
Richmond, Kentucky 40475-3163
(859) 622-6519   Fax (859) 622-5018

Dear _____,

During the Spring 2011 semester, EKU Libraries and the Teaching & Learning Center (TLC) are offering a professional learning community (PLC), "Being a Successful Journal Editor." As facilitators of this community, we would like to extend an invitation to you to be a participant in this community because you are currently a journal editor or have expressed an interest in developing an online journal in EKU's institutional repository, Encompass.

Participants in the "Being a Successful Journal Editor" PLC will:
- Have an opportunity to engage in discussions about a new or existing journal
- Learn strategies related to creating a broader readership
- Discuss trends and issues related to scholarly communication and open access
- Learn how to host an online journal through Encompass, EKU's institutional repository.

The PLC facilitators will provide you with:
- Guided discussions
- Guest speakers
- Individualized assistance with your journal if hosted on Encompass
- Snacks.

We anticipate the PLC will meet 5-6 times on alternate Fridays during the spring semester for an hour each session.

Please email Laura Edwards at laura.edwards@eku.edu as to your interest and any questions you might have so we can start planning our professional learning community.

Sincerely,

Laura Edwards,
Electronic Resources Access Librarian

Linda Sizemore,
Government Documents & Law Library Team Leader

Hal Blythe, Co-Director
Teaching and Learning Center

Charlie Sweet, Co-Director
Teaching & Learning Center

Eastern Kentucky University is an Equal Opportunity/Affirmative Action Employer and Educational Institution

Appendix B

Journal Editor PLC
Schedule & Special Events

February

2/4: Introductions/Share Your Journal

> Share your journal and any challenges you face as an editor
> Discussion point: what makes a great journal

2/18: Journal Editor Panel Discussion

> Panelists: Dr. Vic Kappeler, editorial board member for *Criminal Justice Review*, and
> George Brosi, editor of *Appalachian Heritage*
> Discussion point: role of editors and editorial board members

March

3/4: Dirty Business of Running a Journal

> Discussion point: management strategies

3/18: Scholarly Communications with special guest Lee Van Orsdel

> Lee Van Orsdel, dean of university libraries at Grand Valley State University and member of the
> steering committee for Scholarly Publishing and Academic Resources Coalition (SPARC), speaks
> nationally and internationally on scholarly communications issues.

> *Tentative*: 10 AM Campus-Wide Presentation
> *Tentative*: Dinner with Lee, either Thursday 3/17 or Friday 3/18

3/28 – 4/1: Scholarship Week

> 3/28: Encompass & Selected Works (11:15 AM)
> 3/29: *Brain Rules* of Scholarship, by Brain Rules author John Medina (12:30 PM)
> (for more Scholarship Week events, see HTTP://WWW.TLC.EKU.EDU/WORKSHOPS/)

April

4/1: Broadening Your Readership

> Discussion point: strategies for wide distribution of your journal

The Faculty-Led, Library-Supported Journal

Appendix C

Questions for Journal Editor Panelists
February 18, 2011

◇ How authors choose a journal for their submission

◇ On multiple submissions of the same article to different journals

◇ How authors should write a cover letter

◇ How authors should prepare papers for submission

◇ How editors assign papers to referees

◇ How referees evaluate articles

◇ How editors make publication decisions

◇ How authors should interpret the feedback of the referees and editorial decisions

◇ How authors should prepare the resubmission cover letter and response

◇ The types of collaboration that are permitted in an individually authored article

◇ How/when should authors obtain copyright permissions

◇ How a paper presented in a conference or on the Internet might affect submission to a journal

◇ How authors should engage in proofreading/copyediting

◇ Behind the scenes in the editorial office: questions about liaison, deadlines, inquiries from authors etc.

The California Geographer and the OA Movement:

Using the Green OA Institutional Repository as a Publishing Platform

Michael Biondo & Andrew Weiss

California State University, Northridge

The Faculty-Led, Library-Supported Journal

2 IN THIS CHAPTER

Theme

Transitioning a Journal from traditional publishing to Open Access

Highlighted Service

Journal hosting & publishing

Software/Platforms Utilized

DSpace & Open Journal Systems

Resources

Discussion of the benefits and challenges in the transition to OA

Publishing in open access has been largely dominated by Gold OA journals. Publication in these journals, which in some cases have developed as the leading scholarly journals in their respective disciplines, provides immediate dissemination of information, a greater likelihood of citations for authors, and costs less than traditional publishing venues (Wagner, 2010). Lesk (2012) estimates that publisher Elsevier spends about $10,000 per article published, while the Public Library of Science (PLoS), a prominent Gold OA journal, spends only about $1,500 per article. PLoS' fee-based approach is a vital part of the open access movement even as it erects economic obstacles for researchers who lack sufficient funding to pay publishing fees. Total costs are clearly cheaper than their traditional counterparts, but those costs are essentially shifted from readers onto authors.

On the other side of the OA movement, Green open access repositories have traditionally been used for gathering previously published scholarly materials—usually pre-prints, post-prints, and the occasional final version from compliant publishers. Yet one recent strategy of institutional repositories has been to move away from being passive gatherers of self-archived content to becoming active promoters of new scholarship, especially in the creation of Web-based journals. This is occurring at significantly reduced costs as well. Cornell University's *Arxiv*, for example spends approximately $7 per article to gather work in physics, mathematics, computer science, quantitative biology, quantitative finance, and statistics (Lesk, 2012). Peer review and other services still remain the responsibility of the journals.

The California State University, Northridge (CSUN) has joined this growing movement by providing space in its open access institutional repository, *ScholarWorks*, for *The California Geographer*, a journal currently edited by CSUN faculty. From May 2012 to April 2013, CSUN *ScholarWorks*, based on the open source IR software DSpace, has grown from roughly 200 items to nearly 2,200 (California, 2013). Growth has been evenly distributed between ETDs, which were mandated in May 2012, faculty publications, and several campus-based open access journals, including the English Department's student journal, a journal of Chicana/o studies, newsletters and pamphlets in the Biology Department, and *The California Geographer*.

Publishing The California Geographer to a Shrinking Audience

The California Geographer serves as the flagship publication of the California Geographic Society. Through 52 volumes and nearly 400 articles, the journal had been published entirely in print form. However, in 2012 society members decided to move to an electronic-only version. The main reason to move to purely digital was to alleviate the growing costs of paper-based publication. According to the current editor and treasurer, Steven Graves, professor of geography at CSUN, yearly printing costs for the journal reached about $2,500, with approximately $1,400 going toward the copyeditor and $1,100 going toward the printing and mailing of the journal. Continuing to provide print journals was increasingly seen as an unsustainable practice. E-versions would be cheaper to produce and distribute, cutting out both printing and postage costs. Second, the society believed that e-versions of their work would be much more environmentally friendly, one of their core values as a geographic society (Graves, 2013).

The most pressing issue for the society, however, has been ensuring the journal's accessibility to a wider audience. For the past decade *The California Geographer* had been available as a print journal with digital versions added to the online content aggregator EBSCOhost databases. The problem was that the journal was bundled with the company's highest-priced access package, *Academic Search Premier*. As a result, the online articles were available neither to the CSUN campus itself nor about half of the other 22 campuses in the California State University system. Much of the journal's readership, including CSUN faculty and students, was unable to access the journal except in print form. Ironically, this limited access occurred despite the fact that the society had never transferred copyright to EBSCO. Their agreement merely allowed the company to distribute it online through a limited license agreement.

Moving The California Geographer to Open Access

Moving to open access turned out to be a relatively simple process. Once the editors had learned of CSUN *ScholarWorks*, its overall access and preservation philosophy, and its online search capabilities, the society's board of directors voted to move the journal to open access. As owners of the copyright, they were not fettered with drawn-out negotiations to return transferred rights. Additionally, the board decided to keep the current agreement with EBSCO in order to continue receiving revenues, however diminished they might be.

ScholarWorks staff next took over the task of digitizing the print journals and cataloging them at the article level within the repository. It was considered easier to digitize the journals in-house as well as to secure any digital files from the journal editors than to deal with acquiring digital files from EBSCO directly.

Procedure

ScholarWorks staff obtained a print issue of each volume and began digitization with an Epson 10000 XL flatbed scanner. The resulting high-quality TIFF files were batch-processed in Photoshop, and merged and converted into multi-page PDFs. The digitization of the journal took approximately six weeks. This resulted in the scanning of over 5,500 pages and the creation of 400 individual PDF items. One-time costs are estimated at $50 for each item submitted to *ScholarWorks* during the period of time April 2012–March 2013 (this includes all items as well as *The California Geographer*). This is significantly cheaper than traditional or Gold OA publishing, though still about seven times higher than the Green OA repository *Arxiv* (see Figure 1).

Benefits and Impact

According to *Library Journal's Periodicals Price Survey 2012*, the average price per title in geography was $1,348 (Bosch and Henderson, 2012). By choosing to forgo the traditional publishing model, which results in higher costs in both financial and environmental terms, the journal has become significantly more accessible and therefore more sustainable. Although the journal will continue to be edited by the members of the editorial staff, time and cost no longer need to be sunk in printing costs. The benefit of the savings offsets the eventual loss of royalties from EBSCO, which totaled roughly $850 in 2012. Including all costs associated with the print version of the *California Geographer*, which were about $2,500, the society was losing nearly $1,700 to publish and distribute the journal.

By choosing to forgo the traditional publishing model, which results in higher costs in both financial and environmental terms, the journal has become significantly more accessible and therefore more sustainable.

By placing the journal in CSUN *ScholarWorks*, the society benefits from a robust digital preservation infrastructure supported by the California State University's Chancellor's Office Digital Library Services. DSpace's handle system provides each journal article with a permanent uniform resource indicator (URI), which functions like a digital object identifier (DOI). By adding the journal to the IR, the society also receives permanence and stability for its publication without incurring the high cost of purchasing its own server, storage, and backup.

The move from print to digital has a direct impact on the library itself. The Oviatt Library is currently transitioning away from the traditional model of stacks and individual study carrels toward a "Learning Commons" model of collaboration, multi-purpose use, and group-centered learning. As a result, interior space is a valuable commodity. The movement of journals, serials, and reference works from print to digital open access allows the library to free up space that can be used for student-centric activities. Librarians at Oviatt recently completed a thorough weeding of traditional reference materials, and the stacks and shelving that once housed print publications such as *The California Geographer* are scheduled to be removed to make room for its new Learning Commons. Print journals will be moved to Oviatt Library's Automated Storage and Retrieval System (ASRS).

Drawbacks & Solutions

As mentioned earlier, one of the drawbacks from the move to *ScholarWorks* is the potential loss of royalty revenue that the publication receives from EBSCO for each download. Yet, as we demonstrated earlier, this amount is offset by the costs incurred by maintaining a traditional print model. Furthermore, it appears that only the years after 1990 are provided full-text in EBSCO. The first 30 years are therefore not available as full-text, which results in significantly fewer downloads and subsequent royalties.

A much larger concern expressed by members of the society was disappointment at the loss of a physical copy. The need for a physical copy appears to be drawn along generational lines. New members of the society, in fact, appear to be more comfortable accessing and reading an article on a tablet/iPad. Yet any PDF-based issue or article in *ScholarWorks* can be printed, usually in the exact form in which it was published. In contrast, though PDFs are available through EBSCO, the aggregator's version is primarily accessible only in text-based HTML, which tends to eliminate the character, physical context, and feel of the original print publication. In cases of items with maps and detailed images, this is a drawback. Ultimately, though, for those members of the society who still wish to receive a print version of the journal, the *California Geographer* editorial board could instead use the services of short-run, on-demand-printing, at a fraction of the cost of a traditional full print run.

It must be noted that EBSCO's image scans in the supplied PDFs are also significantly poorer in terms of image quality. *ScholarWorks*, however, allows the journal to add high-quality supplemental files to items within the collection in any file format, including TIFF and JPEG2000. A good example of this added value appears in Volume 39 (1999) with the supplemental "Absurdist Cartographer Map" (see Figure 2).

Originally, this map was mailed out to all print subscribers subsequent to the journal's publication. As it appears in the EBSCO database, however, the map is illegible and therefore unreadable. The text in the image is too small to read yet does not have sufficient resolution for zooming in. By scanning the supplemental map that appeared with the journal in a high-resolution TIFF file, viewers are able to get the full experience of "Dadaist geography" as intended by the author (Kaplan and Nemeth, 1999).

Another drawback stems from relying solely on the DSpace package to "publish" *The California Geographer*. While *ScholarWorks* staff members believe very strongly in creating open access journals, there are still some limitations to using DSpace as the primary publication platform. First, unlike bepress or Open Journal Systems(OJS), which could be implemented and integrated with DSpace, the stand-alone DSpace system does not handle the workflow of a peer-reviewed journal. It is not a full-service publishing platform. Additionally, while some systems can provide a unique "look and feel" for individual journals, we have not yet distinguished the journal from the framework of the IR. Because the journal is in reality a sub-community within the DSpace repository structure, it remains submerged within its hierarchy of community/sub-community/collection. One strategy taken to approximate the functionality of a dynamic table of contents for each volume, then, is to embed permanent links of the individual articles within the collection page.

Future Plans

Long-term planning will be implemented over the course of the 2013–2014 academic year. To accomplish this, a new Digital Publication Implementation Group was established by Oviatt Library Dean Mark Stover in May 2013. The members of this group will oversee digital journal publication as well as provide needs analyses for future projects. Although membership is currently limited to library faculty and staff, the group will reach out to form partnerships with campus departments and colleges interested in establishing or moving to online digital journals.

The first priority for the group will be to pilot OJS at the library. As it is an open source software system compatible with DSpace, it matches our philosophical goals while also supplementing our long-term development model. By pairing an open access publishing system like OJS with DSpace, we can provide dynamic front-end accessibility with stable back-end archiving and storage. This is accomplished by the SWORD protocol, which, in layperson's terms, basically pushes content into the DSpace system from source locations. CSUN already uses SWORD for its online electronic theses and dissertations (ETDs) submission forms. There are also plans to set up SWORD in various colleges and departments across CSUN in order to begin collecting materials for the university's archives. The more drivers available for content submission, the more likely faculty and administrators will participate in adding content to an open access IR (see Figure 3).

> # Since mentioning the possibility of providing a publishing platform, various organizations and departments on campus have become very interested in partnerships.

Oviatt Library will consider plans to restart the currently shuttered university press, *Santa Susannah Press*, as an open access imprint. Multiple projects are on the horizon, including the archiving and publishing of conference proceedings and presentations for the *28th Annual International Technology and Persons with Disabilities Conference*. Since mentioning the possibility of providing a publishing platform, various organizations and departments on campus have become very interested in partnerships.

Conclusions

The implementation and integration of open source, open access platforms such as DSpace and OJS will allow Oviatt Library to continue partnering with institutions such as *The California Geographical Society*, and promoting the dissemination of information openly, economically, and sustainably. Ultimately we see *The California Geographer* as the first jewel in an expanding crown of online electronic open access CSUN publications.

As we have seen with not only ETDs but with any formerly print collection moving to an online environment, the added value from digitization—increased access, cheaper printing costs, full-text searching, and so on—provides new life for the content. CSUN *ScholarWorks* statistics show multifold increases in ETD access. It is not unreasonable to expect similar increases in access to *The California Geographer*. Those who are vision impaired also benefit from the increased availability of the content in an ADA-compliant form, especially in PDFs that have been formatted with optical character recognition software.

Open access publication will surely continue to evolve and the Green open access IR may be poised to take over some of the duties of publishing that have been the primary domain of the Gold OA movement. Lower overall costs for this type of model may signal perhaps that a hybrid Green-Gold OA movement will be our future.

References

Bosch, S., & Henderson, K. (2012, April 30). *Coping with the terrible twins: Periodical price survey 2012*. Retrieved from http://lj.libraryjournal.com/2012/04/funding/coping-with-the-terrible-twins-periodicals-price-survey-2012/

California State University, Northridge. (2013, April 19). *The California Geographer*. Retrieved from ScholarWorks: http://scholarworks.csun.edu/handle/10211.2/2186

Graves, S. D. (2013, April 09). Usage stats for California geographer. (A. Weiss, Interviewer)

Kaplan, D., & Nemeth, D. (1999). Absurdist cartography: The dada millennium map of the United States. *The California Geographer, 39*, 65–69. Retrieved from http://hdl.handle.net/10211.2/2716

Lesk, M. (2012). A personal history of digital libraries. *Library Hi Tech, 30*(4), 593–603. doi: 10.1108/07378831211285077

Wagner, A. B. (2010). Open access citation advantage: An annotated bibliography. *Issues in Science and Technology Librarianship, 60*(Winter). doi:10.5062/F4Q81B0W

Appendix:

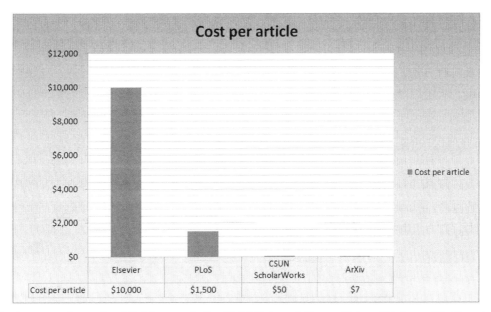

Figure 1: A comparison of publishing costs for Gold OA and Green OA publishers. PLoS costs close to $1,500 per submission. ArXiv costs $7 per submission. CSUN's costs are $50 per submission. Elsevier, however, is estimated at nearly $10,000 per submission. (Lesk 2012)

Figure 2: A comparison of the same sections of the Absurdist Map of the U.S. from the California Geographer, v.39, 1999. The image on the left is EBSCO's version. The image on the right is the supplementary material version in CSUN ScholarWorks.

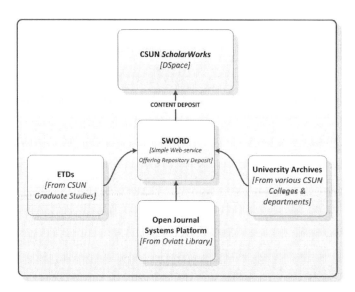

Figure 3: Diagram shows the central importance of the SWORD protocol for facilitating automated content submission into the DSpace repository. By integrating OJS with DSpace, another content driver functioning like CSUN's ETDs online submission process or the proposed University Archives submission form will ensure the IR's continued development.

A Case Study in Open Access Journal Publishing at Syracuse University:
Library and University Press Partnership Furthers Scholarly Communications

Yuan Li, Suzanne E. Guiod, & Suzanne Preate

Syracuse University

The Faculty-Led, Library-Supported Journal

3

IN THIS CHAPTER

Theme

Working with a university press to host and manage journal publishing

Highlighted Service

Online journal hosting & publishing

Software/Platforms Utilized

Digital Commons by bepress & Open Journal Systems

Resources

Division of roles & duties between partners

Syracuse University is driven by its mission, "Scholarship in Action," a commitment to forging bold, imaginative, reciprocal engagements with its many constituent local and global communities. These outward-looking engagements inevitably yield new forms of scholarship and new collaborative arrangements. To that end, open access (OA) journal publishing services are being developed at SU to meet the emerging needs of the campus community through a partnership between Syracuse University Libraries, Library Information and Technology Services (LITS), campus Information and Technology Services (ITS), and Syracuse University Press.

215

These services have been designed specifically to address faculty needs for new publishing venues, especially in interdisciplinary fields. The SU Libraries seek to provide faculty with non-commercial OA publishing venues, and the SU Press seeks to support research, teaching, and outreach at the university.

The SU Library launched its institutional repository (IR) in 2010 and started OA journal publishing services through its IR in 2011. As the number of faculty requests for e-journal publishing support increased, the SU Libraries began to explore a sustainable publishing service model, specifically the possibility of adopting an open source publishing system and collaborating with SU Press and ITS for complementary services. Two new OA journals are now in pilot stages under a joint library-press imprint, currently called Syracuse Unbound.

Using these two new OA journals—scheduled to publish inaugural issues during the 2013-14 academic year—as case studies, this paper will highlight the development of campus partnerships, share the implementation of publishing platforms and distributed workflows, and foster a discussion about innovative and collaborative strategies for SU Library publishing programs.

SU Institutional Repository and Digital Commons

In October 2010, SU launched its institutional repository, called SUrface: Syracuse University Research Facility and Collaborative Environment. The repository was built using Digital Commons (DC), a system developed by bepress, which includes a journal publishing module. Through it, SU Library is able to provide basic publishing services for faculty, students, and researchers interested in starting a new e-journal, hosting and publishing an existing e-journal, or digitizing a print journal. Early projects included a campus magazine and an undergraduate student journal. The services we're able to offer through Digital Commons include hosting a standard e-journal site in SUrface, migrating back issues to the site, helping to draft copyright guidelines, applying for E-ISSNs, helping with indexing and abstracting, and software training and demonstration.

New Demands

In 2011, the library was approached by the director of Imagining America (IA)—a national consortium focused on publicly engaged scholarship—with interest in developing a journal concept. The journal development team included a national group of IA scholars led by two SU professors in architecture and design. The result is *Public: A Journal of Imagining America*. This peer-reviewed journal required editorial expertise, sophisticated design, and user interface customization that the current DC platform was unable to support.

In early 2012, the director of the Syracuse University's LGBT Studies program reached out to the SU Libraries for support and guidance in publishing the *Journal of Diverse Sexualities*, "an open-access, peer-reviewed journal dedicated to publishing scholarship, criticism, and commentary." This publishing model would encourage a broad readership beyond the academy.

216

Although this journal does not require the same level of customization as *Public*, it does require some design and editorial support and the ability to accommodate multimedia elements.

These requests exceeded our existing service capabilities. Subscribers to Digital Commons are allowed to host five journals without additional charges, but beyond that, a per-journal setup fee applies. This added cost could become a challenge for both the SU library and researchers, heightening the need to explore a different model for providing campus publishing support.

Open Source Publishing System Adoption

While Digital Commons provides a centrally hosted and maintained service, allowing libraries to focus staff resources on content acquisition and management, it is not fully customizable. The SU Libraries began looking for a system that was less expensive and more flexible, and as a result adopted Open Journal Systems (OJS), an open source software system developed by the Public Knowledge Project (PKP), that is typically implemented, hosted, and maintained locally. This option offers hosting libraries flexibility and local control, but also requires dedicated technical staff and other resources (e.g., online storage). The best solution for a given library depends on a number of factors, such as the institution's size, technical capacity, and available resources. Working with campus ITS, the SU Libraries added OJS as an alternative to Digital Commons to meet the more sophisticated demands of these publishing projects. ITS provided server space for the OJS system and two pilot journals, as well as assistance with front-end design for one of the journals.

Library-Press Partnership

In addition to exploring open source systems, the library also sought a partner to assist with editorial consultation and production. Because SU Press had recently become administratively part of the library, SU Libraries administration viewed this as an opportunity for mutually beneficial collaboration. The library staff's skills in organizing, describing, managing, disseminating, and preserving scholarship and technical expertise in information management could complement the traditional publishing skills of a university press staff—peer review oversight, manuscript editorial management, design, marketing, and production.

For SU Press, the partnership offered an opportunity to collaborate closely with colleagues at the SU Libraries, to interact directly with SU faculty, and to offer its editorial and design services in a way that would support the dissemination of scholarship generated from within its host institution, a core value at the heart of the mission of most university presses. The partnership also allows the press to experiment with journal publishing without the additional burden of offering subscriptions and sales services. A partnership between the SU Libraries and SU Press to offer quality digital publishing services to faculty seemed natural, as both are charged with making available the intellectual output of scholars. The relationship also enables SU Press to take advantage of the SU Libraries' infrastructure and resources to contain costs.

Under the new partnership model, the SU Libraries provide more sustainable professional publishing services, including technical guidance and support; server space and administration; training and demonstration; digital preservation; E-ISSN application; DOI assignment; metadata consultation, abstracting/indexing services; editorial consulting, professional copyediting; and some design services. Together, building on the ITS infrastructure, the two entities offer a unique suite of scholarly communication services and support for SU faculty, staff, and students in response to the evolving needs of our research community.

The collaborative nature of this undertaking requires clearly defined roles, responsibilities, and expectations. The roles and responsibilities are determined by a combination of project stakeholder input, available expertise, staff capacity, funding, and other specifications dictated by each journal's memorandum of understanding (MOU). Start-up costs are an important consideration, whether in real dollars (for server space, DOI registration, design consultation, Web programming, and editorial expertise) or in-kind staff time.

> **The roles and responsibilities are determined by a combination of project stakeholder input, available expertise, staff capacity, funding, and other specifications dictated by each journal's memorandum of understanding.**

In our pilot phase, the roles are filled by staff from the campus and library IT, SU Press, and faculty departments. The OJS implementation process begins with software installation, server administration, and journal configuration. Campus ITS provides server space for each OJS journal and brings expertise to the interface development effort, while the library is responsible for software installation, server administration, full back-end configuration and minimal front-end customization, metadata consultation, and software training for faculty editors and SU Press staff. Once the software foundation is established, several workstreams emerge—technical, content, policy and procedural, editorial, and author support. SU Press staff has met regularly with the journals' faculty editors to advise on forming editorial boards, writing editorial policies, determining peer review procedures, and designing the look and feel of the journals. Professional copyediting and content layout will be managed by SU Press's editorial and production department. The workstreams are sometimes parallel, sometimes dependent, but all overlap at various points in the process and ultimately contribute to and follow a shared and sometimes complex timeline.

The following functional roles are represented in our pilot project and it is common for one stakeholder to assume several roles. Roles marked with an asterisk use OJS terminology to describe traditional responsibilities as well as elements specific to OJS software such as workflow and system permission levels. This list could be used as a starting point for similar undertakings.

Functional Roles	Stakeholders			
	Faculty Initiator	SU Libraries	SU Press	Campus ITS
Project Managers	•	•	•	•
IT Analysts		•	•	•
Designers (logo, brand, interface)	•		•	
Metadata Librarian		•		
Policy Makers	•		•	
Copyright Consultants		•	•	
OJS Site Administrator*		•		
OJS Journal Managers*	•	•		
Editorial Board	•		•	
Managing Editor*	•			
Section Editors*	•		•	
Reviewers*	•			
Copyeditors*	•		•	
Layout Editors*	•		•	
Proofreaders*	•			

As we researched and developed services and software options, we identified specific stakeholder considerations in order to select the most appropriate platform for a given publishing scenario. Additionally, any resources faculty editors and other requestors bring to bear and their desired level of involvement in the process (as compared with a singular focus on the content) significantly impact the project direction. The capabilities and strengths of each system (OJS and Digital Commons) coupled with faculty needs and resources inform our workflows and the shape of our overall service model. As we investigate, test, and develop a sustainable suite of services, we find that a combination of priorities and other factors help us to decide which platform to use for a given publishing project. The following questions assist in the articulation of requestor needs, priorities, and expectations:

- Is the journal new/born-digital or print-to-online?
- What is the timeline to launch?
- Will it be OA, delayed OA, or subscription?
- Are there dedicated staff/students available and at what time allocation?
- What staff expertise (e.g., editorial, design, technical) exists?
- Is there available funding and at what funding level?
- Does the journal require a personalized domain?
- Are there specific authentication needs (e.g., LDAP, Shibboleth, local, other)?
- Will the journal require an ISSN application/DOI assignment?
- What are the editorial, copyediting, and layout needs?
- What are the design and interface requirements? Does a logo, color scheme, or brand already exist?
- What are the file type requirements and support for ingest and output?
- What level of metadata consultation and creation is needed?
- What are the indexing requirements—OA, proprietary, or both?
- What kind of statistics/reporting options are desired?
- Are there additional tools and functionality needs, such as integrating a blog, wiki, user comments, tagging, etc.?
- What level and frequency of training is required?
- What level of technical support is required?

OJS was the right choice for this pilot program because of the sophisticated design requirements and user interface customization needs of one journal, including data extraction and manipulation, and because both journals would incorporate multimedia content.

Discussion

The library-press partnership has successfully helped our faculty to develop two OA journals and has allowed the SU Libraries to introduce enhanced publishing services to the campus community. The new service model has enabled us to overcome cost constraints on the number of journals we can publish and the customizations we can apply to the journal site, thereby better supporting faculty publishing needs. As our publishing services grow and mature, however, the need to discuss and develop a plan for sustaining these services increases. Possible approaches would include seeking new sources of funding to supplement the library's subsidy from our host institution, and developing fee-based service models for each journal client. In order to justify a growing allocation of library resources to publishing services, the library must demonstrate the academic value of these services.

Fee-based service models can be developed in different ways. A tiered services menu, such as that used by Columbia University's Center for Digital Research and Scholarship (CDRS), could be implemented, and related costs could be shared with departments. Offering print-on-demand services could also be a possible channel for generating revenue. According to Mullins (2012), another possibility for a fee-based service model is to extend library service offerings beyond core campus constituencies—for example, providing publishing services to society-sponsored journals not affiliated with the institution, as in the case of Project Muse.

The demand from faculty and other campus constituencies for OA publishing outlets will only increase, and libraries must find efficient and cost-effective ways to meet those needs by drawing on existing resources, leveraging new and open source technologies, and forming collegial and reciprocal campus partnerships that will broaden the scope and improve the quality of its services. By using new technologies to make scholarship available to a wider audience, and by implementing and maintaining platforms for the open dissemination of peer-reviewed and carefully edited content, this collaboration between SU Library and SU Press advances scholarly communication and furthers Syracuse University's mission of "Scholarship in Action."

References

Hahn, K. (2008). *Research Library Publishing Services: New Options for University Publishing.* Washington, DC: ARL. Retrieved from http://www.arl.org/storage/documents/publications/research-library-publishing-services-mar08.pdf

Mullins, J. L., Murray-Rust, C., Ogburn, J. L., Crow, R., Ivins, O., Mower, A., Nesdill, D., Newton, M. P., Speer, J., & Watkinson, C. (2012). *Library Publishing Services: Strategies for Success: Final Research Report.* Washington, DC: SPARC. Retrieved from http://docs.lib.purdue.edu/purduepress_ebooks/24/

OAJ From A to Z: How to Succeed at Launching an OA Journal (Without Really Trying)

Nick Paulus

Rochester Institute of Technolgy

The Faculty-Led, Library-Supported Journal

4 IN THIS CHAPTER

Theme

Set up, launch, and maintenance of a library-supported Open Access Journal

Highlighted Service

Online journal hosting & publishing

Resources

Sample author guidelines, launch timelines, & step-by-step overview of the process from set up through the launch of a publication

In order to have success in launching a new open access (OA) journal, careful planning is critical. Following a certain sequence of steps and establishing a framework will facilitate a final publication that is both sustainable and beneficial to its discipline.

The first step in launching a new OA journal is to develop a publication strategy that maps the foundation and development of the publication. The successful publication strategy requires a detailed analysis of how the journal will be launched: governance structure, financing, target audience, marketing, peer review, design/layout, timeline for publication, etc. The investigation of these issues will provide a framework for all future steps necessary to launch a journal. The strategy should be considered a living document that can be amended over time and should include pre-production and launch preparation stages.

Pre-Production Stage

The Name of the Journal

The title should give a clear identity to the type of articles that will appear in the publication. Also consider how people will abbreviate your journal. Try to avoid abbreviation combinations that are hard to remember or spell a word that you don't want associated with your journal. If careful thought is given to the title at the beginning stage, you can avoid the need to rebrand your journal at a later date, which is expensive and can be perceived negatively (Huggett, 2011).

Rationale for a New Publication

The reason why a new journal is needed is an important question that needs to be well defined and communicated to your intended audience. This is the foundation and justification for your journal and should address current and future trends in your discipline, examine existing journals and explain how yours will be different, and portray confidence that you can garner high-quality submissions and a large and sustainable audience. The development of a concise rationale will assist in the development of the journal's scope and recruitment of an editorial board.

> # The reason why a new journal is needed is an important question that needs to be well defined and communicated to your intended audience.

The Scope of the Journal

Publishing the scope of your journal in a prominent location on your website is essential. The scope should communicate the goals and content of the publication. It should be considered a marketing message for readers who, after reading the scope, will want to click further into the journal. A well-defined scope will also engage authors to consider submitting an article. The scope of the journal should specify that it is an OA publication and should include a complete list of articles the journal will consider publishing (e.g., original articles, book reviews, review articles, letter to the editors, etc.) (CoAction Publishing, 2010).

Journal Governance Structure

The governance structure typically has an appointed editor-in-chief, who is the publication's final voice on operations and policies Additionally, the editor-in-chief is responsible for developing an editorial board, contributing editorial pieces, marketing, and is the final say on the publication of each article.

The managing editor represents the journal to external entities, including associations, societies, academic institutions, and authors. Managing editors assume responsibility for publishing high-quality material, which is vetted through the journal's review system, and for managing the workflow of articles from submission to publication.

Peer reviewers provide constructive feedback to authors regarding publication and research standards as they pertain to article submissions.

Graphic designers are responsible for the layout and design of the journal cover and layout of articles for publication.

Editors are responsible for copyediting articles as necessary.

Creation of an Editorial Board

Selection of the editorial board members plays a significant part in establishing/enhancing the reputation of your journal. The editor-in chief should strive to recruit well-known, respected, and international members of the scholarly community who have published in a field related to the scope of the journal. The editorial board is responsible for garnering content, marketing, and developing a vision for the publication.

Peer-Review Workflow

Peer review is the traditional assessment method of manuscripts submitted for publication in journals (Grant, 2010). It is also the biggest challenge to the timely publication of a journal. The editor-in-chief is responsible for the formation of a peer-review board. This board usually consists of published experts in the field of the journal's scope. These individuals agree to review submitted articles (typically two articles a year) in exchange for being recognized by the journal as a reviewer. The reviewers are given a deadline (typically four weeks) to review the submission and provide feedback to the managing editor regarding whether to accept, accept with changes, or reject the submission. Two or three reviewers should review each article. The managing editor is responsible for merging the comments from all of the reviewers and forwarding them to the editor-in-chief for final judgment. The judgment should be forwarded to the author who, depending on the verdict, will make revisions before publication. If the paper is not accepted, the author is free to submit his/her paper to another journal. It should be mentioned that peer review will not determine if an article's finding are accurate—it simply determines if the process that lead to the paper's findings were done correctly (Grant, 2010).

This peer-review workflow is littered with time-sucking landmines that cause numerous delays and gray hairs for managing editors everywhere. The problem is that peer reviewers, through no fault of their own, insert an element of unpredictability into your timeline. Peer reviewers are often sent articles six months to a year after they agree to provide their service. Schedules, jobs, and available free time can change in that time period. As a result, deadlines for article review are missed or ignored altogether. Finding enough reviewers to vet an article can be a challenge. Consider asking authors from journals with a similar scope or searching on Google Scholar for authors who have published on a similar topic.

> ...peer reviewers, through no fault of their own, insert an element of unpredictability into your timeline.

Also, because multimedia files are also becoming more popular in journals, managing editors should consider developing guidelines for the review of supplemental multimedia files and an effective system to disseminate these files to reviewers.

Timeline for Publication and a Commitment to Publish

The time commitment for the first issue is far greater than post-inaugural issues due to the administrative groundwork necessary for the inaugural issue. To minimize stress, place a liberal timeline for publication.

Journal Management Software

Open Journal Systems (OJS) is an effective open source journal management publishing system. This system, once installed on your server, provides a full-service journal management and website creation system that makes the dissemination of a journal easy and free. The only fee you will incur is the cost of hosting the site. A list of free/open source journal management systems can be found at http://oad.simmons.edu/oadwiki/Free_and_open-source_journal_management_software.

Archival

It's important to develop an archiving system/policy to ensure that your content is maintained in a sustainable environment. OJS creates archived issues of your journal but should not be confused with archival-quality backups. An example of a suitable archiving system would be an institutional repository similar to DSpace or Digital Commons.

Launch Preparation Stage

With the groundwork finished, you can begin the launch preparation stage, which consists of designing a cover for your journal, applying for an ISSN, developing a layout style for your journal articles, setting a launch date and timeline for publication, issuing a call for papers (CFP), garnering content for your journal, testing all aspects of your website, and launching and marketing your journal.

Cover Design

Some people might think that designing a cover for a journal that hasn't launched yet is like putting the cart before the horse. However, designing a cover and placing the cover on a website is the precursor to obtaining an ISSN.

Obtaining an ISSN

The ISSN can be thought of as the Social Security number of the serials world. Allow two weeks for your application[1] to be processed. The URL of the journal and a mockup of the cover help to expedite the process. If you are using a journal management system, at some point you will be asked to enter the name of the journal and its desired abbreviation. This will allow the software to create a URL for the journal's home page.

Layout and Design of Articles

Before you begin the layout process of the journal articles, it's important to develop a submission guideline for authors. This guideline should define the look and specifications of every element in the publication (from abstract to references). It is also extremely helpful to prepare a downloadable template that authors can employ to easily format their manuscript. Topics addressed in the guideline will vary from journal to journal. The sample on the following page is of an author guideline page created for the *Journal of Applied Science & Engineering Technology* (JASET).

---

[1] http://www.loc.gov/issn/form/

Sample Author Guidelines for the *Journal of Applied Science & Engineering Technology* (JASET)	
Author and affiliations	(Added after blind review)
Abstract	Limit length to 400 words. Define all symbols used in abstract.
Introduction	1. When you open the Template.doc, please ensure that the Formatting Toolbar is visible: To activate it, go to the Microsoft Word View Menu and select the Toolbars' Formatting and Task Pane if it is available in your Windows application. 2. Type over sections of Template.doc or cut and paste from another document and then use markup styles. Markup styles may be accessed in the Task Pane, by selecting "Show: Available Styles" from a dropdown menu. The styles may also be accessed from the dropdown menu in the Formatting Toolbar (e.g., the style at this point in the document is "Numbered List"). 3. Highlight a section of your text that you want to designate with a certain style and then select the appropriate name on the style menu. The style will adjust your fonts and line spacing. 4. The number of pages must be between 5–10 correctly formatted pages including all tables, figures, references, and author biographies, which are only added after the paper is "accepted pending revisions." Do not change the font sizes or line spacing to squeeze more text into a limited number of pages. 5. Use italics for emphasis; do not underline. 6. To insert images in Word, position the cursor at the insertion point and either use Insert | Picture | From File or copy the image to the Windows clipboard and then Edit | Paste Special | Picture (with "Float over text" unchecked). 7. We expect authors to format their papers according to these guidelines.
PROCEDURE FOR PAPER SUBMISSION	
Review stage	Please submit your manuscript electronically for review. Follow the submission instructions located on the article submission page.

Final stage	1. Please submit your final manuscript electronically as a "revision" (this maintains the manuscript number and ongoing revision history) after your paper has been accepted and corrections have been addressed. 2. The author who submits the manuscript will be the "corresponding author." This is the author to whom proofs of the paper will be sent. Proofs are sent to the corresponding author only.
Copyright form	Authors are responsible for obtaining any necessary copyright permissions (located on the Article Submission page).
Figures	For consistency when preparing tables and figures, use a sans serif font such as "Arial" or "Helvetica." RIT cannot extract the tables and figures embedded in your Microsoft Word document. (The figures and tables you insert in your document are only to help you gauge the size of your paper, for the convenience of the referees, and to make it easy for you to distribute preprints.) Therefore, submit in separate files, tables, graphs, and image files, using the naming conventions as follows in Section E, "Electronic Image Files."
Electronic image files	The figures in your paper should be ready for print. Please submit graphic files in the following formats: JPEG, TIFF, PDF, Excel. Use a separate file for each image. File names should be of the form "fig2.pdf," etc. Files should be sized at the intended size of reproduction, or at least 5 inches wide, to maintain optimal readability and resolution. 1. Line figures and tables: Using a scanner, save the images in TIFF format. High-contrast line figures and tables should be prepared with 1200 dpi resolution and saved with no compression, 1 bit per pixel (monochrome), with file names of the form "fig3.tif" or "table1.tif." 2. Photographs and grayscale figures: Images should be prepared with 300 dpi resolution and saved with no compression, 8 bits per pixel (grayscale).
Color figures	Color images should be prepared with 400 dpi resolution and saved with no compression, 8 bits per pixel (palette or 256 color).

The JASET Guidelines[2] continue and address figures and tables, footnotes, abbreviation and acronyms, common mistakes, editorial policy, publication principles, and helpful hints. You can customize your guidelines to your journal's specifications. Consider it a living document and update it as needed.

[2]   http://library.rit.edu/oajournals/index.php/jaset/about/submissions#authorGuidelines

The use of a template does not guarantee that the submitted articles will be formatted correctly. It is the managing editor's job to thoroughly examine each article and make corrections. Another option is to bring the skills of a graphic designer into the process. A skilled graphic designer can lay out a typical journal article in about three to four hours.

Set a Launch Date and Timeline for Publication

Setting a launch date is not as easy as it sounds. You need to garner content for your journal and factor time for peer review, revisions, final layout, final proof for authors, and launch. The timeline for launching a journal might look something like this:

Call for papers	Allow three months for articles to come in (this time will be reduced as the journal gets traction with readers).
Peer review	Allow four weeks for reviewers to return articles (three weeks to procrastinate and one week to review).
Author response/edits to reviewer comments	One week for authors to address the concerns of the reviewers.
Final review of accepted papers by editor-in-chief	One week
Formatting and page layout	One week
Author's final review of formatted article	Two days
Total	Approximately five months

Disseminate a Call for Papers (CFP)

The CFP should explain the focus of the issue and provide a link to the journal and a deadline for submissions. Your CFP should be disseminated to all conferences and seminars with common topics. Additionally, you should ask any trade societies to post your CFP on their website. Upload your CFP to PapersInvited[3] and WikiCFP[4].

Garner Content

Posting a CFP for an inaugural issue should be considered a marketing exercise. The CFP will not garner enough content to publish a journal. Scholars are reluctant to publish in new journals due to the risk of a low impact factor. Your CFP might result in a few submissions, but that is about all you can hope. In general, a CFP will only be effective after the second issue is published. Authors typically need to see a commitment to regular publishing and publishing standards before submitting to your journal.

[3]   http://www.papersinvited.com
[4]   http://www.wikicfp.com/cfp/servlet/event.showcfp?

231

The content for the first two issues will come from your editorial board. It should be a condition that anyone who agrees to serve on the board will be responsible for supplying two articles for publication. Preferably, the board members will agree to author one or both of the articles, but the content can also come from the board members' network of peers.

Test All Aspects of Your Website

Simultaneously with issuing your CFP, you need to test the website to ensure that the submission process goes smoothly. You want to confirm that automated e-mails are generated by the content management system and are worded correctly.

Launching and Marketing for the Journal

After you have the content and it has gone through the review, approval, and design process, you are ready to launch the journal on the Web. It's a good idea to have a number of copies printed to send to submitting authors and to use as marketing pieces at conferences.

Having your journal published on the Web is not enough to ensure that readers and potential authors will find it. A multifaceted marketing strategy that incorporates print, social media, and word of mouth works best. A press release should go out one week before the launch of the journal and should target trade publications and local media. Establish a Facebook page for your journal and post on it at least once a week. Design postcards with your next CFP on it and hand them out at conventions and seminars. Finally, talk about the journal to anyone who might be interested in the topic of the publication.

References

CoAction Publishing. (2010). "Online Guide to Open Access Journal Publishing: Set Up." Retrieved from http://www.doaj.org/bpguide/set-up/3/

Grant, R. P. (2010). "On Peer Review." *Research Information Network*. Retrieved from http://www.rin.ac.uk/blogs/guest/richard-p-grant/peer-review

Huggett, S. (2011). "Heading for Success: or How Not to Title Your Paper." *Research Trends*. Retrieved from http://www.researchtrends.com/issue24-september-2011/heading-for-success-or-how-not-to-title-your-paper/

Open Access Directory. (2012). Free and open source journal management software. *Open Access Directory Wiki*. Retrieved from http://oad.simmons.edu/oadwiki/Free_and_open-source_journal_management_software

Library as
Journal Publisher:
Student Research Journals

IN THIS SECTION

Library Services for Creating and Publishing Student Research Journals

Adrian K. Ho

University of Kentucky

1 IN THIS CHAPTER

Theme

Planning & implementing student research journals

Highlighted Services

Journal consulting, publishing and technical support

Resources

Sample journal staff organization models, checklists to support planning, staffing, and production

Conducting research is an integral part of graduate education. To enhance students' learning and research skills, some institutions have launched journals to publish noteworthy scholarly works by graduate students. As Pearson, VanNest, and Jasinski (2004) explain, a graduate student journal encourages contributors to review the professional literature, promotes publishing of original findings, and creates mentoring opportunities for students (p. 68). Meanwhile, research has gained

This paper was derived from:

Ho, A. K. (2011). Creating and hosting student-run research journals: A case study. *Partnership: the Canadian Journal of Library and Information Practice and Research*, *6*(2). Retrieved from https://journal.lib.uoguelph.ca/index.php/perj/article/view/1516/2242

prominence in undergraduate education. The Council on Undergraduate Research, for example, has held an annual conference since 1987 to highlight and celebrate undergraduate students' contributions to research and scholarship. Educators have contended that it is beneficial to create an undergraduate research journal because it provides the students on the editorial board with opportunities to augment their learning, sharpen their critical thinking, and acquire new skills (Bauer, Ogas, Shakir, Oxley, & Clawson, 2009; Deonandan, Patel, & Winterbottom, 2012; Ware & Burns, 2008).

> **...a graduate student journal encourages contributors to review the professional literature, promotes publishing of original findings, and creates mentoring opportunities for students.**

Thanks to technological advancement, academic libraries have been engaged in scholarly publishing to "bring their values to bear on scholarly communication processes" (Harboe-Ree, 2007, p. 17). A survey conducted by Mullins et al. (2012) reports that almost two-thirds of the respondents' library publishing programs involve collaboration with one or more units on campus (p. 6). Unsurprisingly, the collaborators include academic departments and student organizations that wish to bring to fruition the publishing of student journals. Phillips (2010) applauds academic libraries' publishing initiatives because they facilitate access to their parent institutions' intellectual outputs and help enhance the institutions' stature (p. 156).

As one of the stakeholders in the scholarly communication life cycle, the academic library has built working relationships with constituents on and off campus. Therefore, it has much to offer when it comes to campus-based journal publishing. This paper aims to provide an overview of library services, especially for creating and publishing open access student research journals (regardless of whether they are run entirely by students or led by a faculty member[s]). Its coverage is not meant to be all-inclusive. Resources relevant to the mentioned services are listed in Appendix 1. A list of issues related to this topic are presented in Appendix 2.

Faculty members and students may not perceive the library as a player in the dissemination of original research outcomes, even though the library's endeavors in this area have been documented in the professional literature. Thus, it is important to raise the campus's awareness of what resources and services the library has to offer to support online publishing. The annual Open Access Week is an apt occasion for such a publicity event. However, the promotion has to be ongoing and across the campus. One effective way to achieve this is by word of mouth. Liaison librarians, for instance, can draw faculty members' attention to the services when communicating with their departments. Library administrators can highlight the services at meetings with their counterparts from other units and encourage them to spread the word. Librarians can also take the initiative to contact existing print-only student journals on campus, introduce the services, and explore the possibility of transforming the publications to open access journals. Although outreach activities are time-consuming, they are worthwhile because they help identify potential collaborators and build relationships with them. Additionally, they provide a means for the library to gauge what services for online publishing are sought after from different perspectives. That will assist the library with the allocation of resources for the provision and possible growth of the concerned services.

Assistance With Planning and Organizing

While faculty members can be staunch advocates for the creation of student research journals, enthusiastic students may also take the lead to start up such journals because they wish to increase the visibility of outstanding research conducted by their peers. For students who plan to further their academic pursuits, they may volunteer to assume responsibilities for the journal operations in order to familiarize themselves with scholarly publishing practices and gain valuable credentials. If it is a faculty member who intends to start a student research journal, s/he may have a clear idea with regard to the staffing and necessary resources for the journal operations. If it is students who seek assistance from the library for the launch of a journal, they may not be fully aware of the issues and responsibilities entailed by developing and managing an open access journal. Bittman, Lynch, and Pauls (2007) state that there are a wide variety of tasks involved in running a journal (p. 8). They range from strategic planning and operational oversight to marketing, financial management, and journal site maintenance. They differ in nature and are divided up among a team of individuals who work closely to keep the journal alive. As the *Online Guide to Open Access Journals Publishing* points out, it is crucial that the members of a journal team assume appropriate roles and "understand what activities need to be carried out, who ought to carry them out and how they relate to other activities" (n.d.). To ensure that a student-initiated journal will take off and continue over time, the library ought to get these points across to the students right at the beginning:

- Publishing a journal is a team effort that requires the recruitment of committed fellow students to fill the positions on the team and perform different tasks.

- It is likely that the team members have to acquire new skills in order to carry out the responsibilities they undertake.

- The members have to communicate with each other constantly to facilitate the collaboration.

- There is usually an annual staff rotation due to some members' graduation or departure. Therefore, the outgoing team has to recruit new members to run the journal in the next year. Moreover, departing members should hand over their responsibilities to their successors before the end of their terms.

As part of the education, the library can recommend these useful resources to the students for reference:

- *Developing Open Access Journals: A Practical Guide*
- The *Online Guide to Open Access Journals Publishing*
- Open-Access Journal Publishing Resource Index
- Student Journal Editor Resource Centre

Meanwhile, it is advisable to recommend that the students invite interested faculty members to participate in developing and managing the journal because the latter will be able to offer advice and coach the students from the researcher's perspective. The involvement of faculty may bring about recognition and sponsorship from an academic department or a campus unit. Last but not least, the presence of faculty on the team will be conducive to the journal's success and continuity if they provide oversight of the students' performance. As Froman (2008) cautions, "Without commitment from key faculty members, the journal will not last long" (p. 250).

With at least one faculty member on board, the journal team has to make a decision on how different responsibilities are divided among the members. Common staffing models include but are not limited to:

Editor-in-Chief	Reviewers	Production and Administrative Support (e.g., Copyediting, Marketing, etc.)
Faculty member(s)	Students trained to be reviewers	Faculty members, trained students, and/or liaison librarians
Faculty member(s)	Faculty members	Faculty members, trained students, and/or liaison librarians
Student(s) guided by faculty advisor(s)	Students trained to be reviewers	Faculty members, trained students, and/or liaison librarians
Student(s) guided by faculty advisor(s)	Faculty members	Faculty members, trained students, and/or liaison librarians

Which model a student journal adopts is contingent on factors such as who initiated the creation of the journal, how many faculty members have expressed interest in serving on the editorial board, whether and how many students volunteer for the journal, and the educational level of the students involved. For instance, a subject-based undergraduate journal could have a faculty member as the editor-in-chief and upper-level undergraduate students would be trained as reviewers. A multidisciplinary undergraduate journal, however, could be based on the model that faculty members from various academic departments are appointed as editors-in-chief and reviewers. If the journal is sponsored by a campus unit, the production and administrative support might become the unit's responsibilities. For a graduate journal, one or two students might be assigned as the editor(s)-in-chief and would be mentored by faculty members. Other students on the team would receive training and become reviewers and copy editors. The library and the faculty can work with the journal team to assess the situation, identify the available resources, weigh the pros and cons of different models, and select the one that suits the journal the best. Opportunities may arise for librarians to help coordinate and participate in the student training. Given that each journal has its own mission and characteristics, the adopted model may be none of the four listed above. Nevertheless, it is suggested that the model be evaluated in due course and tweaked as needed to ensure its efficiency and appropriateness.

> **Which model a student journal adopts is contingent on factors such as who initiated the creation of the journal, how many faculty members have expressed interest in serving on the editorial board, whether and how many students volunteer for the journal, and the educational level of the students involved.**

To secure the commitment of the journal team, it is not uncommon that a memorandum of understanding is signed between the library and the team to formalize their publishing partnership. The document clarifies the roles and responsibilities of the two parties and ensures that there will be an ongoing mutually beneficial relationship between them. The terms therein are often determined by the library's service level and the journal's needs.

In addition to assistance with team building, the library can provide input in formulating journal policies. While the faculty members involved are familiar with journal publishing in general, they may not have a solid grasp of open access. This presents the library with a prime opportunity to fill both the students and the faculty in on the economics of traditional journal publishing and the rationale behind open access. Moreover, an introduction to copyright law as well as Creative Commons licenses can illuminate the significance of open access and how publishing is interwoven with teaching, learning, research, and scholarship advancement. Resources from SPARC and the Right to Research Coalition are especially useful and valuable in this regard. A discussion of these topics not only reveals the downsides of subscription-based journal publishing with respect to knowledge sharing, but also highlights how authors' retention of rights in their works can enhance the dissemination, dialoguing, and constructive reuse of their intellectual outputs. Furthermore, it orients the journal team members to their roles as consumers and creators of information in the scholarly communication ecosystem. As

239

the Association of College and Research Libraries (2013) states, such knowledge is important because it is fundamental to being information literate. Cognizant of the impact of access and copyright issues, the journal team will likely place emphasis on maximizing the dissemination and reuse of the published content when laying down policies and practices. Its members will be able to speak of the journal cogently and be prepared to tackle potential authors' queries confidently.

While addressing scholarly communication issues, the library can go further and draw the journal team's attention to such new developments as open peer review, alternative metrics, data management, and researcher identity management. Lapinski, Piwowar, and Priem (2013) assert that librarians can play a critical role in educating campus constituents about article-level metrics and relevant resources. The same is true when it comes to informing faculty and students of other developments in the scholarly communication arena. A variety of guides to these topics are readily available online. If the journal team is interested in integrating these practices into its operations, the library could provide training and offer support as appropriate. Doing so would be an effective way to demonstrate the library's value and leadership in preparing the campus community for open digital scholarship.

...librarians can play a critical role in educating campus constituents about article-level metrics and relevant resources.

An essential part of the planning process is the graphic design of the journal site and the technical setup of the online publishing system. If the library is able to help with graphic design, it may be a boon to the journal team. In case the library cannot help, it can refer the team to appropriate service units on campus for assistance. It can also alert the team to open-licensed resources so that its members can adapt them for the graphic design if they prefer. With regard to setting up the online publishing system, the library introduces the journal team to the system's features, configures its functionality in consultation with the editors, and provides training (and refreshers) to ensure that the team members are able to perform the editorial work using the system. Once the inaugural issue has been published, the library could touch base with the team to discuss if the system needs to be fine-tuned to streamline the operations. What is involved in this stage to a large extent depends on how the library installs the technical infrastructure for publishing. If it has opted for a hosted service approach and offers its publishing services through licensing a vendor's online platform, the vendor will cover some of the graphic design and technical issues on behalf of the library.

Support for Content Management

Furlough (2010) notes that content management services "are frequently cited as a key asset for libraries engaged in publishing" (p. 206). Indeed, the library is able to provide a variety of services before and after the launch of a student journal. For example, the library can apply for an International Standard Serial Number (ISSN) for the journal before (or after) the publication of the inaugural issue. The assignment of digital object identifiers (DOIs) to articles has become an industry standard among journals. If the library is a publisher member of CrossRef and if the journal team decides to assign DOIs to articles, the library can embed itself in the production workflow and perform certain DOI-related responsibilities as long as both parties are able to work out an agreement on issues such as how to fulfill the requirement for providing outbound DOI links for the works cited by the articles and who will pay the fees incurred by new DOIs.

Thanks to its substantial experience with enhancing the discoverability of information, the library has much to offer after the inaugural issue is published. It can add the journal to its online catalog and export the bibliographic record to WorldCat if the library is an OCLC member. Other libraries may import the record into their online catalogs so that their users can find the journal. If the library licenses a vendor's knowledge base to maintain an electronic journal list, it can create an entry for the journal to make it readily accessible to users of the list. Similarly, the library can work with vendors of Web-scale discovery tools to set up metadata harvesting for the journal in order to boost the discoverability of the published articles. As the journal grows and accumulates quality content over time, the library can explore the possibility of having the journal included in academic databases. Besides its array of licensed information resources, the library can also register the journal with online finding aids such as the Directory of Open Access Journals (DOAJ). It can even supply the metadata of published articles to enable article-level searching on DOAJ. Meanwhile, the library could provide assistance with identifying subject-specific online search tools and have the journal content indexed by them. It could also make suggestions for promoting the journal through appropriate avenues such as social media and online communities.

Some services are truly valuable to a new online journal. They include search engine optimization, an RSS feed for newly published content, download rate tracking, periodic delivery of download statistics to editors and authors, and the tracking of the journal site traffic. Data about downloads and site visits inform the journal team of how well its publication is received. It also helps the team determine whether it needs to work on promotion in order to increase readership and recruit more promising manuscripts. The availability of these services is tied to the publishing system. If the library utilizes a vendor's online platform to publish the journal, the vendor will cover at least some of these services. If the library publishes the journal on its own instance of an open source platform, the library probably has to sort out certain technical issues before it can deliver these services.

Last but not least, the library can identify possible means to preserve the journal content for long-term access. Some libraries have their own digital preservation programs and can tackle this issue by themselves. In case the library does not have this advantage, it can look to library consortia of which it is a member for assistance or an opportunity for collaboration. It can also consider participating as a publisher in such digital preservation initiatives as CLOCKSS and Portico.

The content management services support the journal in different ways. They establish its legitimacy, integrate it into the existing scholarly literature, and enhance its discoverability in a sea of online content. They provide data on which the journal team relies to chart its operational activities and future directions. They also ensure long-term access to the journal content in spite of possible disruption caused by technological innovation. The journal team may not think of the need for these services in the first place, but it usually appreciates them once it has realized their importance.

Conclusion

The library is well positioned to educate the team of a student research journal about publishing in an open access environment. It can assist the members with team building, policy setting, and decision-making with regard to the journal operations. The team effort is indispensable in laying the groundwork for the launch and continuity of the journal. The library assumes a different role after the journal has gone live. Its expertise in organizing information can translate into services for managing the published content. In sum, there is a wide range of possible services that cater to the creation and publishing of open access student research journals. As discussed by Perry, Borchert, Deliyannides, Kosavic, & Kennison (2011), what services are offered is predicated upon the library's resources, abilities, and strategic plan. To ensure positive outcomes, Mullins et al. (2012) recommend that positions dedicated to library publishing be created "to provide program champions and improve program continuity and success" (p. 20).

References

Association of College and Research Libraries: Working Group on Intersections of Scholarly Communication and Information Literacy. (2013). *Intersections of Scholarly Communication and Information Literacy: Creating Strategic Collaborations for a Changing Academic Environment*. Chicago, IL: Association of College and Research Libraries. Retrieved from http://www.ala.org/acrl/sites/ala.org.acrl/files/content/publications/whitepapers/Intersections.pdf

Bauer, B. J., Ogas, W. C., Shakir, O. R., Oxley, Z. M., & Clawson, R. A. (2009). Learning through publishing *The Pi Sigma Alpha Undergraduate Journal of Politics*. *PS: Political Science & Politics*, 42, 565–569. http://dx.doi.org/10.1017/S1049096509090908

Bittman, M., Lynch, L., & Pauls, N. (2007). *Best Practices Guide to Scholarly Journal Publishing*. Vancouver, BC: Canadian Association of Learned Journals.

Co-Action Publishing & Lund University Libraries. (n.d.). *Online Guide to Open Access Journals Publishing*. http://www.doaj.org/bpguide/

Deonandan, R., Patel, P., & Winterbottom, R. (2012). A student-run peer-reviewed journal: An educational tool for students in the health sciences. *Advances in Medical Education and Practice, 3*, 1–5. http://dx.doi.org/10.2147/AMEP.S27149

Froman, R. L. (2008). The use of locally published journals to encourage undergraduate research. In R. L. Miller, R. F. Rycek, E. Balcetis, S. T. Barney, B. C. Beins, S. R. Burns, ... M. E. Ware (Eds.), *Developing, Promoting, & Sustaining the Undergraduate Research Experience in Psychology* (pp. 248–252). Washington, DC: Society for the Teaching of Psychology. Retrieved from http://teachpsych.org/ebooks/ur2008/6-6%20Froman.pdf

Furlough, M. J. (2010). The publisher in the library. In S. Walter & K. Williams (Eds.), *The Expert Library: Staffing, Sustaining, and Advancing the Academic Library in the 21st Century* (pp. 190–233). Chicago, IL: Association of College & Research Libraries.

Harboe-Ree, C. (2007). Just advanced librarianship: The role of academic libraries as publishers. *Australian Academic & Research Libraries, 38*, 15–25. Retrieved from http://www.alia.org.au/publishing/aarl/38/ARRL.Vol38.No1.2007.pdf

Lapinski, S., Piwowar, H., & Priem, J. (2013). Riding the crest of the altmetrics wave: How librarians can help prepare faculty for the next generation of research impact metrics. *College & Research Libraries News, 74*, 292–294, 300. Retrieved from http://crln.acrl.org/content/74/6/292.full.pdf+html

Mullins, J. L., Murray-Rust, C., Ogburn, J. L., Crow, R., Ivins, O., Mower, A., ... Watkinson, C. (2012). *Library Publishing Services: Strategies for Success: Final Research Report.* West Lafayette, IN: Purdue University Press. Retrieved from http://docs.lib.purdue.edu/purduepress_ebooks/24/

Pearson, J. A., VanNest, R. L., & Jasinski, D. M. (2004). Promoting publication by producing a student journal. *Nurse Educator, 29*, 68–70. Retrieved from http://journals.lww.com/nurseeducatoronline/Abstract/2004/03000/Promoting_Publication_by_Producing_a_Student.8.aspx

Perry, A. M., Borchert, C. A., Deliyannides, T. S., Kosavic, A., & Kennison, R. (2011). Libraries as journal publishers. *Serials Review, 37*, 196–204. http://dx.doi.org/10.1016/j.serrev.2011.06.006

Phillips, L. L. (2010). Coming home: Scholarly publishing returns to the university. In B. I. Dewey (Ed.), *Transforming Research Libraries for the Global Knowledge Society* (pp. 147–163). Cambridge, UK: Chandos Publishing.

Ware, M. E., & Burns, S. R. (2008). Undergraduate student research journals: Opportunities for and benefits from publication. In R. L. Miller, R. F. Rycek, E. Balcetis, S. T. Barney, B. C. Beins, S. R. Burns, ... M. E. Ware (Eds.), *Developing, Promoting, & Sustaining the Undergraduate Research Experience in Psychology* (pp. 253-256). Washington, DC: Society for the Teaching of Psychology. Retrieved from http://teachpsych.org/ebooks/ ur2008/6-7%20Ware%20&%20Burns.pdf

Appendix 1: Select Resources

Online Forums

LIBPRESS-L Listserv

http://listserv.ucop.edu/cgi-bin/wa.exe?A0=LIBPRESS-L

Libpub Google Group

https://groups.google.com/forum/#!forum/libpub

Planning, Organizing, and Managing

Developing Open Access Journals: A Practical Guide

http://www.developing-oa-journals.org/

(an abridged version freely available at: http://www.developing-oa-journals.org/ Guide_to_developing_oa_journals.pdf)

Library Publishing Services: Strategies for Success: Final Research Report (March 2012)

http://docs.lib.purdue.edu/purduepress_ebooks/24/

Online Guide to Open Access Journals Publishing

http://www.doaj.org/bpguide/

Open-Access Journal Publishing Resource Index

http://www.sparc.arl.org/partnering/planning/

Student Journal Editor Resource Centre

http://studenteditors.org/

Sample Agreements Between Library and Journal

Hosting Agreement for Open-Access or Embargoed Journals (from MPublishing in University of Michigan Library)

http://wiki.publishing.umich.edu/sites/mpublishing/uploads/4/4a/Editors-MPub_ journal_license_OA.pdf

Master Service Agreement—Basic Service Level (from CDRS in Columbia University Libraries)

http://cdrs.columbia.edu/cdrsmain/wp-content/uploads/2009/05/Basic_MSA_
Journals.pdf

Open Access E-Journal Hosting Agreement (from University of South Florida
Libraries)

http://scholarcommons.usf.edu/tlar/10/

Sample Agreements Between Journal and Author

Agreement for Publication and Sharing of Rights (from CDRS in Columbia
University Libraries)

http://cdrs.columbia.edu/cdrsmain/wp-content/uploads/2009/05/
sampleauthoragreement.pdf

Author Publishing Agreement (from MPublishing in University of Michigan
Library)

http://wiki.publishing.umich.edu/sites/mpublishing/uploads/d/d3/Author-journal_
article_license.pdf

Standard Author Copyright Agreement (from University of Pittsburgh Library)

http://www.library.pitt.edu/e-journals/Public/
authorcopyrightagreement-2012-03-28.docx

Suggested Language for Author Agreements (from California Digital Library)

http://www.escholarship.org/sample_author_agreement_final.doc

Scholarly Communication Issues

Article Level Metrics: A SPARC Primer

http://www.sparc.arl.org/bm~doc/sparc-alm-primer.pdf

Copyright in General

http://copyright.columbia.edu/copyright/copyright-in-general/

Creative Commons: About the Licenses

http://creativecommons.org/licenses/

MANTRA: Research Data Management Training

http://datalib.edina.ac.uk/mantra/

Open Access Scholarly Information Sourcebook (OASIS)

http://www.openoasis.org/

Open Review: A Study of Contexts and Practices

http://mediacommons.futureofthebook.org/mcpress/open-review/files/2012/06/
MediaCommons_Open_Review_White_Paper_final.pdf

ORCID: A System to Uniquely Identify Researchers

http://dx.doi.org/10.1087/20120404

Right to Research Coalition

http://www.righttoresearch.org/

SPARC's Author Rights Initiative

http://www.sparc.arl.org/author/

Information Literacy and Scholarly Communication

Common Ground at the Nexus of Information Literacy and Scholarly Communication

http://www.ala.org/acrl/sites/ala.org.acrl/files/content/publications/booksanddigitalresources/digital/commonground_oa.pdf

Intersections of Scholarly Communication and Information Literacy: Creating Strategic Collaborations for a Changing Academic Environment

http://www.ala.org/acrl/sites/ala.org.acrl/files/content/publications/whitepapers/Intersections.pdf

Scholarly Publishing Tutorial (for Information Literacy)

http://liblearn.osu.edu/tutor/scholarlypublishing/

Content Management of Open Access Journals

CLOCKSS

http://www.clockss.org/

CrossRef

http://www.crossref.org/

Directory of Open Access Journals

http://www.doaj.org/

Portico

http://www.portico.org/digital-preservation/

Appendix 2: Issues to Consider

This list aims to help the founder(s) of a student research journal brainstorm and organize. It is by no means comprehensive. Members of a journal team may want to refer to the Student Journal Editor Resource Centre's advice on the important steps in getting started in student publishing: (http://studenteditors.org/important-steps/).

Planning and Policies

1. Ownership

   - Who owns the journal (e.g., an academic department, a student society on campus, etc.)?

2. Continuity

   - What mechanism is in place to ensure the journal's continuity?

3. Faculty involvement

   - How many faculty members are involved in the journal's operations?

4. Title

   - What is the journal title? Has it been used by another journal or publication?

5. Purpose

   - Why has the journal been created? What purpose(s) does it serve?

   - How will it contribute to research and scholarship?

6. Scope

   - What will be the scope or subject area(s) of the journal?

   - Will it cover interdisciplinary works?

7. Authors and readers

   - Who will be eligible to contribute to the journal?

   - Who will be the target readers?

8. Content

   - What kind of article will be published (e.g., original research articles, review essays, opinion pieces, etc.)?

9. Language

   - Will the journal only publish articles written in English?

10. Submission guidelines

    - Will there be a page or word limit per article?

    - What citation style should be used?

    - How should the manuscript be formatted (e.g., double-spaced, line-numbered, etc.)?

    - Will previously published materials be accepted?

    - What content type(s) will be accepted (e.g., texts, charts, tables, graphics, multimedia, supplementary datasets, etc.)?

    - What file format(s) will be published (e.g., .pdf, .xls, .jpg, .mp3, etc.)?

11. Author agreement

- What should be the terms for the author agreement?

- Will the journal publish particular information about authors (e.g., a brief bio, a picture, etc.)?

12. Copyright

- Who will own the copyright of published articles?

- Will the articles be published with a Creative Commons license to facilitate knowledge sharing? If so, which license will be adopted?

13. Frequency/publication schedule

- How many times will the journal be published in a calendar year?

- Will articles be grouped and published together as an issue? Or will they be published on a rolling basis (i.e., they are published individually whenever they are ready)?

14. Numbering

- How will the journal be numbered? By volume and issue (when articles are grouped and published together) or by year and article number (when articles are published individually on a rolling basis)?

- Will articles published in different issues have continuous page numbering?

15. Site design

- Is there a logo, banner, theme color(s), and/or cover image for the journal site?

- What is the timeline for the development and launch of the site?

16. Launch

- When will a call for papers be issued?

- When will the inaugural issue be published?

Staffing and Editorial Workflow

1. Editor(s) and contact person

- How many editor(s) will there be?

- What will be the requirements for the editor position(s)?

- Who will receive and respond to questions and comments about the journal?

2. Journal team

- How many positions will there be on the journal team?

- What will be the responsibilities for the positions?

- How long will the terms be for the positions?

- How many reviewers will there be in total?

- What will be the requirements for journal team members and reviewers?

- How will journal team members and reviewers be recruited and evaluated?

3. Editorial workflow

- What will be the review procedure?

- How many reviewer(s) will be involved in reviewing a manuscript?

- What will be the review criteria?

- If students will be reviewers, what training will be provided to them?

- How many days will a reviewer have for completing a review?

- How much time will be appropriate for the entire editorial workflow?

Production, Promotion, and Preservation

1. Copyediting, layout editing, and publishing

- Who will be responsible for the proofreading, copyediting, and layout editing of accepted manuscripts?

- If translation is required for accepted manuscripts, who will be the translators?

- How much time will be appropriate for the proofreading, copyediting, layout editing, and/or translation?

- Will there be a budget for proofreading, copyediting, layout editing, and/or translation if the work has to be outsourced?

- What information will be displayed in the online article record (e.g., an abstract, keywords, the article citation in a particular style, etc.)?

- Should the system be configured to generate a cover page and an abstract page for the downloaded article?

- Should the system be configured to generate a header and a footer on the content pages of the downloaded article?

- Will a digital object identifier (DOI) be assigned to each published article? If so, who will be responsible for providing the outbound DOI links for the papers cited in an article? What will be the funding source for new DOIs?

2. Marketing

- Who will be responsible for the ongoing marketing of the journal to attract readers and recruit authors?

- What will be appropriate and effective marketing channels for targeted readers and potential authors?

- Will the journal create an RSS feed for newly published articles?

- Will the journal use Google Analytics or a similar tool to track readership?

- Will there be a budget for marketing? Will it be ongoing?

3. Impact assessment

- Will the journal provide article-level metrics?

4. Archiving and preservation

- What will be the plan for archiving and preservation?

The *USFSP Student Research Journal* and the Library's Role as Publisher and Champion

Carol Hixson

University of South Florida St. Petersburg

2 IN THIS CHAPTER

Theme
Case study in the development of a graduate student research journal

Highlighted Service
Online journal hosting and support

Resources
Discusses journals setup and launch, applying metadata, & outreach

Acknowledging and recognizing graduate student research has long been a routine part of academic life at colleges and universities, evidenced by the long-standing requirements for the creation and publication/archiving of master's and doctoral theses and dissertations. More recently, colleges and universities have become much more actively engaged in supporting undergraduate research to develop stronger mentoring relationships between students and faculty, to improve student retention, and to develop strong research and writing skills among undergraduates. Groups such as the Council on Undergraduate Research (CUR), whose mission "is to support and promote high-quality undergraduate student-faculty collaborative research and scholarship" (Council on Undergraduate Research, 2013), hold workshops and conferences to showcase work being done nationally to enhance undergraduate research and to provide support and guidance for such efforts.

At the University of South Florida St. Petersburg (USFSP), a separately accredited master's-level institution within the University of South Florida system, interest in and support for undergraduate as well as graduate student research has been growing. Since 2003 the university has hosted an undergraduate research symposium whose purpose is "to showcase the innovative research and creative work that USF St. Petersburg undergraduate students have produced during the year under the tutelage and with the support of the university's faculty" (Undergraduate Research Symposium, 2013).

Within USFSP, the Nelson Poynter Memorial Library's mission is "to be an active partner in the teaching, research, and learning of the University of South Florida St. Petersburg's students, faculty, and staff" (*Gateway*, p. 4). Two of the strategic goals enumerated in the 2010–2014 library's strategic plan, *Gateway to the World's Information,* were to "support USFSP's undergraduate and master's level research and instruction" and to "increase effective use of technology to improve library services and support a collaborative learning environment, including the creation and preservation of digital collections" (*Gateway*, p. 4). The dean charged several work groups with implementing the strategic plan, including a Digital Collections Team consisting of the library's dean, the head of Public Services, the Special Collections librarian, and the head of Systems. The Digital Collections Team began planning for the establishment of an open-access digital archive for the campus in the spring of 2010. The group selected DSpace because it was open source, was the most widely adopted software in the world for institutional repositories, had a robust user community, was compliant with the Open Archives Initiative Protocol for Metadata Harvesting (OAI-PMH), had the functionality desired by the library, and had been used twice before by the library dean at other institutions.

While the library was laying the groundwork for the digital archive, Dr. Alejandro Brice, a professor in the College of Education, approached the dean of the library in the fall of 2010 looking for support in establishing an online student research journal. During discussions, Dr. Brice and Dean Hixson determined that the planned digital archive met all of the functionality requirements of the proposed student research journal, including that:

- It would provide for articles to be published through online submissions.
- It would allow Dr. Brice, as editor of the journal, to add approved articles without intervention or mediation by the library.
- It would provide a platform that would index, retrieve, and track the usage of its articles.
- It would provide a consistent and unchanging form for citing articles.
- It would provide an open access platform that could be promoted from and linked to appropriate websites and other marketing outlets.

The digital archive would also provide some benefits that were not a requirement of the journal, such as full-text indexing of submissions and the ability to find archived materials by searching on the open Internet.

In early 2011, the library hired an experienced contractor to establish an instance of DSpace hosted by Poynter Library and also provide training to local staff in the system configuration and server backup protocols. The contractor also set up nightly full-text indexing and implemented some requested additions to the Dublin Core metadata element set to allow for tracking peer-reviewed items, along with author status relative to the university. In the spring of 2011, the library implemented the USFSP Digital Archive (http://dspace.nelson.usf.edu/). The mission of the archive is to:

- Promote the scholarship and intellectual activity of USFSP faculty and students.

- Collect and preserve the institutional history and official documents of the university.

- Showcase and provide access to digitized versions of unique scholarly resources.

- Build and strengthen partnerships between USFSP and the broader community.

- Provide a platform to support and utilize a wide range of open educational resources.

Because we are a small library, each member of the team, including the dean, serves as an administrator within DSpace and has the lead responsibility for acquiring different types of content. The dean of the library has the lead responsibility for acquiring student content.

In the first two years, the USFSP digital archive grew to include over 6,000 items of scholarship, community engagement, institutional history, and official documentation in six broad communities and dozens of focused collections. As the first unique content submitted to the archive, the newly formed *University of South Florida St. Petersburg Student Research Journal (SRJ)* launched the USFSP digital archive. The first article in the journal was published through the digital archive on March 29, 2011. In two years, 10 articles were published in the first two issues of the journal.

Technical How-To's and the Editorial Process

Using the DSpace software, the library dean first established a community for student research and within that community a collection for the *Student Research Journal*. In consultation with the journal editor, the dean established a submission and review process in DSpace for the acquisition of new articles. The dean then created a template (Appendix A) for the journal articles that contained all the recurring information for each article, along with prompts for article-specific information. The library dean established the metadata template in consultation with the journal editor, Dr. Brice, and refined it after the first few submissions. In order to facilitate a browse display that mimics a table of contents in an issue of a journal, all articles in a given issue begin with the full title of the journal, followed by issue and article number. The specific title of the individual article only appears as a subtitle (Appendix B). When the number of the issue changes the library dean modifies the template to reflect the new issue numbering.

Within the digital archive, the journal has a homepage (Appendix C), created by the library dean, which links back to a website that the journal editor maintains with information about the journal, the submission process for editorial review, and with a link to the published articles in the archive (Appendix D). Each article gets a separate item record listing all authors, as well as the title, the date of publication, and other descriptive information (Appendix E).

> # One or more faculty members who sponsor each student-authored article also perform the role that peer reviewers play in traditional academic journals by reviewing the content of the article and the writing.

The dean of the library serves on the *Student Research Journal's* editorial board, along with Dr. Brice and the members of the USFSP Research Council (one faculty member each from each college and the library). One or more faculty members who sponsor each student-authored article also perform the role that peer reviewers play in traditional academic journals by reviewing the content of the article and the writing. When the faculty sponsors are satisfied with the quality of the article, they pass the article on to the journal editor. The journal editor formats submissions according to the journal's style guidelines and then submits new articles using the template established in the digital archive. Within DSpace, a submission template consists of three fixed screens for collecting data about the item being submitted, with the data fields being mapped to modified Dublin Core metadata. The data fields collect information about the date, description, creators, titles, keywords, abstracts, standard numbers of URIs affiliated with the item, and more. It is possible to create a collection-specific template where some of the data has been already supplied. The person submitting a new item to the collection must decide whether it is necessary to modify some of the pre-supplied data or accept the values already there. In the case of the *Student Research Journal*, the title field will always need modification to reflect the correct volume, issue, and article number, as well as the title of the specific article being submitted because the template only provides generic prompts for the item-specific data (Appendix F). After the metadata has been supplied, the submission software prompts for one or more affiliated files to be uploaded and then takes the journal editor to a screen where he or he is able to review the metadata and files and make corrections. When the editor, Dr. Brice, is satisfied with the submission and the metadata, he accepts the embedded license, which adds the new article to the archive and automatically assigns a unique and unchanging Corporation for National Research Initiatives (CNRI) handle. The article is dynamically indexed and starts to collect statistics every time the item record describing the article or the file containing the article itself is viewed. Detailed screen shots of the generic submission process can be seen in the step-by-step guide for submitting to the archive, available online (Hixson, 2011).

Next Steps

While the existing 10 articles received more than 5,700 hits from 29 countries in the first two years (see Appendix G for a sample statistics page), the journal faces an uphill battle in getting new submissions. Only three faculty members have sponsored the first 10 articles. Dean Hixson and Dr. Brice have undertaken a number of steps to increase submissions to the archive, including:

- Presenting at the USFSP Undergraduate Research Symposium about the *SRJ* and the power of publishing in it through the digital archive

- Working to establish a library-sponsored student research award with the top submissions receiving a cash prize and award winners being required to publish in the journal

- Proposing a process whereby library faculty could assist college faculty in the review of student papers to ensure proper research and citations have been employed

In April 2013, Dean Hixson and Dr. Brice prepared a joint presentation (Hixson & Brice, 2013) for the symposium outlining the benefits of publication in the journal and the archive, including enabling students to:

- Share the results of research widely

- Get credit for their work and protect their intellectual property

- Contribute new knowledge to a field

- Build a portfolio for work or graduate school

- Get connected with others interested in the same topic

- Secure grant funding for more research

- Highlight individual, group, and institutional achievement

- Improve access to and discoverability of materials

Dean Hixson made presentations to the Deans' Council and the University Research Council to establish an Undergraduate Library Research Award program, sponsored and administered by the Nelson Poynter Memorial Library, to recognize students who demonstrated skill and creativity in the use of library and information resources to original research and scholarship. Applicants would submit original research to be reviewed and judged by a panel of college and library faculty on how well they met established criteria for research and scholarship. Awards were proposed in two categories, one for upper-level course work completed in a single term and the other for theses or projects developed over more than a single term. Awards were proposed in the range of $500–750, with the number of awards to vary from year to year depending on funds and successful applicants. Individuals or teams would need to be currently enrolled

USFSP undergraduates or recent graduates, eligible projects must have been completed for an upper division (3000–4000 level) USFSP credit course, projects would need to be nominated by the instructor responsible for the course, and individuals or teams would need to agree to contribute their projects to the permanent collections of the USFSP Libraries and the USFSP digital archive. Dr. Brice and Dean Hixson are now working to secure funding and to modify the proposal to include publication in the *Student Research Journal* as one of the requirements for award winners.

> ## Applicants would submit original research to be reviewed and judged by a panel of college and library faculty on how well they met established criteria for research and scholarship.

Discussions to gauge interest in and support for the idea of having library faculty assist college faculty in reviewing student research papers for submission to the *SRJ* are in the very preliminary stages. While there are some challenges to overcome, the hope is that the common interest in advancing student research will make it possible to move forward.

Conclusions

The library at USFSP has been accepted readily as a partner in the publishing of student research. The *Student Research Journal* has readers from around the world, simply by virtue of being published in an OAI-PMH based archive that is registered with various indexers and harvesting services. With so many undergraduates and graduate students already actively engaged in scholarly research at the university, finding high-quality content is not a problem. The immediate challenge currently lies in enlisting the support of college and library faculty to serve as mentors and reviewers for the student submissions. The success of the *USFSP Student Research Journal* from the standpoint of ease of publication and finding an international audience has inspired the journal's editor to undertake the establishment of an open access journal for faculty authors in his discipline that will be published exclusively in the USFSP digital archive. The library's role as publisher and champion of scholarly research is assured.

References

Council on Undergraduate Research. (2001). *Fact sheet*. Retrieved from http://www.cur.org/about_cur/fact_sheet/

Hixson, C., & Brice, A. (2013). *Promote and publish your work: A presentation to the USFSP undergraduate research symposium, April 11, 2013*. Retrieved from http://dspace.nelson.usf.edu/xmlui/handle/10806/6415

Hixson, C. (2011). *1st steps for submitting to the USFSP digital archive: A step-by-step guide.* Retrieved from http://dspace.nelson.usf.edu/xmlui/handle/10806/411

Nelson Poynter Memorial Library. (2010). *Gateway to the world's information.* Retrieved from http://dspace.nelson.usf.edu/xmlui/handle/10806/3302

Undergraduate Research Symposium. (2013). Retrieved from http://www.usfsp.edu/research/undergrad-research/undergraduate-research-symposium/

Appendix A

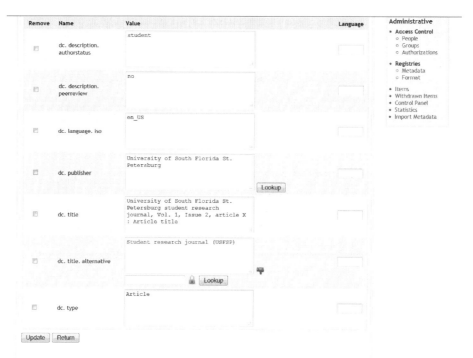

Metadata Template for Student Research Journal

Appendix B

Title Browse Listing for Student Research Journal

Appendix C

Home Page of the Student Research Journal in the USFSP Digital Archive

Appendix D

Web Site Promoting the Journal and Linking to the Published Articles in the Digital Archive

Appendix E

Listing of All Authors and Title on Article Record

Appendix F

Metadata Supplied for Student Research Journal in the Submission Template

Appendix G

University of South Florida St. Petersburg Student Research Journal, Vol. 2, Issue 1, article 5 : The Testing and Design of an Arduino Microcontroller Board for the Study of Proxemics — **Views** 1873

Total Visits Per Month

	October 2012	November 2012	December 2012	January 2013	February 2013	March 2013	April 2013
University of South Florida St. Petersburg Student Research Journal, Vol. 2, Issue 1, article 5 : The Testing and Design of an Arduino Microcontroller Board for the Study of Proxemics	76	518	566	24	90	582	17

File Visits

	Views
Huynh 2012.pdf	1797
Huynh 2012.pdf.txt	2

Top country views

	Views
United States of America	1789
Ukraine	43
Russian Federation	4
China	3
Japan	3
Mexico	3
Germany	2
United Kingdom	2
India	2
Malaysia	2

Top cities views

Advanced Search

Browse

- All of DSpace
  - Communities & Collections
  - By Issue Date
  - Authors
  - Titles
  - Subjects
  - By Submit Date
- This Collection
  - By Issue Date
  - Authors
  - Titles
  - Subjects
  - By Submit Date

My Account

- Logout
- Profile
- Submissions

Context

- Edit this Item
- Export Item
- Export Metadata

Administrative

- Access Control
  - People
  - Groups
  - Authorizations
- Registries
  - Metadata
  - Format
- Items
- Withdrawn Items
- Control Panel
- Statistics

Sample Statistics Page for One of the Journal Articles

Libraries Publishing Other Original Content

Digital Storytelling: The Library as Place of Creation

Mustafa Sakarya

Mercy College

1 IN THIS CHAPTER

Theme
Library supporting the creation of multimedia content

Highlighted Service
Instruction & support for digital storytelling

Software/Platforms Utilized
Microsoft Photostory

Resources
Discussion of collaboration, outreach & technical considerations in supporting multimedia creation

My first big introduction to libraries as places of creation happened in the 11th grade, back in 1980. On the second floor of the high school library was a loft-like space called the Media Center crammed full of metallic, noisy machines, 16mm projectors, phonographs, filmstrips that went "beep," etc. This jumble of analog technology was managed by an amiable librarian, a man we approved of because he would visit our classes wheeling in a rickety device of some kind so we could watch a documentary about crop infestation, the dangers of drunken driving or, of course, that infamous sex education film.

One spring day we trooped in to meet the school's artist-in-residence, a woman who introduced us to the new wizardry of portable video production. I was fascinated by the kitchen appliance–size of the camera and tape recorder and the ability to shoot, erase, and shoot again, as many times as you want. She encouraged us to develop a project using the new medium and, being a huge fan of TV and film, I thought, why not shoot a video instead of writing a term paper for my English class? My teacher fell for the idea, and being a bit naïve, I thought it would be easy. It actually took months of excruciating and painfully unanticipated work. But it paid off. I produced a zany version of O. Henry's *The Green Door*, but more significantly, I began to think of libraries as places where you could create cool things using technology, and learn some useful skills at the same time.

> # [I'm still] hooked to the idea that enabling students to create multimedia-based work can and should become a core function of libraries...

Flash forward 30 years. Now I'm the media librarian at Mercy College, still hooked to the idea that enabling students to create multimedia-based work can and should become a core function of libraries, right next to quiet study, information access, and research instruction. All of these activities can work together to make a richer experience, giving students a full range of 21st century skills. The key is just the willingness to think about information literacy more broadly, to be open-minded and take risks, but above all, be exploratory.

At Mercy College we're encouraged to explore innovative ways of teaching, and the library has supported this initiative in several ways. We've partnered with our Faculty Center for Teaching and Learning, piloted the use of i-clickers and joined learning communities that have coalesced around media-intensive practices such as e-portfolio, game-based learning, and digital storytelling. Digital storytelling, in particular, offers a rich case study of how an academic library develops itself as a place for student scholarship and publication, which in turn demonstrates our value to the college community.

Digital storytelling (DST) is a generic term for a flexible practice of personal story creation told through digital media, popular in the arts and education. In a learning context, students create three- to five-minute multimedia narratives built around a transformative learning experience related to their personal and academic lives, often with an instructional aim. Students perform all the core steps in DST, including writing an effective script; recording voice; gathering, selecting and editing images and video; adding music if desired; screening the story among peers; and finally, after some level of encouragement, publishing the digital story on the school's website, YouTube, or other sites.

When I first heard about DST I saw its potential as a great tool for our first-year students. The first year is a major hurdle at Mercy, a critical turning point where students have to step up their game and negotiate multiple demands and pressures. Freshman Seminar is one of

266

those demands. In Freshman Seminar, students must demonstrate the three competencies of critical thinking, critical reading, and information literacy. As a guest member of the Freshman Seminar faculty learning community, I wanted to assist this group in the development of more impactful assignments for the course, projects that could motivate students, get them excited about creating knowledge, and encourage them to complete the year with something powerful and tangible for themselves and their families.

At that time I found a shared interest in DST from a key member of the Freshman Seminar learning community, Mercy's instructional designer, a skillful storyteller himself. We developed a series of summer workshops to introduce DST to the learning community and selected Photostory as our editing platform. Photostory is freely available from Microsoft and very easy to use, requiring only five basic steps (import images, add titles, add narration/customize motion, add music, export/share). The simplicity of Photostory allows the user to focus on developing a narrative, rather than on learning complex software. And while it can only work with still images and not full-motion video, Photostory can incorporate two tracks of audio, enabling a layering of music beneath the voice, which opens up rich, creative possibilities. On the downside, Photostory can only be used in PC/Windows environments.

Our teaching approach for the workshops loosely followed the *seven elements* structure pioneered by Joe Lambert and the Center for Digital Storytelling (Lambert, 2009). Participants are placed in the round, sharing their ideas as part of a story circle. This is followed by a presentation on the seven elements of effective storytelling and then a technical walk-through of the editing software. The remainder of the day is devoted to production, finally concluding with a celebratory screening of the stories. The workshops were a hit! Within a trusting and engaging work atmosphere, faculty learned about each other's backgrounds, struggles, and dreams, and saw the enormous potential for this tool. Several instructors decided to integrate DST the following semester.

To make it easier for other Freshman Seminar instructors to begin using DST, a small group from the Freshman Seminar learning community developed a pilot assignment called *The Most Important Lesson Learned*. Its approach revolved around the making of a short, digital memoir spoken in each student's voice, expressing a key life lesson learned. We hoped the assignment would enable students to take a critical view of their lives, and from it gain insight expressed in the form of a digital story. For assessment purposes, the digital story would provide a vehicle through which students could demonstrate the required competencies, as well as testing their organizational and technology skills. The appendix to this article includes the rubric we developed for *The Most Important Lesson Learned* assignment, tailored to the critical thinking and information literacy requirement.

While we were making headway, there were still some significant logistical hurdles to overcome. Foremost was the need to schedule librarian and/or instructional designer visits into classes in order to provide both a conceptual overview of DST and hands-on training with Photostory. As facilitators we critique scripts, point students toward image databases, provide coaching on effective speech and diction, and assist with anything else needed to help students complete their stories. Students also needed access to laptops, microphones, and other technology outside of class. With IT's assistance, library loaner laptops were loaded with Photostory and additional headsets were made available. And because audio-visual service resides in the library, we were able to leverage technical staff to provide live assistance and spaces for private recording and editing. A digital storytelling libguide (http://libguides.mercy. edu/digitalstorytelling) was created to provide quick reference to technology tutorials, sample stories, and other helpful resources (see the appendix for the libguide screenshots).

It was especially important to steer students as much as possible toward royalty-free images and music. As librarians, we promote the ethical use of information and require that students cite all relevant images and sounds in MLA format, generally at the end of their stories. Our digital storytelling libguide includes a tab that lists useful copyright-free sites such as jamendo. com and pics4learning.com (see the appendix for a screenshot). Our libguide also gathers other helpful digital storytelling websites, such as the University of Houston's *Educational Uses of Digital Storytelling* http://digitalstorytelling.coe.uh.edu/, with its tremendous array of helpful resources.

Digital storytelling has grown at Mercy College from an initial base of four instructors in Fall 2010 to nearly 20 assigning DST to their students in Spring 2013. It has also expanded by discipline, from Freshman Seminar to Honors English and Graduate Education, with surprising success in health-related areas including occupational therapy and veterinary technology. Part of its success lies in its flexibility. DST is discipline and technology agnostic, adaptable to almost any academic setting, and students can use a variety of editing or computer system to create stories.

With growth comes the challenge of providing support. Additional librarians have become trained in DST and we hope to construct a small multimedia lab in the library to provide a dedicated space for students working on not just storytelling but other media-based practices such as e-portfolio. Another challenge is Microsoft's recent decision to discontinue updates for Photostory. While still available for download, Photostory may become glitchy as the PC/ Windows environment evolves. Finding an alternate free and easy-to-use editing platform is no easy task. Our plan is to switch to either Windows Movie Maker or a Web-based system such as wevideo.com. Unfortunately, cloud-based systems such as wevideo are limited in storage capacity, unless one opts for paid versions. To explore these challenges, a passionate faculty learning community has formed around DST. And to demonstrate DST's value to college administrators, the learning community is exploring and developing assessment tools and rubrics to measure DST's effects on various literacies (see the appendix for rubric examples).

> ## ...students are genuinely engaged and excited by Digital Story Telling as a form of scholarship, which can be effective as writing but more direct.

But the bottom line is that students are genuinely engaged and excited by DST as a form of scholarship, which can be effective as writing but more direct. The assignments have ignited student imagination and interest, encouraged learning and cultural bridging. Discussions and surveys from students after DST have indicated that most felt empowered by the use of their voices and personal experience, by the freedom of choosing to tell their own unique stories. While some students expressed uncertainty and nervousness at the start of projects, by the end almost all identified DST as being the most rewarding assignment of their semester, and the screening of stories, the best day.

Digital stories represent a vital record and history of the college journey from the point of view of its most important user. As DST continues to grow at Mercy College, the library is well suited to find ways to archive, organize, and publish the stories generated by students each semester. Some students willingly publish on YouTube and others sign releases to enable us to feature their stories on the library website (see the appendix for our currently used release). The capacity to store large numbers of stories will require working with IT to leverage use of a recently acquired Kaltura streaming media server. We've also discussed producing our own library-related digital stories as a form of marketing and community outreach.

The horizon looks bright for digital storytelling, a term that may disappear as authoring with media becomes the status quo in education. Like writing, DST is a form of powerful academic discourse. Libraries can provide resources and instruction to further its growth and development. By enabling students to produce and publish their learning experiences, the library can deepen its role as a place of reflection and creativity, which is just a new take on an ancient idea. Libraries are places to read, write, and learn, and now we can add record, edit, and publish. That's something I learned in my old high school library a long, long time ago.

Reference

Lambert, J. (2009). *Digital Storytelling Capturing Lives, Creating Community*. Berkeley, CA: Digital Diner Press.

Appendix

The following are samples of student digital stories produced at Mercy College:

Guardian Angel, by Francis Roman

http://youtu.be/pOPKxx4kThE

DisAble the Label!!!, by Yolanda Stewart

http://youtu.be/80rumAs1d8k

Turning a Problem Into a Purpose, by Brandon Mejia

http://www.youtube.com/watch?v=-FJeC_t3O4w&feature=youtu.be

Screenshots of Mercy College's Digital Storytelling Libguide:

Libguide home page

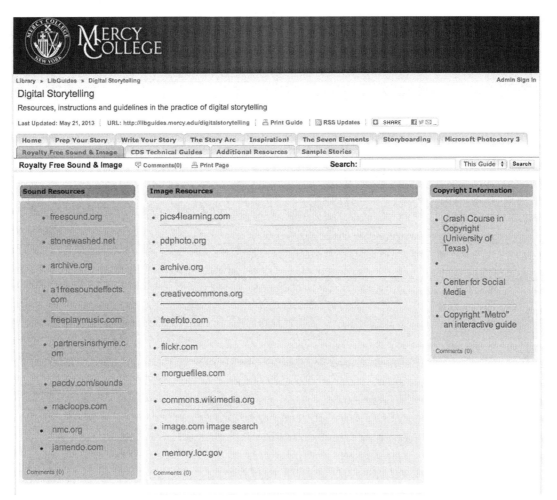

The Royalty Free Sound and Image tab of the Digital Storytelling Libguide

Sample rubric based on the "seven elements" approach of the Center for Digital Storytelling:

CATEGORY	4 Points	3 Points	2 Points	1 Point
1. Purpose of Story	Establishes a purpose early on and maintains a clear focus throughout.	Establishes a purpose early on and maintains focus for most of the presentation.	There are a few lapses in focus, but the purpose is fairly clear.	It is difficult to figure out the purpose of the presentation.
2. Point of View	The point of view is well developed and contributes to the overall meaning of the story.	The point of view is stated but does not connect with eachpart of the story, although an attempt is made to connect it to the overall meaning of the story.	The point of view is stated but no attempt is made to connect it to the overall meaning of the story.	The point of view is only hinted at, or is difficult to discern.
3. Dramatic Question	A meaningful dramatic question is asked and answered within the context of the story.	A dramatic question is asked but not clearly answered within the context of the story.	A dramatic question is hinted at but not clearly established within the context of the story.	Little or no attempt is made to pose a dramatic question or answer it.
4. Choice of Content	Contents create a distinct atmosphere or tone that matches different parts of the story. The images may communicate symbolism and/ or metaphors.	Contents create an atmosphere or tone that matches some parts of the story. The images may communicate symbolism and/ or metaphors.	An attempt was made to use contents to create an atmosphere/tone but it needed more work. Image choice is logical.	Little or no attempt to use contents to create an appropriate atmosphere/tone.
5. Clarity of Voice	Voice quality is clear and consistently audible throughout the presentation.	Voice quality is clear and consistently audible throughout the majority (85-95%) of the presentation.	Voice quality is clear and consistently audible through some (70-84%)of the presentation.	Voice quality needs more attention.

6. Pacing of Narrative	The pace (rhythm and voice punctuation) fits the story line and helps the audience really "get into" the story.	Occasionally speaks too fast or too slowly for the story line. The pacing (rhythm and voice punctuation) is relatively engaging for the audience.	Tries to use pacing (rhythm and voice punctuation), but it is often noticeable that the pacing does not fit the story line. Audience is not consistently engaged.	No attempt to match the pace of the storytelling to the story line or the audience.
7. Meaningful Audio Soundtrack	Music stirs a rich emotional response that matches the story line well. Images coordinated with the music.	Music stirs a rich emotional response that somewhat matches the story line. Images mostly coordinated with the music.	Music is ok, and not distracting, but it does not add much to the story. Not coordinated with images.	Music is distracting, inappropriate, OR was not used.
8. Quality of Images	Images create a distinct atmosphere or tone that matches different parts of the story. The images may communicate symbolism and/or metaphors.	Images create an atmosphere or tone that matches some parts of the story. The images may communicate symbolism and/or metaphors.	An attempt was made to use images to create an atmosphere/tone but it needed more work. Image choice is logical.	Little or no attempt to use images to create an appropriate atmosphere/tone.

273

Release form used to gain student permission to publish digital stories:

I hereby authorize_____College and those acting as authorized representatives of _____
College to:

1. Record my likeness and voice on a video, audio, photographic, digital, electronic or any other medium.

2. Use my name in connection with these recordings.

3. Use, reproduce, exhibit or distribute in any medium (e.g. print publications, video tapes, CD-ROM, Internet) these recordings for any purpose that_____College, and those acting as authorized representatives of the College, deem appropriate, including promotional or advertising efforts.

I release_____College and those acting pursuant to its authority from liability for any violation of any personal or proprietary right I may have in connection with such use. I understand that all such recordings, in whatever medium, shall remain the property of _____College. I have read and fully understand the terms of this release.

Name:

Address:

Street

CityState   Zip

Phone:

Signature: Date:

Parent/Guardian Name (if under 18) :

Date:

Parent/Guardian Signature (if under 18):

Date:

Content and Collaboration II: Opportunities to Host, Possibilities to Publish

Andrew Wesolek & Michael Spooner

Utah State University, University Press of Colorado

2 IN THIS CHAPTER

Theme

Niche publishing through an institutional repository

Highlighted Service

Online book publishing & multimedia components

Software/Platforms Utilized

Digital Commons by bepress

Resources

Examples of different ways to structure an online monograph within an IR

The integration of the Utah State University Press and USU Libraries enhanced access to scholarly materials in a variety of ways. The press utilizes USU's institutional repository, the Digital Commons, to facilitate the open access distribution of its works subsequent to a 12-month embargo. Additionally, the collaborative environment created by shared space within the library fosters innovation. The library benefits from the extensive knowledge of the press and applies it to its nascent library-based publishing efforts. The press has also adopted some of the open access ethos prevalent in library philosophy and practices and applied it to high-quality peer-reviewed and immediately open access online scholarly works. More information on the development of this collaborative relationship may be found in "Content and Collaboration I: A Case Study of Bringing an Institutional Repository and a University Press Together" on page 171.

Launched in October 2008, Utah State University's institutional repository (http://digitalcommons.usu.edu), an instance of Digital Commons by bepress, is thriving. With the aim of capturing the intellectual output of the university and making it openly available to the world, the repository currently houses more than 36,000 records. Where full-text is available, those records have been downloaded nearly 1.6 million times, with 900,000 of those downloads occurring within the past 12 months. Nearly 20% of Utah State's faculty have submitted at least some of their work for deposit in the Digital Commons.

The repository provides the infrastructure to *host* scholarly articles when permissible, but also to *publish* unique scholarly materials created at USU. These include all graduate theses and dissertations completed at USU after 2008, conference proceedings, posters, lectures, seven open access journals, grey literature, and now new types of born-digital open access monographs. This distinction between hosting and publishing is important, yet still developing.

We consider hosted materials to be those that have been published via traditional avenues, and then made openly available in some form through the repository. However, the repository also "publishes" in the sense that it provides a platform to make materials that may be intellectually important but unavailable or inappropriate for publication via traditional venues available and openly accessible to the public. Providing this type of access should not be conflated with the service of disseminating materials that traditional presses provide. The latter is more an active pushing out of scholarship through advertising, marketing, and other sales techniques. Without reliable sources of revenue, the repository cannot actively push out materials. Instead, it facilitates public accessibility. So, while both presses and libraries "publish," this activity differs per community of practice.

> **The relationship between the press and the repository allows for the open access hosting of the backlist of the press, while providing the collaborative space and varying perspectives to facilitate public access to current and future unique publications.**

At Utah State, the relationship between the press and the repository allows for the open access hosting of the backlist of the press, while providing the collaborative space and varying perspectives to facilitate public access to current and future unique publications. More information on the hosting of the press's backlist and the negligible impact on sales may be found in "Content and Collaboration I: A Case Study of Bringing an Institutional Repository and a University Press Together" on page 171.

Publishing Efforts

The hosting of USU Press monographs, in addition to the repository's other hosted materials, has been tremendously successful. However, we are also beginning to use our repository as a platform to publish fully open access scholarly materials. Due to budgetary and labor considerations, the repository cannot publish works with the full suite of value-added services that the press does. However, this limitation may also be seen as an opportunity for the repository. Our lack of reliance on reliable sources of revenue allows us to fill an important role: the publication of niche materials that may be of scholarly importance but out of scope for traditional journal or monograph publishers.

To date, we have published three unique monographs, all three of which are diverse in both scope and structure, thus providing a range of models for future publications. The unifying strand between these examples, though, is that they were developed to be traditional linear monographs. At the initial stages of their development, no thought was given to their full potential as born-digital open access works. Our hope is that by establishing a range of potential modes of publication for existing texts through the IR we can encourage our faculty to experiment with these possibilities at the early stages of monograph production. These examples, then, represent a step in the transition from traditional monographs to born-digital post-monographic texts.

Our first publication, *An Introduction to Editing Manuscripts for Medievalists* (http://digitalcommons.usu.edu/lib_mono/1/), is both highly specialized and relatively short. This makes it economically unattractive to traditional publishers and university presses. By publishing through the IR, though, we can provide a specialized textbook by a recognized authority to the hundreds of graduate students worldwide who will use this text as part of an advanced course in medieval manuscripts. Indeed, in less than a year since publication the work has been downloaded 183 times.

This work shares many characteristics with a traditional monograph in e-book form. We published it and continue to host it as a single PDF that is intended to be read linearly. Again, the repository does not have the resources available to provide copyediting or (at this stage) formal peer-reviewing services. As such, we rely on authors to submit a complete edited manuscript that we will publish as is. Our in-house graphic designer does add a decorative cover page to the works, but the scalability of this option remains to be seen.

We also publish texts that were conceptualized in a traditional linear sense but can be transformed into highly dynamic and socially responsive works by tailoring them to suit our IR. USU is quite happy with bepress's Digital Commons. The system is reliable and highly attractive to Google and other search engine crawlers, and bepress handles all of the technological support for the repository. However, the outsourcing of tech support does entail a bit of rigidity in the system. In the following examples, we have worked within the rigid structure to break a traditionally conceived monograph into logical segments. This enhances the overall discoverability within the structure of the bepress repository.

277

The Foundations of Wave Phenomena (http://digitalcommons.usu.edu/foundation_wave/), for example, was conceived in a traditional sense (i.e., as a monograph to be read linearly), but publication through the repository has allowed us to reconceptualize it to draw on the strengths of the vehicle of publication. To this end, we structured the work such that each module (traditional chapter) stands independently, yet is deeply connected with the other modules. Rather than a linear work to be read from start to finish, this transformed text exists as an interrelated web of concepts, where users can enter and exit at points of their choosing, as well as easily trace linked prerequisite concepts, supplemental materials, and practice problem sets.

In essence, the aim of a text is to transmit a complex concept from the author to the reader by way of a set of interrelated sub concepts. When confined to a traditional structure—i.e., a physical book—these sub-concepts progress linearly. Here, though, we are able to present these sub-concepts as a web—one in which the reader may enter and exit at points of his or her choosing, investigate supplemental materials where necessary or ignore them when they are not. This approach has the added benefit of attracting Google and other search engine crawlers to the concepts outlined in each module to a much greater degree than if those chapters remained part of a traditional book. So, rather than attracting users to the text as a whole, crawlers identify and make findable each of the sub-concepts contained within that work.

> # ...we are able to present these sub-concepts as a web—one in which the reader may enter and exit at points of his or her choosing

To accomplish this within the bepress system, we must first obtain an edited but unpublished monograph from an author. We then work with the author to divide the work into logical segments or modules. We will then determine which modules are prerequisite for understanding other modules within the work, which allows us to conceptualize the interrelated linking of modules. We will also work with the author to identify relevant appendices, additional materials, problem sets, or external resources that enhance understanding of each module.

After working with the author to develop a thorough conceptualization of the work, we upload it into the repository. Given the structure of the Digital Commons, each "book" actually exists as a "book gallery." So, in the above example, we create a "book gallery" for the *Foundations of Wave Phenomena*, then upload each module as a "book." Once all modules have been uploaded, we add "additional files" (such as those mentioned above). Here, we will also make a prerequisite module downloadable. If multiple prerequisites are necessary, we can add additional links to them in the Comments field.

Figure 1 illustrates our use of the book gallery structure to introduce the text and explain the navigation of modules.

FOUNDATIONS OF WAVE PHENOMENA

04 Linear Chain of Coupled Oscillators

Charles G. Torre, *Department of Physics, Utah State University*

Download Full Text (2.4 MB)

Problem Set 2 (398 KB)

03 How To Find Normal Modes.pdf (900 KB)

Read Online

Included in
Physics Commons

SHARE

Description

As an important application and extension of the foregoing ideas, and to obtain a first glimpse of wave phenomena, we consider the following system. Suppose we have N identical particles of mass m in a line, with each particle bound to its neighbors by a Hooke's law force, with "spring constant" k. Let us assume the particles can only be displaced in one-dimension, label the displacement from equilibrium for the jth particle by q_j, $j = 1, \ldots, N$. Let us also assume that particle 1 is attached to particle 2 on the right and a rigid wall on the left, and that particle N is attached to particle N−1 on the left and another rigid wall on the right.

Publication Date 2012

Keywords linear chain, coupled oscillator, chapter 4, four

Disciplines Physics

Comments
Chapter 4

Recommended Citation
Torre, Charles G. "04 Linear Chain of Coupled Oscillators" (2012). *Foundations of Wave Phenomena*. Book 19.
http://digitalcommons.usu.edu/foundation_wave/19

Figure 2 illustrates one module of the work, which has actually been uploaded to the digital commons as a "book." Note the additional problem set and link back to the prerequisite module, "How to Find Normal Modes."

279

Publishing through the repository has the added benefit of allowing us to integrate multimedia components that would be impossible in a traditional work. Our recently published project, Latino Voices in Cache Valley, offers a wonderful example of a work that might not be publishable by a traditional press due to its limited marketability, but which offers a wealth of added scholarship through its multimedia components. This challenge for the press is an opportunity for the repository to make this scholarship available to the world. In addition, digital publication allows us to incorporate audio and video oral histories and presentations given by the authors.

These texts lay a foundation for a promising future. It is important to remember that these two previous examples were not conceived to be non-linear digital texts, but were modified at a later stage of development. Looking forward, though, we can imagine connecting with authors at an early stage in the production of their work. We can then imagine creating truly non-linear texts that incorporate video lectures or labs, or perhaps captured and archived conversations between readers and authors that clarify content, or perhaps link to other relevant content, thus crowdsourcing the deep integration of the text into the broader scholarly dialogue.

Our initial publications, along with the collaborative space shared with the press, offer exciting opportunities moving forward. Without a reliable revenue stream generated by book sales, we cannot provide the value-added services as the press. However, we can potentially leverage the skills of both librarians and the press to locate and manage external peer reviewers and build bridges between authors who desire added value—print on demand comes to mind—and independent contractors that can provide these services. Indeed, bringing our university press and institutional repository together provides us with a collaborative pathway forward to both facilitate accessibility to scholarship and create new modes of openly accessible scholarship.

References

Bak, J. M. (2012). *An introduction to editing manuscripts for medievalists.* Retrieved from http://digitalcommons.usu.edu/lib_mono/1

Torre, C. G. (2012). *Foundations of wave phenomena.* Retrieved from http://digitalcommons.usu.edu/foundation_wave/http://digitalcommons.usu.edu/foundation_wave/

Spooner, M., & Wesolek, A. (2013). *Content and collaboration I: A case study of bringing an institutional repository and a university press together.* Retrieved from [insert link]

Williams, R., Ortiz, E., & Spicer-Escalante, M. L. (2012). *Latino voices in Cache Valley.* Retrieved from http://digitalcommons.usu.edu/latino_voices/

Creating Digital Library Content for Integrated Course Development

Erika Bennett, Kim Staley, & Jennie Simning

Capella University Library

3 IN THIS CHAPTER

Theme

Collaboration and workflow in creating online course guides & resources

Highlighted Service

Creating custom research guides

Software/Platforms Utilized

LibGuides & Adobe Captivate

Resources

Sample outreach materials and the details of a collaborative workflow

apella University Library is a completely virtual library supporting a broad range of degree programs from bachelor to doctoral level. Because it serves as the library for a completely online institution, publishing digital content is an extremely important aspect of our outreach, instruction, and reference services. Most unique is our systematic process of content creation for online courses, including creating point-of-need research guides and instructional media, as well as collaborating with faculty to integrate information literacy-focused assignments into the online courseroom.

Since the Capella Library instituted LibGuides in 2010, they have become our biggest forum for digital content publishing. In a few short years our libguide use has grown to nearly 500,000 hits per year. In addition to libguides, we also create Adobe Captivates and other digital instructional content for integration within the online courseroom. Last year our instructional materials were assigned over 2,000 times throughout the curriculum.

> # Most unique is our systematic process of content creation for online courses, including creating point-of-need research guides and instructional media...

While the creation of digital content in LibGuides and Adobe Captivate is not unique in itself, our ability to incorporate faculty input and feedback at all stages of creation and implementation has led to guides and other learning objects (see Other Digital Publishing Examples) that are highly customized to specific courses and highly utilized by the student population. We have been able to realize a high rate of usage largely thanks to being involved in the course development process right from the beginning.

Course Development and the Library

Capella University has a very robust and tightly organized course development process. In fact, Capella University was awarded the 2010 CHEA Award for Outstanding Institutional Practice in Student Learning Outcomes by the Council for Higher Education Accreditation. This was due to the fact that its entire curriculum has carefully defined learning outcomes and competencies, and all learning competencies carefully align from program to assignment level.

In 2008, Capella University approved information literacy as its sixth curriculum-wide learning outcome. At this time we were able to make a case to the Course Design department that library involvement in course development was essential to ensuring that this learning outcome was met in all new and revised courses. From that point forward It has become standard practice by the course development project managers to invite a librarian, along with faculty subject matter experts (SMEs), instructional designers, curriculum specialists, media creationists, and faculty chairs to the kickoff meetings for all new and revised courses.

Course development kickoff meetings provide us with the built-in opportunity to promote our LibGuides creation service to faculty and open a discussion on how the libguide (or other library-published content) can be integrated into the course as an essential point-of-need resource for assignment completion. They also provide us insight on how to better leverage our already existing libguides, research tutorials, and other digital content.

Digital Content Publishing Process

Kickoff Meetings

Our digital content publishing process often begins at kickoff meetings by starting a conversation with the faculty SME about the course. The attending librarian begins the conversation by giving an overview of our current library services and emphasizing any information literacy competencies being integrated into the course. The librarian then asks the faculty SME:

- Which library or information research skills do you want students to demonstrate in this course?

- At what point during the course will they demonstrate the skill?

- How will you assess whether they have the skill?

- What should the librarian's role be in this process? (Inspired by Miller, 2010)

Based on the answers we receive to the above questions, and other discussions held during the kickoff meeting, we prepare a written follow-up report for the faculty SME and the instructional designer who will work most closely with the SME to develop the course (see Figure 1). This report summarizes our conversation in the meeting, includes any recommendations for existing library guides that could be integrated into the course, and offers to create course- or assignment-specific research guides based on their need.

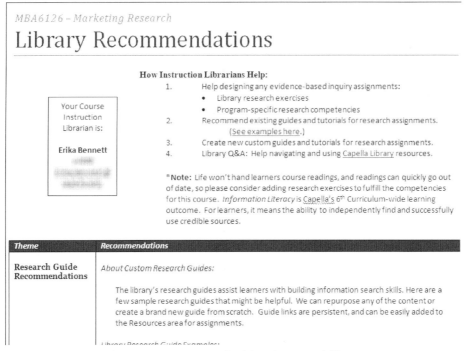

Figure 1. Library Recommendations report. Capella librarians send library resource suggestions to the members of each course development team.

All course stakeholders are actively encouraged to contact our faculty support inbox or their liaison librarian directly for continuing questions, collaboration, assignment design, or learning tool creation. The liaison librarian for the course will then check back in with the course development team several times during the six- to ten-week development cycle to review assignments, build new guides, and give general library-related advice.

Content Development and Faculty Input

When a member of the course development team asks us to create a custom research guide or other learning object for their course, we begin by asking the faculty member and instructional designer for as much information as possible to ensure that we can get a good start on the material and that we can accommodate their request before their course development deadline.

Once content creation starts, the librarians will send the guide or learning object to faculty periodically for review and input. The vast majority of librarian-faculty communication, collaboration, and feedback is done through the library's dedicated faculty support inbox within Capella's customer relationship management (CRM) system (allowing us to easily track all faculty interactions) or via conference call with the faculty and instructional designer.

Faculty feedback is most useful at strategic points in the creation process to ensure that we are still on the same page and all expectations are being met. For example, we typically solicit feedback once the framework of a libguide is complete (tabs, box headings), but not too much content has been written; once a significant amount of content has been populated into the libguide; and once before we publish the guide live and it is ready to be linked within the course.

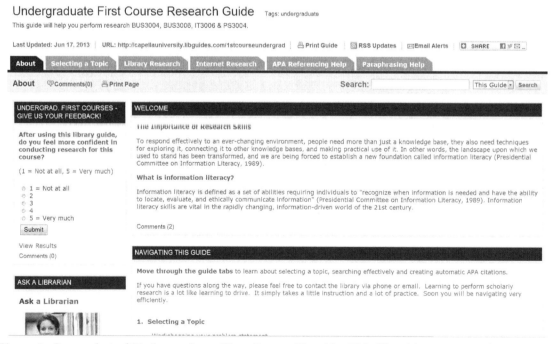

Figure 2. Screenshot of Undergraduate First Course libguide. This libguide was created to help new learners navigate the research-based assignments in their first course.

A good example of collaboration with faculty on libguides creation is our First Course Undergraduate guide (see Figure 2). We learned that the Undergraduate First Course was being revised at the beginning of the quarterly cycle, so we promoted our services at the team kickoff meeting, soliciting interest from the chair of the program. She expressed the desire to hold weekly conference calls between her faculty and the subject librarian. We created a site map of the libguide using bubbles to represent each page of the guide, which allowed us to build consensus about the topics and learning competencies.

Once the skeleton of the guide was established, the subject librarian fleshed it out and revised it based on faculty feedback from the weekly conference calls and in conjunction with ongoing revisions to the course. The final touches included fixing the navigation hierarchy to ensure the title formatting matched the courseroom, and embedding documents within the libguide to support assignments. This last step proved more difficult than anticipated, as faculty liked the libguide so much that they kept asking for additional pages and content to support aspects of the course that went outside the original scope.

We have found that partnering with faculty to develop guides and other learning objects, as described above, typically increases the number of hits on the guide. Whether this is because the co-creation process helps faculty members feel more ownership, or because they realize the helpful potential of the guide and promote its use more heavily in the online courseroom, is unclear. In either case, this collaborative strategy often builds better digital guides and better relationships between faculty and the library.

Workflow Process

Our content creation process can be summed up in the following steps:

1. Establish our expertise as helpful.
2. Clarify our roles and processes.
3. Build awareness of the problems of unsupported learning outcomes and information literacy integration across the curriculum.
4. Agree upon the deliverables.
5. Create the product.
6. Incorporate input on the alignment, content, and fit.
7. Revise and publish our learning resources (LibGuides, Captivates, etc.).
8. Review the language that supports the guides in the courseroom.

Other Digital Publishing Examples

Normally, our assignment support work focuses on building LibGuides or Adobe Captivates, because those don't require extra budget allotment for interactive designers. In those cases, we internally develop learning resources to support research competencies in a manner that saves the course media budget. In other cases, the faculty may allot us some of their course media budget to get more complex interactive media built.

For instance, we worked with the MBA chair and instructional designers to create a larger piece called Business Information Sources (Capella, 2010). The school leadership allotted us the media hours needed to create a flash-based accordion piece that allows students to explore information about different areas of the business literature (see Figure 3). The allotted media hours meant that we could focus on creating the content and hand off the majority of the layout design to interactive designers.

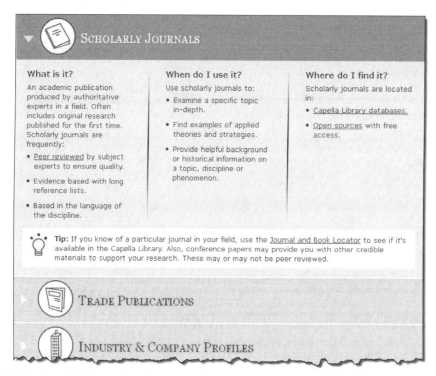

Figure 3. Business Information Sources. This is an accordion-style media piece created by a collaboration of librarians, instructional designers, and the MBA chair.

In 2011, we combined our labor-intensive embedded librarian model with our aging, PRIMO-recognized basic information literacy and library skills website. To do this, we pulled the content of the website into our virtual campus and updated it based on information literacy standards and the FAQs from our embedded experience to create a unified new skills website (see Figure 4). It includes interactive media, video tutorials, and navigational assessments that arrange the content according to student knowledge gaps. (For further information, see Shumaker, 2011. We are Site 5.)

Creating this information literacy and library skills website was a long process with many people involved. To begin, the information literacy librarian worked with a curriculum specialist to define the learning outcomes of the site. A project manager was selected to coordinate meetings and keep everyone on track. Two librarians were responsible for writing all of the text content of the site, the integrated media content, and the assessments. The librarians worked closely with both instructional design and interactive design to present the content in an effective and user-friendly way. This site has proved successful and nearly every new First Course (first required course in any program) since 2011 has included the new website in its curriculum.

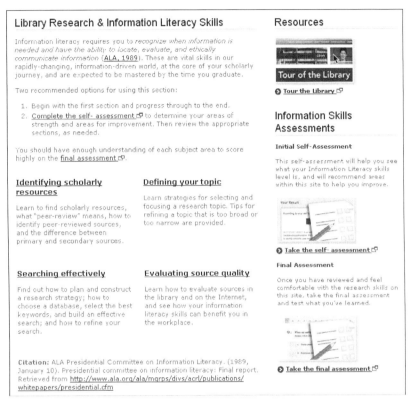

Figure 4. Library Research & Information Literacy Skills site. This main page includes links to the four major skill areas as well as to pre- and post-assessments.

In general, the creation of these complex media-driven learning objects often involves much more collaboration between the librarian, instructional designer, and interactive designers than a basic libguide or Adobe Captivate; but the basic publishing process is similar. The librarian and instructional designer work with the faculty to ensure a good understanding of their information literacy needs, the librarian writes the content, and the instructional and interactive designers build the media and collaborate with the librarian and faculty member to present the content in a way that most effectively facilitates learning.

We plan to base our rubric on the one our interactive design department uses, which judges both the critical thinking level and the design effectiveness.

Our Next Steps

As we continue to promote the inclusion of library resources into courses, we have been working toward a universal measurement rubric that can help us score the quality of any given learning object. We plan to base our rubric on the one our interactive design department uses, which judges both the critical thinking level (based on Bloom's taxonomy) and the design effectiveness (based on interactivity, learning outcome alignment, etc.). We will score each of our learning objects based on these criteria and assign sunset dates to help prioritize regular revisions.

The last five years have provided us with many challenges, successes, and further opportunities to expand our digital publishing role within the college curriculum. Though we have integrated library research and information literacy resources into a number of courses, we will continue to use the course development process to advocate for the ultimate goal that every course will include the necessary research or information literacy resources our learners need to be successful students and lifelong learners.

References

Capella University. (2010). Business information sources. Retrieved from http://media.capella.edu/coursemedia/mba_central/bizinfo/bizinfo.html

Miller, I. (2010). Turning the tables: A faculty-centered approach to integrating information literacy. *Reference Services Review*, 38(4), 647–662. http://dx.doi.org/10.1108/00907321011090782

Shumaker, D. (2011). Models of embedded librarianship: Addendum 2011. Special Library Association. https://www.sla.org/wp-content/uploads/2013/01/ModelsofEmbeddedLibrarianshipAddendum2011.pdf

An Experiment in Progress: The MSU Student Comic Art Anthology

Ruth Ann Jones

Michigan State University Libraries

IN THIS CHAPTER

Theme

Outreach & process for publishing student work

Highlighted services

Print on Demand with the Espresso Book Machine

Resources

Example submission requirements, and discussion of pricing, online vendors and marketing efforts

In Autumn 2011, the Michigan State University Libraries (http://lib.msu.edu/) acquired an Espresso Book Machine (EBM), a print-on-demand installation allowing us to print trade-quality paperback books. Over the last 18 months, we've had a steady flow of faculty and students coming to print materials they've created: seminar workbooks, job-hunting portfolios, and conference programs, to name just a few. We've also done a modest business in printing public domain works from the On Demand Books (http://www.ondemandbooks.com/) catalog. The service models we've developed are described in Kyle Pressley's chapter "Client-Driven Workflows and Publishing Models" on page 127 in this collection.

The EBM also makes it possible for MSU Libraries to publish our own works. Our first efforts have centered on reprints from our own collection, primarily rare cookbooks from our Cookery & Food Collection (http://specialcollections.lib. msu.edu/html/materials/collections/cookery_coll.jsp). We've also reprinted several works related to our institution, including an early history of MSU, a memoir on college life from an early graduate, and a mid-century etiquette book for students.

During the first year of our EBM service, library staff often brainstormed on ways to use the print-on-demand capability. One recurring suggestion was to collaborate with other campus units to publish student writing. There are many possible genres and candidates for partnerships: a poetry volume, working with the Department of English; student reflections on study abroad experiences with International Studies and Programs; sports writing with the School of Journalism, and more.

Detail from "This Isn't a Movie" by Gabriel P. Cooper.

In the fall of 2012, I proposed that the library produce our first student anthology as a solo project. This would be an opportunity to iron out the wrinkles in a first-time effort, and give us a completed volume to show potential partners. This was also our first effort to create new content for the EBM instead of reproductions or customer work. The content—comic art by students—was a natural choice, as MSU's Special Collections (http://specialcollections.lib.msu. edu/) are widely known for comic art.

Preparing to Publish

In addition to the Espresso Book Machine, MSU Libraries had significant resources to draw on for this project. The mechanics for promoting a call for submissions were already in place, thanks to the frequent public events we offer, and our active social media presence: MSU was recently ranked #22 in the list of 100 Most Social Media Friendly College & University Libraries for 2013 (http://librarysciencelist.com/100-most-social-media-friendly -college-university-libraries/).

The MSU libraries also have some experience running student competitions. From 1998 to 2010, the library held an annual MSU Student Book Collection Competition, with winning collections on view at a public event and the top winner entered into the National Collegiate Book Collecting Contest. Beginning in 2010, an MSU Student Art Competition (http://lib.msu.

edu/artcontest.jsp) was created, with prizes funded by an endowment from a generous donor. Each year, two works are acquired by the library and displayed in public areas of the library, which enhances our space and gives exposure to student artists.

The library's print office is managed by a staff member with excellent graphic design skills. The book design was handled in-house, which allowed us to produce a 92-page book within three weeks of finalizing the content.

A final resource was my own experience in publishing. Before becoming a librarian, I worked in ALA's publishing division for six years, and handled marketing for the ALA Books imprint (now ALA Editions). Publishing technology and the book market have changed dramatically since then, but familiarity with the traditional publishing model has been useful.

The MSU Student Comic Art Anthology

Once the library administration gave permission, *The MSU Student Comic Art Anthology* was a go. The first three priorities were:

- Developing submission guidelines

- Recruiting a jury to select works from the submissions

- Advertising the call for submissions

The submission guidelines clearly had to be ready before the competition was announced. We had decided not to limit the themes or subject matter, so the guidelines were merely technical, based on EBM production specifications. I also wanted entrants to know who the jury members were, so securing commitments from three faculty members had to be finished early on.

With those two pieces ready, the competition was announced in late October 2012, with a submission deadline of January 18, 2013 (http://lib.msu.edu/cartooncontest.jsp). We were pleased to receive a total of 30 submissions from 17 artists.

Selecting Content

The next task was to select material to publish from the larger group of submissions. The process went smoothly, but in retrospect, this area will need more attention in future publications.

The three jury members recruited in October were Randy Scott, curator of the library's Comic Art Collection (http://specialcollections.lib.msu.edu/html/materials/collections/comicart_coll.jsp); Ryan Claytor, the faculty member who teaches MSU's one cartooning course in the Department of Art, Art History, and Design; and Samuel Thomas, a recent retired faculty member from the Department of History, whose research interests include editorial cartoons.

Submissions were compiled with the artists' names removed, and distributed to the jury before we met to discuss the entries in person. I attended to facilitate, but did not vote on individual entries. The discussions were cordial, and the two jury members with a background in comic art shared useful background and insights on what made a given work successful or not. At the same time, they were very interested in hearing the third faculty member's perspective. The three selectors were able to reach a consensus in every case, and the resulting volume is a delightful mix of artistic styles, subject matter, and narrative techniques.

What would I do differently next time?

I'm not sure it was necessary to have all three selectors be knowledgeable about comic art, or in Professor Thomas's case, a related genre. While Professor Claytor's background as a teacher of cartooning was extremely helpful, Professor Thomas's contributions were just as valuable   and my sense was that his reactions were not so much based on his editorial cartoon research as on decades of evaluating student writing.

Expanding the field of potential selectors (and allowing more time to recruit) would address an important issue: the potential conflict of interest in having a faculty member judge a pool of submissions that included some of his own students. This was hard to avoid if the jury had to be made up of comic art experts, but not ideal. The fact that the three selectors were able to reach a consensus about every entry suggests

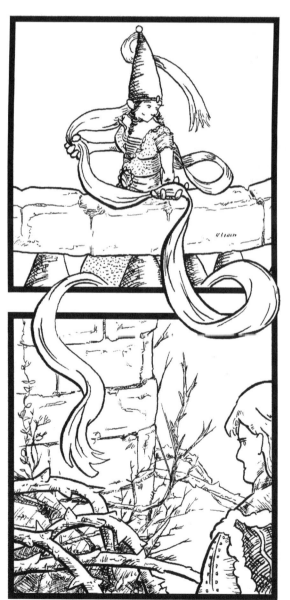

Detail from "Rapunzel" by Ryan Esch.

that they were able to approach each work on its merits. Nevertheless, in the future, I would like to invite jury members from a wider range of disciplines.

Detail from "The Grackle" by Leslie J. Anderson.

Production and Pricing

All editorial chores and book design were handled within the library, so the direct production costs included only the cost of printing books on the Espresso Book Machine. For internal pricing, we use a cost estimator tool provided by Xerox, which handles EBM sales and maintenance. (See Kyle Pressley's chapter, "Client-Driven Workflows and Publishing Models" on page 127 for more on the estimator tool.)

The great benefit of print-on-demand publishing is the ability to produce very low quantities of trade-quality paperback books. The downside is that there is no economy of scale for multiple copies. The internal price for our 92-page paperback, with a color cover and black & white interior, is $7.64.

For commercial publishers, paper, printing, and binding usually account for about 20% of the retail price (Dreher, 2002). A unit cost of $7.64 would price out to about $38, which would most likely represent a longer volume with color inserts, hardcover binding, and dust jacket. However, the cost of preparing an offset press for any print job means it is rare to print fewer than 1,000 copies at a time.

For now, our working assumption is that the purpose of publishing our own books—whether reprinted or original—is to promote the library on campus, in the community, and in the profession; and to help to preserve rare material by making affordable reprints available to libraries. Thus, prices are set as low as possible, to cover only our direct printing costs and fees for selling on Amazon, plus a token $1 toward indirect costs. In the case of the comic art anthology, the $1 was waived, as this particular volume is potentially of greater interest to students than the historical volumes in our reprint series.

> ...the purpose of publishing our own books—whether reprinted or original—is to promote the library on campus, in the community, and in the profession; and to help to preserve rare material by making affordable reprints available to libraries.

The MSU libraries are currently registered as an individual seller on Amazon.com, a category representing sales of fewer than 40 units per month (Sell on Amazon, n.d.). Individual sellers are charged a $0.99 selling fee per transaction. For those with higher sales volumes, the Professional Seller category offers a flat selling fee of $39.99 per month, which becomes cost effective when selling more than 40 units a month.

The selling fee is accompanied by a referral fee of 15% of the retail price and a closing fee of $1.35 per item sold. Both of these fees are the same for Individual and Professional Sellers.

Opening panel from "Chewski Goes Sledding" by Matt Dye.

The Individual and Professional selling categories are both offered under the heading "Sell on Amazon," which does not include fulfillment services. Amazon adds a shipping fee for each book, handles the payment transaction with the customer, and sends shipping information to the seller. The sellers ship books from their own locations, so books in this program are not eligible for Amazon's free shipping for orders over $25. Amazon credits the seller's account with the retail price of the book plus the shipping fee, less the selling fee, the referral fee, and the closing fee. Amazon also offers the "Fulfillment by Amazon" option, in which Amazon fulfill orders generated either by its own website or the customer's website [http://services.amazon.com/fulfillment-by-amazon/benefits.htm]. Fulfillment by Amazon has its own fee structure.

Detail from "Treasure Island" by Marie Lazar.

With these figures, it's possible to identify the break-even point for books sold on Amazon and set the retail price accordingly. For *The MSU Student Comic Art Anthology*, the break-even would be a retail price of $11.64. The actual retail price was set at $12.00, which yields a princely 22-cent profit after Amazon fees and production costs are subtracted. The anthology's Amazon listing is http://www.amazon.com/MSU-Student-Comic-Art-Anthology/dp/1626100012/.

Of course, Amazon is not our only sales outlet, and it is the most expensive in terms of fees. The book is also sold through shop.msu.edu (http://shop.msu.edu/product_p/lib-21.htm), an online storefront for MSU-related products, and at the library's Copy Center (where customers can also see the book being printed if they wish). Copies were sold at the MSU Comics Forum in March and can be sold at future events. The prominence of MSU's Comic Art Collection means that we are regularly requested to attend both public and campus gatherings with displays and examples from the collection.

Thus far, promotion for the new book has been limited to the free coverage I can arrange. The anthology was featured in the MSU student newspaper, *The State News* (http://statenews.com/article/2013/03/spartan-made-comics-featured-in-new-book), and in a local alternative paper, *The Lansing City Pulse*. It was a section leader in the University's news website, *MSU Today* (http://msutoday.msu.edu/news/2013/msu-libraries-publishes-anthology-of-student-comic-art/), and was featured in the online alumni newsletter in April.

The number of books sold so far has been somewhat disappointing: 22 copies in the first 10 weeks, including Amazon, shop.msu.edu, the Comics Forum, and our over-the-counter sales in the library. However, the media coverage has been stronger than I'm usually able to generate for new initiatives, resources, services, and events at the library. The perennial challenge of public relations is that it's impossible to quantify the value of that exposure.

There are promising sales opportunities still ahead. The campus bookstore has agreed to feature *The MSU Student Comic Art Anthology* prominently during football season this fall, when alumni visit campus in the thousands. Approaching local off-campus bookstores will be a priority this summer, with the goal of placing the student anthology and our most significant historic cookbook reprints on sale. September will see the publication of our first comic strip reprint volume: a two-year run of the Golden Age strip *Tim Tyler's Luck*, by Lyman Young. With a small critical mass of comics-related publications, it will be possible to consider paid advertisements for the books in the MSU alumni magazine and in online venues such as *Comic Book Resources* (http://www.comicbookresources.com), *The Comics Journal* (http://www.tcj.com), and the Comic-Con *Pulse* (http://comicon.com/pulse).

Conclusion

Will publishing become so lucrative that MSU Libraries no longer faces budget constraints? Unlikely, but early reactions to *The MSU Student Comic Art Anthology* clearly indicate that this type of project can be a source of positive media attention, opportunities for collaboration, and even advertising for our Espresso Book Machine service.

References

Dreher, C. (2002). *Why Do Books Cost So Much?* Retrieved from http://www.salon.com/2002/12/03/prices/

Sell on Amazon: Start Selling Online Fast. (n.d.). Retrieved from http://services.amazon.com/selling/pricing.htm

The MSU Student Comic Art Anthology. Cover design by Theresa Moore.

Contributor Gabriel P. Cooper with a fresh copy of The MSU Student Comic Art Anthology, newly printed on the Espresso Book Machine at right.

A Production Process for Library Help Videos

Shawn Vaillancourt, Kelsey Brett, Katie Buehner, Andrea Malone, & Ayla Stein

University of Houston

5 IN THIS CHAPTER

Theme

Assessment & workflow for writing & producing video content

Highlighted Service

Tutorial videos for a variety of library services

Software/Platforms Utilized

YouTube

Resources

Shared production criteria, workflow, & checklist

When it comes to the editorial process, video content does not differ fundamentally from other published content. Videos must be vetted and edited with a scrupulous eye to ensure quality of construction and validity of content. The University of Houston Libraries govern their video program using a procedure designed to track videos through development, production, and distribution. This rigorous editorial process frees librarians from agonizing over logistics and technical issues so they can spend the bulk of their efforts on content development.

In 2010, the University of Houston Libraries posted their first video to YouTube. This first video, produced by the Marketing Committee, was an orientation video that gave an overview of the libraries' locations, collections, and services. In three years, the libraries have posted approximately 90 videos, added over 100 subscribers, and received more than 40,000 views. In 2011, the Help Videos committee was created to oversee the migration of an older set of how-to videos into YouTube (e.g., How to use Interlibrary Loan, How to use Course Reserves) and to manage new video creation. Despite the committee's best efforts, videos often stalled in production or languished post-publication. It became clear that a standardized publication process was needed, so that the committee could maintain production consistency, delegate responsibilities, vet prospective videos, and ensure quality.

> **To manage new video creation...[i]t became clear that a standardized publication process was needed, so that the committee could maintain production consistency, delegate responsibilities, vet prospective videos, and ensure quality.**

Maintain Production Consistency

Because the libraries intended to create many videos over a period of time, it was necessary to establish a consistent viewing experience for patrons. For example, each video now uses the same basic color scheme, and is branded with the libraries' wordmark.

Production consistency is not limited to the video itself; consistency is also of vital importance in the hosting environment. For instance, all UH Libraries' videos are posted to our YouTube channel, tagged with a common set of metadata, and are Creative Commons licensed.

One of the hidden benefits of production consistency is that it eliminates the need to start from scratch with every new video. For example, the libraries produce approximately 20 videos every year for the university's reading series, Poetry & Prose. In 2011, a reusable color scheme, standard font, and branding was formulated for Poetry & Prose videos. This saves hours of editorial work, as editors can simply copy and paste the template and drop in the new footage.

The last, and perhaps most important element of production consistency, is that each video should be designed around a clearly defined outcome. Many of the videos that stalled in production did so because they either had no stated outcome or because they tried to accomplish too many outcomes in a two-minute time frame. Consistent outcomes have the potential to be multi-purpose, or to fuel learning across multiple videos. In this way, librarians are not limited to teaching one concept or procedure per video, but can layer learning through a series of videos. The Libraries' "Developing Keywords" (http://www.youtube.com/watch?v=Ui-iFnS-9hs) and "Search Using Keywords" (http://www.youtube.com/watch?v=1tUqc4gnxc8) videos illustrate this principle.

Delegate Responsibilities

The video publishing process typically involves several librarians or staff members. This created two specific problems at UH: the same people made all the videos, and it was difficult to train or involve additional collaborators. Our solution was to create three primary production roles—producer, director, and editor. The producer is the individual (or individuals) who proposes the video and writes its initial script. The producer may or may not be a committee member. Directors and editors are always members of the committee, because their responsibilities require a specialized skill set and/or depth of experience. The director is responsible for keeping the production moving forward or on schedule, and the editor puts the video together.

This system meant that producers focus on crafting effective outcomes and content, while the committee concentrates on providing expert advice and technical support. The committee shoulders the responsibility for developing the necessary hardware and software skills instead of trying to train every librarian who proposed a new video. Most of all, it meant that each participant had a clear understanding of their responsibilities and expected investment in any video project.

> **The hours required to produce a quality video are significant, and that time should not be wasted producing videos that no one will watch or that are ineffective.**

Vet Prospective Videos

While video is an excellent communication medium, it is not the appropriate tool for every situation. The hours required to produce a quality video are significant, and that time should not be wasted producing videos that no one will watch or that are ineffective. Therefore, it is necessary to vet video ideas before dedicating staff time and resources to the production process.

Sometimes, the best way to vet a video is through "self-weeding." At Houston, several librarians experienced this after failing to produce videos introducing our discovery platform. A brief reflection on our attempts revealed that we could not establish a clear outcome, target audience, or promotion platform for the proposed videos. Also, it was difficult to conceive of a video that provided meaningful coverage of any of the platform's features within our target length of one to two minutes. Instead, we produced a short series of videos that modeled the use of specific features (e.g., RSS feeds and citation tools; http://www.youtube.com/playlist?l ist=PLbiKDGQR5r5RZVv1atijlQJUucBreMN5). However, there have also been times when a video concept never fully materialized, and the committee has discarded it.

Now producers must complete several requirements in a checklist (Appendix 1) in order to ensure that vetting occurs before video production begins. The checklist requires producers to complete essential steps, such as writing a script or stating a learning objective, before the video reaches later—and more time-intensive—stages of production. If a producer struggles to complete parts of the checklist (e.g., unable to secure visuals that effectively illustrate the script), then video production ceases via self-weeding. Producers receive support for problem-solving from members of the committee or other experts for relevant portions (e.g., the Libraries' Instruction Team for developing learning outcomes). Despite best intentions or conscientious effort, some videos will never make it past the drawing board. Vetting is a vital part of the publishing process, and while it can foster disappointment, it can also end cycles of failure or halt an unsupportable project before it starts.

Ensure Quality

Many YouTube videos are simply unwatchable because of their sound and/or video quality. In consultation with a member of the School of Communications faculty, the University of Houston Libraries invested in some basic, affordable equipment that would mean that our videos would be both seen and heard, including a HD video camera with audio inputs, two microphones, and the creation of a green screen room. In addition to this equipment, the libraries' Learning Commons is home to a recording studio that can be used to create crisp, professional spoken audio tracks. Many universities have such a space available for campus media production, even if it is not located in the library proper. In the end, the greatest content in the world can be ruined by a cheap microphone or a grainy image. A standardized production process is an excellent opportunity to establish uniform benchmarks of product quality.

The production process has standardized the basic task flow for video creation, which has allowed committee members and producers to focus on content creation and placement. The committee is using assessment data to adjust the publication process as needed. The committee's Video Assessment Plan outlines four criteria for the assessment of video efficacy:

1. Find: Users should easily be able to locate videos, especially at point-of-need.
2. Watch: Users should stay engaged throughout the video.
3. Learn: Users should learn a process, concept, or about using products or services at their disposal.
4. Promote: Library staff will use videos in their instruction and reference work, both in person and online.

Currently, the group is working to shorten all video introductions to less than three seconds based on data mined from YouTube analytics. This change responds to evaluation of the second criteria, Watch, as it should decrease the initial fall-off in viewership many of our videos experience in the first seven to ten seconds.

The UH Libraries also continues to develop its production process through meeting with producers to solicit feedback concerning their experiences with both creating and utilizing videos. Our last feedback session affirmed that producers find the process useful overall. However, they made several suggestions for improvement. Several librarians asked for a set of best practices to assist in the early stages of video development. One librarian commented that, "It would be nice to know from the onset that videos are most useful if they don't exceed this amount of time, and they meet these goals."

> No editorial process is self-contained; instead, it is built on levels of expertise that work together to produce the best possible publication.

In addition to supporting producers' needs, the committee's role as the in-house experts is important to the process. One librarian stated that, "We went into our videos clearly wanting something very short and concise and I don't think that is what everyone goes into the video with. So if you have someone whose role is to proofread and cut down, I think that it is helpful."

No editorial process is self-contained; instead, it is built on levels of expertise that work together to produce the best possible publication. The University of Houston Libraries' video production process has simplified the creation of effective help videos through the implementation of basic editorial principles and practices. The process will continue to evolve as the committee solicits feedback and evaluates assessment data.

Appendix A

Video Production Checklist

Name of Video:				
Producer:				
Director:				
Editor:				
Learning Objective(s):				

		PRODUCER	DIRECTOR	EDITOR
PRE-PRODUCTION		Create a file repository in the 'O drive		
		Write script		
		Create storyboard		
		Collect all graphics and still images needed for the video		
PRODUCTION		Create live video	Film all live video	Create screen captures
		Create voice over	Assist with voice recording	
POST-PRODUCTION		Proof the video		Edit Video
		Request any changes		Implement changes requested by producer
PUBLISHING		Tag video	Save & share embedd code	Upload video to YouTube
		Describe video	Create captions	Obtain Creative Commons license
		Assign video to playlist		Add video to requested playlists

Publishing in the Archives

Open (Flu) Season: A Case Study of The American Influenza Epidemic of 1918: A Digital Encyclopedia

Julie Judkins

University of Michigan Medical School

IN THIS CHAPTER

1

Theme
Building a digital encyclopedia & conducting an open peer-review

Highlighted Service
Curating a digital archive

Software/Platforms Utilized
Wordpress & Digital Library eXtension Service (DLXS)

Resources
Example usability testing procedures & survey

The *American Influenza Epidemic of 1918: A Digital Encyclopedia* (*AIE*) (2012) is an undertaking by the University of Michigan's Center for the History of Medicine (CHM) in partnership with the University of Michigan Library's MPublishing division, to create an open source digital collection of archival, primary, and interpretive materials related to the history of the 1918 influenza pandemic in the United States. This virtual collection, powered by the University of Michigan's Digital Library eXtension Service (DLXS), documents the experiences of diverse communities in the United States in the fall of 1918 and winter of 1919 when influenza took the lives of approximately 675,000 Americans. The National Endowment for the Humanities (NEH) awarded the project a prestigious "We the People"

Publishing in the Archives

designation for its contribution to the teaching, study, and understanding of American history and culture.

The *AIE* was officially released to the public on October 10th, 2012, at a celebratory event held in the University of Michigan's Harlan Hatcher Graduate Library Gallery. To date, the website attracts an average of 100 unique users a day. An active Twitter feed (@1918FluArchive) complements the website.

Project Background

The materials in the *AIE* collection originated as research for two government-commissioned reports. In 2005, the Defense Threat Reduction Agency contacted CHM and asked the staff to conduct a study of "escape communities," or places that experienced few influenza cases and no deaths during the 1918 pandemic. A formal report (Markel, Stern, Navarro, & Michalsen, 2006) focused on a historical evaluation of the non-pharmaceutical interventions employed by seven communities[1] was delivered to DTRA in early 2006. Following the DTRA study, in 2007, the CDC tasked CHM with conducting a quantitative historical study of American cities during the pandemic. Expanding their original project a great deal, CHM researchers studied 50 diverse cities across the United States. At the project's end, they concluded that cities that acted early, implemented a layered response, and kept health measures in place for longer fared better, experiencing lower influenza and pneumonia mortality rates. Their final report, published in *JAMA*, is the basis for the United States government's pandemic preparedness policy (Markel et al., 2007).

Recognizing the importance of the materials collected during the DTRA and CDC projects, CHM staff members originally intended to pursue publication of a print-based encyclopedia based on their research. However, when it became clear that the comprehensive volume they envisioned would be cost-prohibitive, the CHM staff decided to adapt the project for a digital format. With the guidance of colleagues in the University of Michigan's Scholarly Publishing Office (later renamed MPublishing), the CHM staff began to prepare a digital encyclopedia drawing on their research and subject expertise. Funding for the project was provided by CHM, the CDC, and an NEH Preservation and Access grant.

Project Features

The *AIE* collocates an estimated 50,000 pages of digitized reproductions of archival materials gathered by CHM staff at over 140 national institutions. It is intended for a wide-ranging audience that encompasses high school and college students, historians and social scientists, epidemiologists and public health practitioners, journalists and writers, as well as casual Internet users interested in the period.

---

[1]   The communities studied include: the San Francisco Naval Training Station (Yerba Buena Island, California); Gunnison, Colorado; Princeton University (Princeton, New Jersey); the Western Pennsylvania Institution for the Blind (Pittsburgh, Pennsylvania); Trudeau Tuberculosis Sanatorium (Saranac Lake, New York); Bryn Mawr College (Bryn Mawr, Pennsylvania); and Fletcher, Vermont.

The *AIE* is the first digital encyclopedia to document the social, cultural, public health, and human dimensions of the most devastating infectious health crisis to occur during the post–germ theory era and it is the first to highlight the responses of over 50 American communities. In addition to archival materials, the website offers interpretative documents that serve as templates for self-guided research projects. The most notable set of interpretative documents are the 50 "city biographies" written by CHM's research team. These essays explore the responses taken by 50 of the most populous cities during the fall of 1918 and winter of 1919 as influenza ravaged their communities. The essays present the social and cultural context of each city and explore the issues that became significant as the epidemic unfolded over the fall and winter. Each essay is approximately 2,000 words and provides not only a portrait of the city during the epidemic—steps taken to prevent infection and the spread of disease, death totals, and introduction to major officials—but also the current state of the city at the time. Interactive timelines complement the essays.

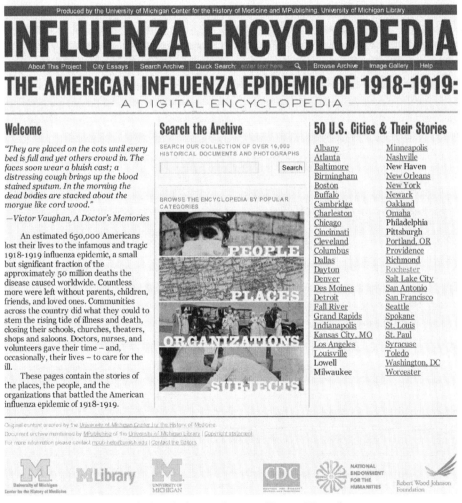

Writing History in the Digital Age Open Peer Review

In Fall 2011, one year before the *AIE*'s public launch, a preliminary case study appeared in the open peer review edition of *Writing History in the Digital Age*, a born-digital, open access book edited by Jack Dougherty and Kristen Nawrotzki. The six-week open peer review process, which generated 945 comments across all contributed articles, was a valuable opportunity to interact with scholars involved with similar projects and a chance to gauge future public reactions to CHM's then forthcoming digital encyclopedia.

During *Writing History*'s open peer review process, hosted on the project's WordPress website under a Creative Commons Attribution-Non-Commercial 3.0 license, members of the general public were invited to comment on the publication in general, on individual essays, and on specific paragraphs within each essay. All comments required an author to submit his or her full name and e-mail address (kept private), to minimize flaming and facilitate communication with the editors. The *AIE* case study received 10 constructive reader comments. Digital Curator Julie Judkins made an additional four comments in response to questions. Responses to the *AIE* case study centered around three broad themes: inquires about technical specifications, appreciation of the *AIE*'s open source format, and reactions to the *AIE* as a pioneering piece of historical scholarship.

Although support for open access projects might be expected within the confines of an open access experiment like *Writing History*, the CHM development team was nevertheless gratified to read readers' enthusiasm for projects like the *AIE*. In response to the *AIE* case study, Abbey Lowe wrote, "It was interesting to see this type of archival research that is intended, not to be insular only for academic or scholarly uses, but also hopes to reach the public sphere in terms of health related issues. This led me to think about how collaboration [...] brings relevancy to work that, although actively pursued by a few, can now be accessed and used by communities." As champions of open access content and believers in the power of shared research, the *AIE* team is pleased that users find CHM's work relevant outside of its original intent. We hope projects like *Writing History* and the *Library Publishing Toolkit* galvanize this exciting trend in scholarly communication.

Participating in the *Writing History* open peer review process was a catalyst for the *AIE*'s final stages of development. Receiving a reaction to the encyclopedia while it was still in progress allowed the development team to prioritize necessary actions in the months before the public launch. Given the novelty of a project like the *AIE*, future users were as interested in the technical and legal aspects of the project as the encyclopedia's archival content. An FAQ regarding copyright and citation methods was added to the final *AIE* website in response to questions asked by *Writing History* commenters (Appendix A). The concerns and questions raised during the open peer review also helped refine the user testing protocol used prior to the *AIE*'s public release (Appendices B and C) and inspired a presentation at the American Library Association's 2012 Annual Conference (Judkins & Thomas, 2012).

> **Receiving a reaction to the encyclopedia while it was still in progress allowed the development team to prioritize necessary actions in the months before the public launch.**

Reflecting on the open peer review process ("General comments on the book," 2011), *Writing History* participants observed that essays appearing later in the electronic book received fewer comments than those appearing at the beginning. This might explain why the *AIE* case study, positioned in the book's final section well below "the jump," did not draw as many comments as other essays. Although this technical aspect had no impact on the value of the comments received (quality over quantity should be the watchword in such endeavors), those interested in pursuing similar open peer review projects might reflect on how interfaces should be designed to encourage conversation on a more egalitarian level.

User Testing

In early August 2012, two months before the website's public release on October 10, the first users outside the development team tested the fledging *AIE* website. Initial user testing was carried out prior to the website's official release to ensure the most polished final product at the launch event.

Jonathan McGlone, Digital Publishing Project Manager at the University of Michigan Library, was the primary author of the *AIE* user testing protocol (Appendices B and C), developed in collaboration with CHM's Assistant Managing Director Alex Navarro and Digital Curator Julie Judkins. Questions were developed in respect to McGlone's prior experience with user testing, guidance from Suzanne Chapman and Sonali Mishra of the Michigan Library User Experience Department, and concerns brought forth during the *Writing History* open peer review process. Two practice tests were conducted with volunteer staff members prior to the official tests and adjustments were made to the protocol as needed.

Because the prototype website was not accessible to the public and required a credentialed log-in, all user tests were conducted in person with testers from Metro Detroit. Every effort was made to recruit the most diverse pool of testers possible, despite the limitations. Candidate testers were recruited from colleagues with backgrounds in medical history and/or archives, interested members of the community, and librarians working at the University of Michigan's Taubman Health Sciences Library. All communication with testers prior to the tests, from recruitment to scheduling, was conducted by e-mail.

> **...those interested in pursuing similar open peer review projects might reflect on how interfaces should be designed to encourage conversation on a more egalitarian level.**

The testers' response to the prototype website was largely positive. Testers liked the website's design, found the content interesting, and said the website was easy to navigate. Negative comments prompted a change to the way document images were displayed and fonts and graphics were adjusted on the homepage to facilitate comprehension. User testing also revealed a bug in search capabilities from the homepage that was corrected prior to the website's release.

Conclusion

The *AIE* is a living document by design. The development team looks forward to increasing the digital encyclopedia's value in the coming years as new technologies and collaborations arise. We hope the *AIE* will prove useful to historians today and well into the future. Our goal is to maintain an innovative database that will inspire other scholars to share their research in a similar manner, making it accessible to a larger audience. Although the future of publishing is a moving target, the *AIE* development team looks forward to participating fully in this inspiring time for digital humanists and librarians alike.

References

American Influenza Epidemic of 1918: A Digital Encyclopedia (2012). J. A. Navarro, A. Stern, H. Markel, & M. S. Cetron (Eds.). Retrieved fromhttp://www.influenzaarchive.org/

General comments on the book (2011). In K. Nawrotzki & J. Dougherty (Eds.), *Writing History in the Digital Age Open Review*. Retrieved from http://writinghistory.trincoll.edu/general-comments/

Judkins, J. (2011). Case Study of the American Influenza Epidemic of 1918: A Digital Encyclopedia. In K. Nawrotzki & J. Dougherty (Eds.), *Writing History in the Digital Age Open Review* (Part 6: New Ways to Tell ~~Old~~ New Stories). Retrieved from http://writinghistory.trincoll.edu/new-ways/the-american-influenza-epidemic-of-1918-judkins/

Judkins, J., & Thomas, K. (2012, June 25). *Welcome to the Digital Revolution. Where Are Your Libraries?* [PDF document]. Presentation at the Annual Meeting of the American Library Association, Anaheim, CA. Retrieved from http://ala12.scheduler.ala.org/node/1706

Markel, H., Lipmann, H. B., Navarro, J. A., Sloan, A., Michalsen, J. R., Stern, A. M., & Cetron, M. S. (2007). Nonpharmaceutical interventions implemented by US cities during the 1918–1919 influenza pandemic. *Journal of the American Medical Association, 298*, 644–654.

Markel, H., Stern, A. M., Navarro, J. A., & Michalsen, J. A. (2006). Historical Assessment of Nonpharmaceutical Disease Containment Strategies Employed by Selected U.S. Communities during the Second Wave of the 1918–1920 Influenza Pandemic. Defense Threat Reduction Agency, U.S. Department of Defense.

Open peer review essays (Fall 2011). (2011). In K. Nawrotzki & J. Dougherty (Eds.), *Writing History in the Digital Age Open Review*. Retrieved from http://writinghistory.trincoll.edu/evolution/open-review-contents-fall-2011/

Appendix A

FAQ

Where did these materials come from? Where can I find them?

Please see our list of Acknowledgements.

Why can't I download every image?

Although the majority of materials in the AIE are out of copyright or otherwise in the public domain, some are not. Any materials protected by copyright cannot be downloaded.

Please use any images you download from our site for personal or scholarly use only. If you wish to distribute these materials in print or electronically, you must receive permission. You can contact mpub-help@umich.edu for more information.

If I want to use images or text, may I do so?

These pages may be freely searched and displayed. Permission must be received for subsequent print or electronic distribution. For more information, please read the University of Michigan Library access and usage policy, or contact

mpub-help@umich.edu.

Is there an official citation for the encyclopedia?

The preferred citation of our site is as follows:

["Name of Article or Item," if applicable] *American Influenza Epidemic of 1918 - 1919: A Digital Encyclopedia*. http://www.influenzaarchive.org. Date accessed.

Is there an official citation for items in the archive?

The preferred citation for items in the archive, such as a newspaper article, should look like:

"Grade Schools Will Not Open Here Tuesday." *The Dayton Daily News*. December 9, 1918. 1, 12. American Influenza Epidemic of 1918 - 1919: A Digital Encyclopedia. http://www.influenzaarchive.org. October 10, 2012.

Can I contribute photographs or other similar original materials to the archive?

You may inquire about contributing materials by using the information provided on the Contact the Editors page. Submitting materials does not guarantee that they will appear on the website as we must abide by our collections policy and copyright restrictions, as appropriate. We appreciate your interest in contributing to our project!

Appendix B

Talk Aloud Protocol for American Influenza Encyclopedia Usability Testing (Takes about 45 min - 1 hour to complete)

Background: The AIE Project Team is conducting usability testing of this online resource in order to get direct feedback on use of the tool and ideas for improvements. We are asking that faculty, staff, and students assist us in this work, and their input is essential. The procedure below was established to get their key input efficiently and then allow them to proceed with their day.

1. Moderator should greet and thank the participant

2. Conduct them to the testing area.

3. Introduce the note taker. Give the participant an overview of why we're doing this, ask if they have any questions.

4. Notetaker: Assign the user a code name, your [intervewer] last name with a number. For example, if Jonathan was working with a tester and she was his second tester, the code would be McGlone2.

5. Provide a brief training for the participant on the use of the resource and an overview.

6. Ask the participant to use the AIE to do the following:

    a. Ask the participant to find a newspaper article mentioning the United States Public Health Service ["Correct" answer: Organization -- United States Public Health Service].

    b. Ask the participant to find (San Francisco) Mayor James Rolph, Jr.'s papers ["Correct" answer: James Rolph, Jr. Papers, 1911-1930 (MS 1818) at the CA Historical Society]

    c. Ask them if there is anything they would like to search for.

7. Ask the participant to think out loud as they work with the resource, make decisions, and perhaps get stuck doing what they want to do. Set them at ease: remind them we

are testing the website, not them, that they can't make mistakes here, and we want their honest feedback -- it won't hurt our feelings.

8. Note taker should begin taking notes as soon as the tester begins working with the site.

9. Offer assistance as needed, but let them work out problems if they can. Don't let them struggle or become frustrated. Each person will be different so remain aware of their progress and how it is going with them.

10. Follow up on tasks if it isn't clear they successfully completed it -- if they said they completed it, but it is not clear if they really did, ask them "so, you got it?"

11. Observations will include misconceptions, vocabulary, problems, and aspirations. Make quick notes on these.

12. After the tester has finished, the moderator should follow up the session with the AIE Usability Questionnaire. While you are making observations, you may already have answers to these questions, and if so there is no need to ask again.

13. Thank the tester and be sure to ask and answer any questions they may have.

Appendix C

AIE Talk Aloud Protocol Usability Questionnaire

Participant code name _____

1. What'd you think?

2. On a scale of 1 to 5 (1 being easy, 5 being difficult), rate the level of difficulty you encountered when searching and finding your documents?

3. If you used the browse feature, what'd you think? Was it easy or difficult to browse your given topic?

4. In what ways would this resource be of use to you? How do you envision using this in your research? Would you ever use it?

5. Were there any areas in which difficulties arose?

6. Would you recommend this resource to other people?

7. What advice would you give for improving this resource?

Digitizing an Oral History from Analog Audio Cassettes and Typewritten Documents: A Case Study

Matthew M. Best

SUNY Erie Community College

2 IN THIS CHAPTER

Theme
Selection of materials and choosing equipment for digitization

Highlighted Project
Audio digitization

Software/Platforms Utilized
DSpace, LibGuides, & Audacity

Resources
Discussion of material selection & recommended standards

This case study examines the steps taken by the Library Resource Center (LRC) at Erie Community College (ECC) to digitally reproduce the analog content of an oral history created by James E. Shenton entitled *A Verbal History of Erie Community College*. Mr. Shenton was instrumental in the college's inception in 1946 and served as the college's president from 1963 to 1974. As such, his audio memoirs of his time at ECC serve as a primary source detailing the beginnings of the college and the effort to create the first community colleges within the State University of New York system. Mr. Shenton recorded his oral history in 1982 and died in 2003. The ECC LRC staff approached the digitization of Mr. Shenton's oral history in 2010. We did so with no budget and no established infrastructure for performing digital content creation projects. Instead, the staff relied on combinations of loaned and readily available hardware, commercially available and open source software, and published best practices for digitizing archival materials.

Material Selection

The LRC staff began materials selection in September 2010. We selected Mr. Shenton's oral history as the subject of our first digitization project primarily because of its enduring value and unique characteristics. ECC's archival storage room houses the oral history's analog master. It consists of six analog audio cassettes, a one-page typewritten outline, and a 55-page typewritten transcript. The transcript is legible, but the sound of Mr. Shenton's voice telling his story was in danger of being lost to an outmoded media format: the analog audiocassette tape. The LRC staff agreed that digitizing the oral history would prevent loss of information due to obsolescence and deterioration of the original analog audio format.

The LRC staff also took the physical condition and extent of the oral history into consideration during material selection. In October 2010, the LRC staff examined the entire content of the oral history to validate its condition and overall completeness. We considered the oral history to be a manageable candidate for digitization because it consists of only eight physical units. We believed that its inherently limited physical scope could potentially reduce the labor required to digitize it and provide a greater chance that users would fully experience the project upon its completion. The LRC staff considered other archived items for this foray into digitization before we settled on the oral history. Student newspapers, yearbooks, photograph collections, college catalogs, scrapbooks, etc., were also available in the college's archival storage. However, we did not characterize these items with the same value or risk of loss as the oral history.

> We considered the oral history to be a manageable candidate for digitization because it consists of only eight physical units... its inherently limited physical scope could potentially reduce the labor required to digitize it and provide a greater chance that users would fully experience the project upon its completion.

The Federal Agencies Digitization Guidelines Initiative (FADGI) (2010) recommends the use of digital repositories for long-term storage of digital files and metadata (p. 82). Following this recommendation, the LRC staff selected the SUNY Digital Repository (http://dspace. sunyconnect.suny.edu/) as the location for long-term storage and access to the digital files created for this project. As a member of the State University of New York system, ECC can add content to the SUNY digital repository at no charge. Once content and metadata is loaded into the repository's online DSpace software application, the application automatically indexes and makes the content available via the Internet.

With a digital repository selected, the LRC staff chose SpringShare's content management software application, LibGuides (http://springshare.com/libguides/), for the creation of an appealing and accessible online exhibit of the content within the repository. Utilizing LibGuides required no additional cost to the LRC because it already maintained subscription access to the application for the creation of online subject-based research guides.

The material selection process continued with an assessment of the oral history's copyright. The LRC staff conducted the initial assessment using Peter B. Hirtle's (2013) "Copyright Term and the Public Domain in the United States" as a reference. Hirtle's document indicates that the oral history is likely part of the public domain because ECC's LRC originally published it between 1978 and March 1, 1989, without copyright notice or subsequent copyright registration within five years of publication. An examination of the oral history's content indicates a 1982 publication date, and no copyright notices appear within any of its parts. Title, author, and keyword searches at the U.S. Copyright Office's Search Copyright Records database (http://www.copyright.gov/records) on October 27, 2010, revealed no indication that a subsequent registration was completed within five years of the publication of the oral history or afterward. Given these circumstances, it is our best assessment that *A Verbal History of Erie Community College* is part of the public domain. This assessment is further justified by Section 405 of the Copyrights Act (2011).

> **Title, author, and keyword searches...revealed no indication that a subsequent registration was completed within five years of the publication of the oral history or afterward.**

The final stage of material selection, metadata assessment, began at the end of October. FADGI (2010) recommends collecting existing metadata before beginning any digitization activities. FADGI also notes that it is extremely beneficial to export existing metadata from other systems to a production database before digitizing (p. 76). Several instances of metadata appear within the content of the oral history and in some instances exist within ECC's library catalog records. The LRC staff collected initial descriptive metadata from these resources (the *who, what, when,* and *where* of the oral history) in a spreadsheet for use throughout the project. LRC staff agreed to collect additional metadata as it became available and required during each subsequent stage of the project. The staff referred to FADGI guidelines (p. 70–79) for further understanding of the importance of metadata and detailed explanations of metadata types.

Equipment Selection

In November, the LRC staff established the necessary equipment in the form of hardware, software, and file formats that were required to capture the oral history digitally. Lacking a budget, the LRC staff utilized loaned, readily available, and open source resources (see the appendix to learn more about the LRC staff's selected equipment, means of acquisition, and URL links to additional information about each selection).

Digital Capture: Audio

During the audio capture, LRC staff played the six analog master audio cassettes through a loaned RCA SCT-510 stereo cassette tape deck. The staff used a loaned 3.5mm male-to-RCA stereo audio cable to create an RCA line-out connection from the tape deck to the 3.5mm line-in of a Microsoft/Intel high-definition audio device. The Microsoft/Intel high-definition audio device acted as an analog-to-digital audio converter; it was installed in a personal computer consisting of an Intel Pentium dual-core CPU E2200 (2.20 GHz, 2 Gb RAM, Windows Vista Enterprise). Access to the high-definition audio device was a serendipitous occurrence for the LRC staff. It could be configured for high-resolution analog-to-digital audio conversion and was part of the factory-installed equipment in a staff member's office computer.

The LRC staff digitally recorded the audio with the free, open source software application Audacity Digital Audio Editor v. 1.2.6. The staff created digital master recordings with a sample rate of 96 kHz, 24-bit bit depth, and exported them in WAVE (.wav) file format while maintaining the initial sample rate and bit depth. These specifications and the use of the high-resolution, uncompressed WAVE file format represent archival digital audio reproduction recommendations in 2010 (Fleischhauer, 2010, p. 36). The LRC staff applied no editing, effects, or filtering to the high-resolution digital master recordings. We derived production recordings from the digital masters. The LRC staff edited the production recordings lightly in Audacity to remove or reduce extraneous noise and silent passages that are present in the original analog recordings. Using the LAME MP3 encoder plug-in for Audacity, we exported the production recordings in MP3 (.mp3) file format at 128 Kbit/s, constant bit-rate, mono. The LRC staff selected the low-resolution, compressed MP3 file format to ensure successful dissemination via slower Internet connections without dramatically affecting the quality of the audio reproduction.

Digital Capture: Text

The LRC staff scanned the text of the original outline and transcript digitally using a loaned Epson Perfection 3490 PHOTO scanner. The scanner resolution was set to 300dpi and a 12-bit bit-depth. We selected these specifications based on calculations made with the Image Quality Calculator (http://images.library.uiuc.edu/calculator), an online tool maintained by the library at University of Illinois at Urbana-Champaign. The Image Quality Calculator is designed to calculate the minimum recommended resolution necessary to capture all of the details of a printed manuscript when scanned optically and saved in an uncompressed image file format. The LRC staff exported the page images as uncompressed black-and-white TIFF (.tif) files using a loaned copy of ABBYY FineReader 10 Professional Edition software. We also used ABBYY FineReader 10 to perform optical character recognition (OCR) on the page images to create editable and searchable text. Subsequently, the LRC staff merged and exported the page images and searchable text in the compressed Portable Document Format (.pdf) file format.

Archival and Public Access

In July 2011, following the digital capture of the oral history's audio and text, the LRC staff uploaded the uncompressed files and their compressed derivatives with their corresponding metadata to the SUNY digital repository. Direct access to these files and metadata is available as a collection in the repository at http://hdl.handle.net/1951/52520. The LRC staff used the LibGuides' content management application to create an online exhibit that links to the files and showcases their historical context. Access to this online exhibit is available at http://

> **The online exhibit allows users mediated access to the oral history's low-resolution, compressed files located in the SUNY digital repository.**

libguides.ecc.edu/ecchistory within the ECC LRC website (http://library.ecc.edu). The online exhibit allows users mediated access to the oral history's low-resolution, compressed files located in the SUNY digital repository. While viewing the online exhibit, users can stream the oral history's audio and read its textual content. Links to related resources and additional information are also available in the online exhibit. Downloading the audio and text is possible, but not necessary. Additionally, if users desire access to the oral history's uncompressed, high-resolution master files, the online exhibit contains links to their location within the SUNY digital repository.

Discussion

Digitizing *A Verbal History of Erie Community College* was successful. The LRC staff digitally preserved and provided wide access to the oral history's aural and textual content while defining its historical context. In addition, we achieved a means of long-term, off-site digital storage of the content. The do-it-yourself nature of the project is a point of pride for the LRC staff, but it is not without its drawbacks. Learning and experimenting with best practices added substantial time to the project. Securing acceptable hardware and software for the project with no funding also took time and was risky. The condition, quality, and operation of such equipment directly affect a digital project. Borrowing such equipment provides little means of creating a sustainable infrastructure for future digital projects. Under these circumstances, we only achieved our goal by being cautious, methodical, and a little lucky. The LRC staff started this project with no budget and no infrastructure, but we had a tremendous story to share. Ultimately, we hope this digital project promotes awareness of ECC's unique history and honors James E. Shenton's remarkable legacy as a man who helped forge the college, worked within the college, and went on to successfully lead the college.

References

Copyrights Act, 17 U.S.C. §405 (2011).

Federal Agencies Digitization Guidelines Initiative (FADGI) – Still Image Working Group. (2010). *Technical guidelines for digitizing cultural heritage materials: Creation of raster image master files.* Rev. ed. Retrieved from http://www.digitizationguidelines.gov/guidelines/ FADGI_Still_Image-Tech_Guidelines_2010-08-24.pdf

Fleischhauer, C. (2010). Format considerations in audio-visual preservation reformatting: Snapshots from the Federal Agencies Digitization Guidelines Initiative. *Information Standards Quarterly, 22*(2), 34–39. doi:10.3789/isqv22n2.2010.07

Hirtle, P. B. (2013). Copyright term and the public domain in the United States. Retrieved from http://copyright.cornell.edu/resources/publicdomain.cfm

Appendix

Equipment Selection for the Digitization of A Verbal History of Erie Community College

Core Equipment	Means of Acquisition	URL For Additional Information
Personal computer: Intel Pentium Dual-Core CPU E2200 (2.20 GHz, 2Gb RAM, Windows Vista Enterprise), color video monitor, mouse	Readily available in the LRC's offices	http://ark.intel.com/products/33925/Intel-Pentium-Processor-E2200-1M-Cache-2_20-GHz-800-MHz-FSB
Audio Reproduction Equipment	**Means of Acquisition**	**URL For Additional Information**
RCA SCT-510 Stereo Cassette Tape Deck	Loaned by participating staff member	http://support.radioshack.com/support_audio/66124.htm
3.5mm male to RCA Stereo Audio Cable	Loaned by participating staff member	http://www.mediabridgeproducts.com/store/pc/3-5mm-To-RCA-Stereo-Cable-c146.htm
Labtec LCS-1070 Amplified PC speakers	Readily available in the LRC's offices	N/A
Microsoft/Intel High Definition Audio Device (analog to digital audio converter)	Factory installed in the personal computer described in Core Equipment	http://www.intel.com/design/chipsets/hdaudio.htm
Audacity Digital Audio Editor v. 1.2.6 with LAME MP3 encoder plug-in	Open-source software download, no cost	http://audacity.sourceforge.net/ http://lame.buanzo.com.ar/ http://lame.sourceforge.net/
Uncompressed, high-resolution file format: WAVE (.wav); Compressed, low-resolution file format: MP3 (.mp3)	Created by Audacity Digital Audio Editor	http://www.digitalpreservation.gov/formats/fdd/fdd000001.shtml http://www.digitalpreservation.gov/formats/fdd/fdd000105.shtml

Text Reproduction Equipment	Means of Acquisition	URL For Additional information
Image Quality Calculator	Publicly accessible via Internet	http://images.library.uiuc.edu/calculator/
Epson Perfection 3490 PHOTO scanner	Loaned by participating staff member	http://www.epson.com/cgi-bin/Store/support/supDetail.jsp?oid=58609
ABBYY FineReader 10 Professional Edition: OCR software for text recognition and document conversion with OCR and PDF features	Loaned by participating staff member	http://finereader.abbyy.com/
Uncompressed, high-resolution file format: TIFF (.tif); Compressed, low-resolution file format: PDF (.pdf)	Created by ABBYY FineReader 10	http://www.digitalpreservation.gov/formats/fdd/fdd000022.shtml http://www.digitalpreservation.gov/formats/fdd/fdd000030.shtml

Publishing Reprints: Repurposing Free Online Tools

Allison P. Brown & Joe Easterly

SUNY Geneseo

3 IN THIS CHAPTER

Theme

Selection & production of reprinted books

Highlighted project

Production of public domain reprints from an archival collection

Software/Platforms Utilized

Adobe Indesign, Createspace, & Open Monograph Press (OMP)

Resources

Shared documentation of selection & production procedures

In 2012, Milne Library at SUNY Geneseo began exploring a two-pronged publishing model that combines for-profit reprint sales with freely downloadable copies. We collected a list of rare and unusual titles from the library's special collections as candidates, with the goals to make them more widely available through digitization and online access, to preserve them in both electronic and print formats, and to use the experience to reflectively develop administrative and production workflows in pursuit of more efficient publishing services for our wider campus and community. In the process we explored and developed expertise in the platforms we chose—in this case Open Monograph Press (OMP) for managing and distributing the electronic format, and Amazon's CreateSpace™ for the print.

The players in the project were the assembled Publishing Team, a committee which manages Milne's publishing activities, the Electronic Resources & Digital Scholarship Librarian, the Special Collections Librarian, the Access Services and Information Delivery Services Librarian, and the Evening & Weekend Manager, who has previous experience with book layout and design. So far, Milne's reprints initiative has produced five titles, which are currently available on Amazon.com and Open Monograph Press (go.geneseo.edu/omp). With each reprinted title our processes have been refined and updated.

We utilized CreateSpace™, which is generally intended for self-publishers and for original content, to reprint public domain works. We utilized OMP as a project management and file hosting tool, which also has capabilities for hosting many users and roles and the peer-review process. The former was chosen for its ability to distribute easily through Amazon, lack of setup fees, usability, and fair royalties. OMP was chosen because—though we adopted it early in development—its varied capabilities have a lot of potential, and we wish to actively participate in its development.

We recruited other members of our library staff to review candidate reprint titles, and to write a brief summary which would accompany and enhance the reprint they selected. OMP makes it easy to to manage the review process for library staff, and makes it easy for library staff to submit written summaries through the same interface. This not only opens up the intricacies of the publishing process to the larger library body but increases staff awareness of the titles in Milne Library's Special Collections. These staff-written summaries make the reprints more accessible within both library and publishing settings. Lastly, it has prompted those of us involved in managing Milne's publishing activities to develop educational resources related to publishing for use by library staff, and for broader audiences as we market our publishing services to the campus community.

We intend this article to share the workflow and documentation we have developed as an illustration of repurposing readily available publishing tools to engage in relatively small-scale publishing projects. What is shared here is our documentation of the processes of selection, production, and uploading to both CreateSpace™ and Open Monograph Press. Our instructions have been generalized to remove specific references to staff, file locations, and our institution's catalog, but represent the framework that will hopefully aid other libraries in identifying potential projects and services. Our documentation assumes a basic understanding of the Adobe Creative Suite applications.

Selection, Scanning & Producing the Production-Ready Files

A. Select				B. Digitize			C. Design		
Candidate List	Selection	Metadata	Assess	Interior Scan	Exterior Scan	Template	Layout	Proof
Publishing Team		Managing Editor		IDS		Layout Designer		Managing Editor

A. Select Book

1. Criteria

Eligible books for reprint must be all of the following:

- In the public domain
- Not held by other libraries in New York
- Not already available digitally
- Not available as a reprint
- Cannot be unpublished, e.g., manuscript or letters
- Must be complete and readable
- Over 20 pages, to qualify for print production

2. Review Process

While the selected books are being digitized, any library staff member may select a book to review and summarize from the specified list of candidate titles (See Milne Library's example list of candidate titles[2]). This summary should be between 200 and 500 words, and will appear as the product description on Amazon.com, and either on the back cover, or as part of a colophon inside the book. The summary should review, introduce, and entice general readers to pick up the book.

[2]   http://tinyurl.com/ltjxvpj

3. Stage Selected Book for Reprinting

a. Gather publication metadata

CreateSpace™ and Open Monograph Press both require key pieces of metadata for processing. This data should be entered into these catalogs by the time the book has been scanned.

- **Local Collection/OCLC Number**: The record for the book in the local collection should be located, and used to provide the metadata needed.

- **Title**

- **Primary author**: Even if there is no primary author, CreateSpace™ requires one to be recorded.

- **Editor**: Our project lists the library as editor (e.g. "Milne Library at SUNY Geneseo")

- **Other original contributors**

- **Date of publication, publisher:** Enter original publication date in full format (eg. January 1, 1914)

- **Description**: A proofread version of the submitted/written summary

- **BISAC Code**: This standard is available at through the Book Industry Study Group website[3].

- **Author Bio**

- **Series**

- **Page count of book interior (excluding cover)**

- **Trim Size**

B. Digitize Book

1. Determine Digitization Strategy

Fragile and brittle books should be reviewed by an archivist prior to digitization for any specific guidelines on processing and handling.

Generally, the cover should be scanned on a flatbed scanner, and the interior using a production book scanning appliance. Each page of the book should be reviewed to determine if certain illustrations or pages should be scanned individually, and the appropriate production staff should be notified. Even if informally, begin thinking about how digitization will affect the reprint's design.

---

[3]   http://www.bisg.org/what-we-do-0-136-bisac-subject-headings-list-major-subjects.php

2. Scan Book Interior

The book interior should be scanned using the scanning specifications listed below. The interior should be scanned as a multi-page PDF. This PDF, along with the original book, should then be submitted to the staff member responsible for book design. *Note: In our workflow this step is completed by our Information Delivery Services Department using an overhead book scanner. The settings we choose are based on the book's interior content and generally have higher contrast settings as the majority of the content is black and white text.*

- All: 400dpi, no despeckling

- Text only: Black & White

- Simple B&W illustrations: Black & White

- B&W photos: Grayscale

- Color photos: Color

3. Scan Book Exterior

The book cover should be scanned on a flatbed scanner as uncompressed TIFFs, in the CMYK color space at 600 dpi.

C. Design Book

Considerations for the designer

1. All design components should be in CMYK or Grayscale color space.

2. All book exterior elements should have the same color profile (e.g., US Web Coated (SWOP) v2), and interior elements should have the same color profile (e.g., US Web Uncoated v2).

3. No spot colors should be used in the design — any spot colors should be converted to process color by double-clicking on the swatch to edit its settings.

4. No raster graphics (especially for the book exterior) should have partially or fully transparent elements. These graphics should be flattened onto a background layer which is the same color as the page background, or whatever page elements that appear behind the graphic. While this can increase file size, it addresses a potential bug in the CreateSpace™ printing and proofing process. Vector graphics do not seem to be affected by this bug.

5. Wherever practical, all design elements for the book exterior should be at the same resolution (600 DPI recommended), or vector.

6. For both maximizing efficiency and respecting the intent of the original work (as a reprint series), the overall design of the book exterior and interior should reflect the original work.

1. Design Book Interior

a. Initial proof of scanned .pdf file

Ensure that the quality is workable and no information has been cut off or distorted.

b. Touch up of pages as needed.

Use Adobe Photoshop to edit pages that need major adjustments. To edit the page images without having to reinsert each page into the original file, in Adobe Acrobat use the Touch Up Object Tool under Advanced Editing in the Tools menu. For each page, right-click to choose "edit", which will open the scanned page in Photoshop. After completing the desired edits, save the document and return to the PDF in Acrobat. The PDF will reflect the changes.

c. Determine trim size

Use the printer's specifications and the original trim size[4]:

Note: getting close to the original trim size is ideal, but more importantly the proportions are what you will want to pay attention to. A few things to consider:

- A book's interior that is designed to be more 'square' make look strange on a taller, skinnier trim size.

- If the book is over 150 pages, the margin requirements change, so there is less printable space on the page and the original text may need to be scaled down smaller than anticipated.

- If you are working with scanned cover images staying close to the original is best for the quality.

- These are CreateSpace™'s listed Trim Sizes. They recommend 6" x 9", as the most popular (also see Sacramento Public Library's publication guide[5] for a great intro to industry standards of trim sizes)

	Trim (in.)	White Paper Pg. Count	Cream Paper Pg. Count
	5 x 8	24 - 828	24 - 740
	5.06 x 7.81	24 - 828	24 - 740
	5.25 x 8	24 - 828	24 - 740
	5.5 x 8.5	24 - 828	24 - 740
Most Popular »	**6 x 9**	**24 - 828**	**24 - 740**
	6.14 x 9.21	24 - 828	24 - 740

---

[4]   https://www.createspace.com/Products/Book/#content4

[5]   http://tinyurl.com/pp3wbtj

6.69 x 9.61	24 - 828	24 - 740
7 x 10	24 - 828	24 - 740
7.44 x 9.69	24 - 828	24 - 740
7.5 x 9.25	24 - 828	24 - 740
8 x 10	24 - 440	24 - 400
8.25 x 6	24 - 220	24 - 200
8.25 x 8.25	24 - 220	24 - 200
8.5 x 11	24 - 630	24 - 570
8.5 x 8.5	24 - 630	24 - 570

d. Create an InDesign document

Note: A well-scanned book can be edited and resized in Acrobat as is described in 1b. We chose to also use InDesign as it provides more tools for working with tilted images and arranging the PDF images on the page.

- Create a new document in InDesign at the chosen trim size. To begin, only a 2-3 page document is needed.
  - Ensure the margins are set at the printer's specifications to avoid placing text outside the printable area

Margins

Gutter margins are by the book's binding. You'll want a wider margin for longer (thicker) books. See the table for what to set your inside margins to.

Outside margins are the page edges opposite of the binding, and the top and bottom margins. All live text and images must have an outside margin of at least .25" -- but we recommend an outside margin of at least .5"

Page Count	Inside Margin	Outside Margins
24 to 150 pages	.375"	at least .25"
151 to 400 pages	.75	at least .25"
401 to 600 pages	.875"	at least .25"
More than 600 pages	1.0"	at least .25"

Does your book contain images?
If you want your images to bleed to the edges of your book, ensure that they extend at least .125" beyond the final trim size from the top, bottom and outer edges and submit your PDF .25" higher and .125" wider than your selected trim size to accommodate the full bleed area.

Keep in mind all live elements must be at least .25" away from the trim lines, so if your file is formatted to be full bleed all live elements should be .375" away from the edge of the page.

- Insert one or two pages using the rectangle frame tool and placing the PDF file (command d) to see what resizing will need to be done.
- Using a master page create guides for the placement of the text within the page to make sure each page is uniform

e. Import pages

i. Each page can be placed manually if desired, but if all the pages are in a single PDF document use the plugin from Zanelli.[6] With this tool, run from Adobe ExtendScript Toolkit, pages can be automatically imported, resized, and placed:

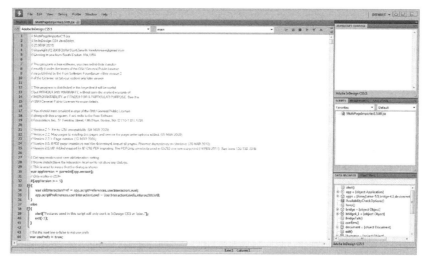

ii. In the top lefthand corner set the target application as "Adobe InDesign' and hit the play button. A "clear runtime error?" box may pop up, but just hit continue.

iii. A window with import options will pop up:

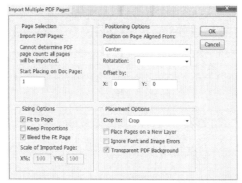

iv. If the trim size can accommodate the size of the image, uncheck "Fit to Page", or percentage can be specified under "Scale of Imported Page". The position on the page can also be altered according to the particular book's needs, but "Center", or "Center, relative to spine" are sufficient for most reprints.

Note: there is also a tool within InDesign (Window > Utilities > Scripts > PlaceMultiPagePDF), but in my experience this script does not offer placement or sizing options.

---

[6]   http://tinyurl.com/ycbyd9h

f. Make adjustments

- The pages will be placed, but may need to be moved to fit exactly in the guides that have been set up. If the scan is quite uniform, the images straight and the text/images within the set guides, this process may be skipped over.

- Any skewed or tilted pages can be adjusted using the free rotate tool. Select the content of the image rather than the frame and hover over the corner for the tool to appear. Rotate the image so it fits into the guidelines.

g. Proof & export

- Double-check for errors

- Export two PDF files:

- File > Adobe PDF Presets > [High Quality Print]
  - Name this document "[Book Title] Interior"

- File > Adobe PDF Presets > [Smallest File Size]
  - Name this document "[Book Title] E-book"

2. Design Book Cover

a. Download a template *through Create Space[7] appropriate for the trim size and pagination. This will be a zipped file with a PDF and PNG version of your template.*

- OR use the page count to calculate the spine width[8] and create your own[9]

b. Create an InDesign document

- Create a document with no margins at the same size as the downloaded template (usually 19" x 13").

- Place the CreateSpace™ template (the PNG-formatted template tends to work better) on the master page and place guides that correspond with the trim edges, bleed, and spine

- Place and arrange cover elements. *Note: CreateSpace™ does not print spine content on titles with less than 130 pages.*

- Run a preflight on the document to ensure the images are CMYK and there are no other errors. Window > Output > Preflight

d. Export the document as a PDF

- File > Adobe PDF Presets > [High Quality Print]

---

[7]   http://tinyurl.com/lvbh99e

[8]   http://tinyurl.com/mb6yklv

[9]   http://tinyurl.com/kq7aofa

e. Create the e-book cover

- In a new InDesign document sized the same as the interior trim size, create an e-book front cover and back cover by copy/pasting the cover elements onto two separate pages. Export these pages as a PDF (Smallest File Size) and insert the pages at the beginning and end of the e-book PDF document.

3. Review Files

- The final files should be reviewed internally before being uploaded to CreateSpace™: a submission entry in OMP should be created and the Managing Editor should be notified to review the files.
- Make any appropriate fixes and updates.
- Re-export files if any changes have been made, replacing or renaming the incorrect files.

4. Update Metadata

- Note the final page count and trim size for the file setup in CreateSpace™.

Upload Files in CreateSpace

A. Submit File			B. Catalog			C. Finalize		
1	2	3	4	5	6	7	8	9
Prepare	Upload	Prelim Catalog	Accept	Send to Production	Fully Catalog	Upload final file	Specify DL Settings	Approve
Series Editor			Series Editor			Layout Editor		

A. Setup Record in CreateSpace™

Note: As of March 2013, there is a known bug in the "Expert Setup" for CreateSpace™ titles, which wipes any publication date data once the files are submitted for review. Until this is resolved, use the "Guided Setup"

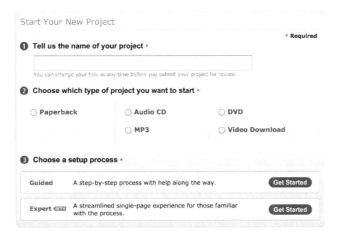

1. Title Information

Information about the work is recorded here and should reflect the information gathered from the local or OCLC record in the selection process. This information can not be changed after publication, so all metadata should be ready and proofed prior to proceeding. Pay special attention to the following entries:

a. Other contributors

From CreateSpace™: "You have the option of adding contributors for your work, including more authors, illustrators, editors, and translators, among others. These contributors will be listed on your product's eStore and Amazon product page, with their role."

When entering additional contributors:

- Do not use all capital letters. For example, use John Smith, not JOHN SMITH.

- For contributors with only a single name, use the last name field.

- To enter names with multiple initials, make sure to use both the first and middle name fields. For example, J.B. Smith should be entered as:
    - First Name: J.
    - Middle Name: B.
    - Last Name: Smith

- List other contributors as credited in the book, or if original design work was included, note the designer.

b. Series title

- If the book is from the Genesee Valley Historical Collection the series should be listed as "Genesee Valley Historical Reprints". General collection items do not need a series entered.

- Click the box marked "This book is part of a series" and enter the series title.

c. Publication date

- Enter original publication date in full format (e.g. January 1, 1914). If the chief source of information for the work (or other authoritative sources) provides only the year, record the month and day as January 1.

d. Description

- In CreateSpace™ the Description can be entered under the "Distribute" category even in the early stages of creating a record.

- The appropriate description will be saved with the book's metadata. The description should specify that the book is a reprint by noting "Reprinted by Milne Library, SUNY College at Geneseo", as well as the original date (e.g. "Originally published in 1896...").

2. ISBN

Unless previously specified otherwise, choose **Free CreateSpace™-Assigned ISBN**.

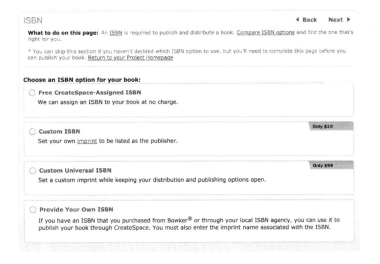

3. Set up Descriptions in CreateSpace™

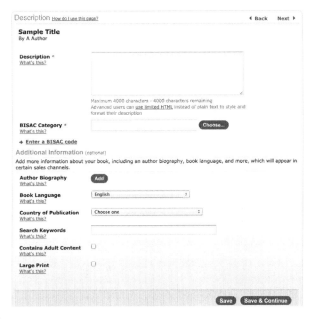

a. Description

This description should be between 200 and 500 words, and will appear as the product description on the book's Amazon.com page, and either on the back cover, or as part of a colophon inside the book. The summary should review, introduce, and entice general readers to pick up the book.

b. BISAC category

Enter the appropriate BISAC Codes supplied by the submitting library staff member. These codes/categories are available from the Book Industry Study Group website[10], or from CreateSpace™.com.

"Book Industry Standards and Communications (BISAC) categories are used by the book-selling industry to help identify and group books by their subject matter. Choose the BISAC category that best fits your book." (CreateSpace.com)

CreateSpace™ will offer choices of categories to choose from (For example: "Cooking>General" or "Fiction>Short Stories").

c. Search keywords

Add relevant search keywords as desired.

B. Upload Files in CreateSpace

1. Interior

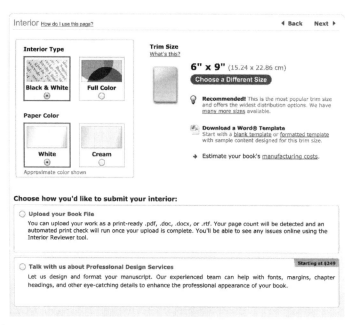

a. Interior type

In most cases, the interior type should be black and white.

b. Paper color

In most cases, the paper color should be white.

---

[10]   http://tinyurl.com/46qx8q2

c. Trim size

Based on the decision made in the design process, select the designated trim size. The final trim size will be listed with the book's compiled metadata or can be found in the final PDF file.

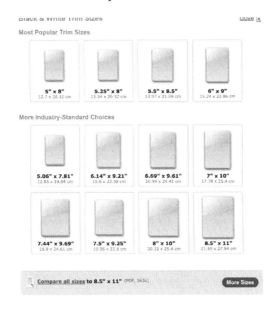

d. Upload interior PDF

This should be the proofed and approved High Quality PDF exported from InDesign.

2. Upload Cover

a. Submit book cover

In most cases, you should choose "Upload a Print-Ready PDF Cover", and upload the cover PDF created earlier in this workflow. Design support and templates options are available through CreateSpace™.

339

b. Submit for review

CreateSpace™ has a 48 hour file review period, after which an email will be sent to notify that the file is ready, or that changes need to be made. In many cases, the review will take less than 48 hours.

3. Review Proof in CreateSpace™

a. File review

CreateSpace™ will notify by email when the file has been accepted, sometimes with alerts. Most files will show an error like "overset images" since often the blank edges of the .pdf file will overset the printer's minimum margins. The digital proofing process will provide the opportunity to ensure that no text is actually outside of the printable area.

b. Proof your book

- Printed Proof: A printed proof can be ordered, but unless there are detailed illustrations or a complicated layout the digital proof should suffice.
- Digital Proof: Be sure to check all aspects of the interior and cover.

C. Distribution & Sales in CreateSpace™

1. Channels

Our program utilizes only Standard Distribution.

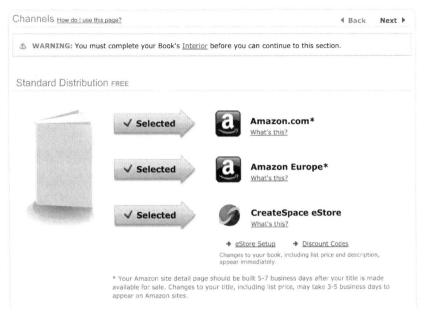

2. Pricing

Pricing for Black and White reprinted titles are set between $5.99-$9.99, whichever price provides approximately $2 in royalties on Amazon. For original titles, such as the recently published title Tagging Along by Stuart Symington, Jr.[11], we calculate a $5.00 or higher royalty depending on the content or author contract.

11   http://www.amazon.com/dp/1484153138

3. Manage Sales in CreateSpace™

CreateSpace™ allows you to track royalties per title and overall. A minimum of $100 is needed to request a royalty payment through the website

Publishing the E-book in OMP

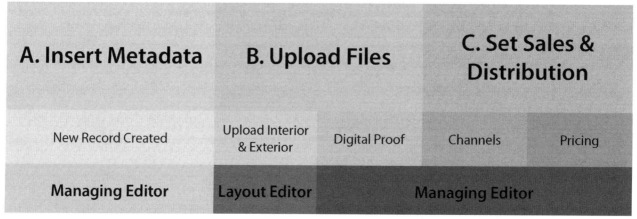

1. Prepare the submission

    a. Log in to Open Monograph Press and, from your dashboard, initiate a new submission.

    b. Choose Monograph for "Type of Book"

    c. Select Appropriate Series

    d. Check all items on the Submission Checklist

    e. Save & Continue

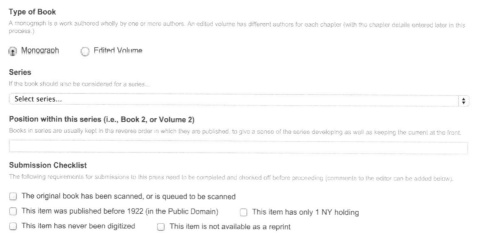

2. Upload the file

Upload e-book PDF file by clicking "Upload File". Hit "Save and Continue".

Start New Book Submission

| 1. PREPARE | 2. UPLOAD | 3. CATALOG | 4. NEXT STEPS |

SUBMISSION FILES   ⬆ Upload File

Name   Element

No Files

Encountering difficulties? Contact for assistance.

Cancel   Save and continue

3. Preliminary Catalog

a. Type complete book title/subtitle. Utilize the Prefix entry for titles that begin with "A" or "The".

b. Fill in supplied book summary if available (this can also be updated when the book is fully cataloged).

c. Add the original author under contributors and remove yourself

   ◦ *Note: for reprints we list a noreply email for the author*

d. Scroll to the very bottom of the Catalog tab and hit the "Finish Submission" button.

4. Accept Submission

a. Return to the Dashboard, where you will find a notice with the book title you submitted and the message: "A new monograph has been submitted to which an editor needs to be assigned." Click the message to access the workflow

b. Click "Accept Submission" *Note: If a staff member or other reviewer is involved, the submission is sent to Internal Review*

343

5. Send to Production

In the Editorial tab click "Send to Production"

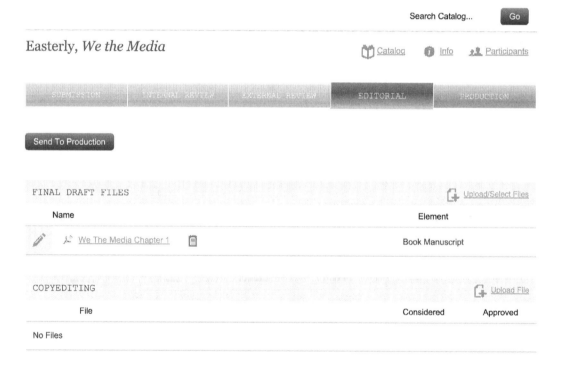

6. Fully Catalog the E-book

    a.   Click the link above the workflow labeled "Catalog" to fully catalog the entry.

    b.   Under the Monograph tab:

        i.   Check the "Create a catalog entry" box

        ii.   Add appropriate categories: generally a genre or a general subject heading

   iii. Ensure the proper series is selected

   iv. Ensure the title, subtitle, and author are entered correctly

   v. Submit the book summary if it was not entered during the submission phase

   vi. Hit save at the bottom of the screen

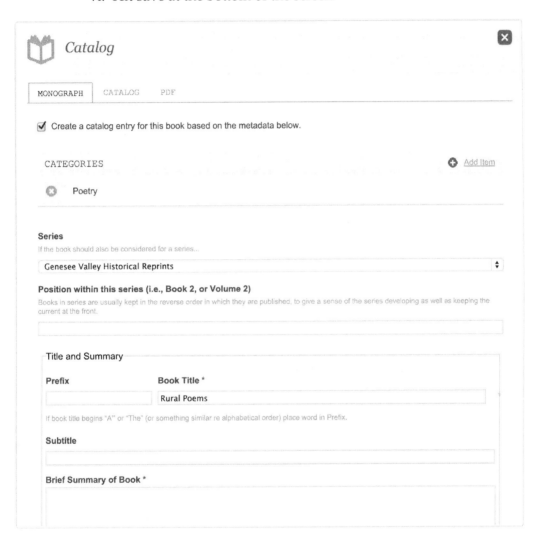

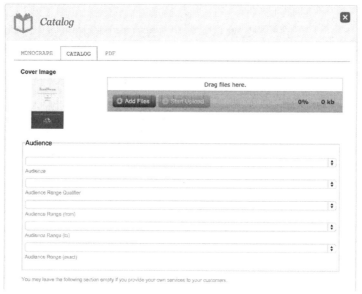

c. Under the Catalog tab:

    i. Upload the e-book cover as a PNG file approximately 600 px in height

    ii. Further down on that same page, add the publication format as "PDF" under name and choose "Digital" from the dropdown menu. Name the format by the book name followed with "(Free PDF)".

7. Upload Final File

a. Under the Production tab in the main workflow area, upload the file by clicking the "Proof" checkbox under the Publication Format section. When uploading, also name the file by the book name followed with "(Free PDF)".

346

b. To assign a final proof to another member of the editorial staff, select Assign, add the member's name and select the file from the dropdown menu. This will invite the staff member to look over the files and provide comments before the final publication.

8. Set Download Terms

    a. Return to the Cataloging link above the Editorial tab and click on the PDF tab

    c. Click the pencil icon to the left of the file name and choose "Set Terms"

    d. Choose Open Access and Save

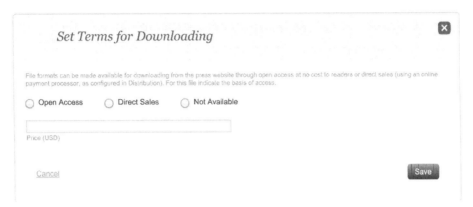

9. Approve

    a. Return to the production tab and next to the Page Proof file, click the "Approve" box.

    b. Above that, if not already checked, under "Publication Format" check all boxes: "Proof", "Catalog", & "Available".

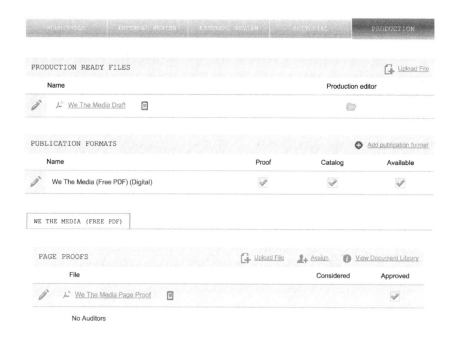

c. Return to the main press page and view the entry in the catalog to review it for quirks & errors:

   ◦ Cover image

   ◦ Title/Author/Synopsis

   ◦ File download

d. Under Management > Catalog, the entries can be added to the homepage feature & new release list by clicking "Feature" link to the right of the catalog entries and clicking the star icon and/or the exclamation point.

For more information and detailed documentation of Open Monograph Press, see the Public Knowledge Project's website: http://pkp.sfu.ca/omp_documentation.

Consortia & Inter-Organizational Cooperation

349

Scholarly Publishing in the Digital Library of the Caribbean (dLOC)

Laurie N. Taylor, Brooke Wooldridge, Lourdes Santamaría-Wheeler, Mark V. Sullivan, Benjamin Hebblethwaite, & Megan Raitano

University of Florida & Florida International University

1 IN THIS CHAPTER

Theme
Collaboration to develop a platform & system to digitize, curate and publish archival and original material

Highlighted Service
Hosting & management of archival materials, journals and other resources

Resources
Examples of and references to robust tools and methods of digitization & online publication management

The Digital Library of the Caribbean (dLOC) began in 2004 as a cooperative international digital library to provide open access and preserve materials from partner institutions. dLOC established a Scholarly Advisory Board to inform ongoing growth and activities. Over the years since its founding, dLOC has grown to include 35 content-contributing partner institutions, over one million user views per month, and over 1.8 million pages of all types of historic through current materials, including museum objects, archival documents, photographs, rare books, maps, scholarly journals and books, data sets, videos, and more.

dLOC developed stronger and richer connections to the scholarly community, resulting in new forms of digital scholarship now being

351

published through dLOC. dLOC was able to become a publisher of new digital scholarship because of a strong governance model with a clear mission and vision, robust technologies, and clear communication among constituents.[1] With those supports in place, when scholars approached dLOC with ideas for new scholarly publications, dLOC was able to provide a clear response, laying the groundwork for future publications which thus far have included online versions of previous print-only journals (e.g., *MaComère* and *Jamaica Journal*), curated online exhibits (e.g., *About Face* and *Island Luminous*), curated edited collections or archives (e.g., *Vodou Archive*), digital acquisition and publishing of archival materials (e.g., *Planters' Punch*), teaching resources (e.g., lesson plans and bibliographies), digitized versions of previously printed materials, and more.

About the Digital Library of the Caribbean (dLOC)

The Digital Library of the Caribbean (dLOC) officially began in 2004 at a meeting focused on a solution to a longer planning process revolving around preservation and access to materials held by institutions across the world with importance for Caribbean studies. At the 2004 meeting, the founding partners (Archives Nationale d'Haïti; Caribbean Community Secretariat; National Library of Jamaica; La Fundación Global Democracia y Desarrollo; Universidad de Oriente, Venezuela; University of the Virgin Islands; Florida International University; University of Central Florida; and University of Florida)[2] developed plans for creating, governing, and sustaining a shared digital library program that focused on preservation, access, capacity building among all partners, and leveraging of all work for future growth and enhancements (Rogers & Wooldridge, 2011). Prior to 2004, the founding partners and other institutions in the Caribbean had undertaken many collaborative initiatives, often coordinated with the Association of Caribbean University, Research and Institutional Libraries (ACURIL). The founding partners were informed and able to create a governance model and plans that were equitable and that supported all partners for both immediate needs and future goals. The robust governance model includes dLOC partners as "full participants in governance, formulating collection policy, and addressing membership and sustainability issues" (Rogers et al., 2011).

In 2005, the dLOC partners were awarded a grant from the U.S. Department of Education. The grant provided four years of funding to create dLOC as the central hub infrastructure for creating, growing, and leveraging digital projects and collections focused on the Caribbean. As a socio-technical hub, dLOC is comprised of the technologies, people, and organizations that all support the effective and appropriate development and use of technologies in service to the overall programmatic goals and mission. Together, the dLOC partners developed the technology for the SobekCM Digital Content Management System and related tools for digitization, digital curation and publishing, online publishing tools, digital library tools for libraries to create and manage collections, and digital library tools for users to use materials with feature-rich tools.[3] This socio-technical hub with the SobekCM open source repository software, open source software for digitization, onsite expert training with materials developed for partner workflow needs, and partner collaboration was all part of the overall system that brought together collections from various institutions in a single space, meeting immediate needs for preservation and access, while building capacity in terms of technologies as well as local experts to perform needed work and to lay the foundation for new opportunities in the future (Wooldridge, Taylor, & Sullivan, 2009; Sullivan & Ochoa, 2009; Renwick, 2011).[4]

> The partners created a sustainability plan to leverage capacity, minimize ongoing costs, develop a full business model, and create funding plans to ensure dLOC could continue with minimal funding and could best utilize all funding available.

During the early years, dLOC partners frequently discussed the need to ensure ongoing sustainability with the awareness that the purposes for scholarly work require that scholarly communications and publishing is permanent, or as close to permanent as possible. The partners created a sustainability plan to leverage capacity, minimize ongoing costs, develop a full business model, and create funding plans to ensure dLOC could continue with minimal funding and could best utilize all funding available. The sustainability plan has been operational since 2011 (Wooldridge et al., 2011).

The dLOC model supports all partners participating fully in governance and retaining all rights to their materials, and only granting permissions to dLOC. The equitable nature of the dLOC model supports partners and conversations with publishers, authors, and other rights holders about having their materials available as open access in dLOC. Similarly, partners collaborated on the technical infrastructure which supports branding and recognition for all materials in the citations and metadata, wordmarks images for partners that display to the left of the item when items are viewed, and customized collection interfaces for partner collections that have full search and other capabilities to showcase contributions for each partner. Partners collaborated on the development of these technical supports to maintain their needs for recognition and attribution. dLOC partners have found these to also be of great value for supporting collaboration with authors, publishers, affiliated institutions, and other rights holders.

With the strong central infrastructure in terms of technologies, people, and policies, dLOC partners digitize materials in their holdings, curate born-digital materials, and collaborate with publishers and scholars to digitize, curate existing digital materials, and support the creation of new works of digital scholarship.

dLOC Publishing Overview

With dLOC partners representing different types of institutions, including libraries and many others, dLOC partners support multiple types of publishing. To publish in dLOC, the rights holder (often a publisher or author) completes a grant of permissions[5] to allow dLOC to display the work as open access and to preserve the work. With permissions in place, dLOC partners support publishing the work by digitizing materials from print, curating born-digital materials, and collaborating for new scholarly works using various technologies. The four major publishing areas for dLOC are:

1. Publishing digitized and curated born-digital materials from partner holdings

2. Publishing re-born digital print publications where the print versions are not held by partners (often done with journals and newspapers where the publishers contribute the materials for inclusion in dLOC), which is also a process for digital acquisition with the digital files acquired and the materials then made open access

3. Supporting the creation of scholarly curated digital collections and exhibits, with these similar in many ways to print scholarly editions, edited collections, and exhibit guides with physical exhibits

DIGITAL LIBRARY OF THE CARIBBEAN
BIBLIOTECA DIGITAL DEL CARIBE
BIBLIOTHÈQUE NUMÉRIQUE DES CARAÏBES
w w w . d l o c . c o m

4. Creating new, alternative scholarly works

Re-born Digital Publishing and Digital Acquisition

When dLOC partners collaborate with publishers to publish journals online in dLOC which have previously only been published in print, some appear immediately and others after an embargo period to support publisher needs in adapting business models. Journals published in print with added online publishing in dLOC include *MaComère, Jamaica Journal, Sargasso,* and others.

In addition to journals, dozens of newspaper publishers publish their newspapers through dLOC's *Caribbean Newspaper Digital Library.* For this publishers send born-digital printer files for newer newspaper issues. Publishers also submit digital files of older and historic newspaper issues, with those

354

files created through digitization conducted by the publishers. dLOC then serves as the digital publishing venue and archive for the newspapers, supporting publisher needs as well as the greater benefits of online archives for these publications.

In some cases, institutions and others with physical materials are unable to cover costs for digitization of materials. dLOC partners have collaborated on projects that utilize traditional library acquisition budgets to cover the cost of digitization, with the resulting digital files being a digital acquisition where the materials are then available as open access in dLOC.

Scholarly Curated Digital Collections and Exhibits

In addition to publishing specific titles (like journals, newspapers, and other serial and monographic publications), dLOC's robust technical infrastructure supports specialized collections, with this required for partner collections and also supporting thematic collections, curated collections, exhibits, etc. dLOC's central infrastructure, shared training, resources, and collaborative network provide the necessary support and capacity for publishing scholarly curated digital collections and exhibits.

One example of a curated digital collection is the *Vodou Archive*. This scholarly curated digital collection stems from Hebblethwaite's work on Haitian Creole. Hebblethwaite et al. (2012a) collected primary resources and translated them into English for scholarly research. He needed a way to support access to additional resources as he continued his research and collected resources. Hebblethwaite realized that dLOC offered the desired print-style functionality for context and curatorial control, and that dLOC offered many enhancements over a print edition. Hebblethwaite collaborated with dLOC partner institutions to begin developing the collection, which initially held materials he had created that could not be included in the book. With a functioning collection, Hebblethwaite was awarded an NEH Collaborative Research grant for the "Archive of Haitian Religion and Culture: Collaborative Research and Scholarship on Haiti and the Haitian Diaspora" (2012b). With the grant underway, Hebblethwaite is collaborating with a diverse project team of scholars, students, librarians, archivists, and other researchers in developing the collection.

Other scholar-curated digital collections in dLOC include thematic and topical collections, to which many scholars contribute. In some cases, they are curated by specific scholars. In other cases, they are curated by the dLOC Scholarly Advisory Board, as with the *Teaching Guides & Materials Collection*.

Scholar-curated digital collections focus on adding materials to the collection as well as the scholarly critical apparatus. Scholarly-curated online exhibits focus on a limited set of materials presented with the exhibit narrative and substantive design elements. These exhibits may be connected directly to specific digital collections, as with the *Efrain Barradas Mexican and Cuban Film Posters Collection* and *Exhibit*. The exhibit features a selection of materials in the collection through 2009, whereas the collection continues to grow as new materials are acquired and digitized.

Conclusion: Digital Scholarly Publishing and Alternative Scholarly Works

Scholar-curated digital collections and exhibits as well as new and alternative scholarly works published by dLOC enrich and expand on the resources in dLOC. dLOC also supports new forms of digital scholarship and several new experimental or alternative scholarly works are in development.

dLOC supports the technical and editorial review processes for digital publishing to ensure the quality of published materials.[6] Editorial review for improvement is supported through review and recommendations from the Scholarly Advisory Board, dLOC team experts, partner experts, scholar curators, and the full dLOC scholarly community network. In addition to review for improvement, scholarly publications also undergo peer review for validation.[7] dLOC partners are currently developing a process to ensure robust peer-review support is in place and available for any work published by dLOC.[8] This is needed to ensure that scholars are not disadvantaged for their work simply because they select a format that is less traditional or an alternative scholarly form. Full and equitable support reflects dLOC's core value and goals.

> **Acting as both a digital library and digital publishing system provides an exponentially greater return on investment, enriches and expands library collections, expands opportunities for scholar collaboration and engagement...**

dLOC's digital publishing shows how a digital library, when designed with the necessary technical and social supports, can expand to support new opportunities in digital publishing. Acting as both a digital library and digital publishing system provides an exponentially greater return on investment, enriches and expands library collections, expands opportunities for scholar collaboration and engagement, and promotes core values, including the value and importance of open access publishing by academic libraries.

End Notes

[1] For governance and communication, see http://www.dloc.com/dloc1/bylaw; and for technologies, see http://www.dloc.com/sobekcm and http://www.dloc.com/dloc1/digit.

[2] For all current dLOC partners, see http://dloc.com/partners.

[3] For more about the SobekCM Digital Content Management System software and related tools, see http://www.dloc.com/sobekcm. For more on how SobekCM supports the digital scholarship lifecycle, see http://www.dloc.com/sobekcm/lifecycle. For more on how SobekCM supports broader impacts by

supporting outreach, promotion, and integration with scholarly publishing and teaching, see http://www.dloc.com/sobekcm/broader.

⁴ For more on the dLOC training, see http://www.dloc.com/info/training.

⁵ Template documents for the grant of permissions are available in dLOC: http://www.dloc.com/AA00004147. Also, the *dLOC Manual* includes an appendix *Guide to Permissions & Copyright/Public Domain Review* that provides an overview of the permissions model and process for requesting, receiving, and tracking permissions: http://www.dloc.com/AA00002865/00004/pdf. Also, the *dLOC Manual: Introduction* provides an overview of permissions and rights: http://www.dloc.com/AA00002865/00014/pdf.

⁶ Technical review follows standard reviewing practices for the appropriateness of technologies in terms of fit, best practices for technologies in terms of standards compliance with the use of the selected technology, and best practices in terms of digital access and preservation with selecting technologies that are standard based using open standards and so can be guaranteed to be supported in the future for long-term access and digital preservation.

⁷ Editorial review processes are currently less formalized and are tailored for specific projects and needs. A full system is in development for application across all projects.

⁸ For more information on the full, systematic review process in development, see http://www.uflib.ufl.edu/committees/fprc/

References

Hebblethwaite, B. (2012b). "Archive of Haitian Religion and Culture: Collaborative Research and Scholarship on Haiti and the Haitian Diaspora." Grant awarded by the National Endowment for the Humanities. Retrieved from http://www.dloc.com/AA00008614

—. (2012a). *Vodou Songs in Haitian Creole and English = Chante Vodou and Kreyòl Ayisyen ak Angle.* Philadelphia, PA: Temple University Press.

Renwick, S. (2011). Caribbean digital library initiatives in the 21st century: The digital library of the Caribbean (dLOC). *Alexandria 22*(1), 1–18. Retrieved from http://dloc.com/AA00010694/ and http://hdl.handle.net/2139/12622

Rogers, J., & Wooldridge, B. (2011). Collaborative digital collections: Caribbean solutions for effective resource-building and successful partnerships. *IFLA* (2012, April 1). Retrieved from http://dloc.com/AA00008776/

Sullivan, M. V., & Ochoa, M. (2009). Digital library of the Caribbean: A user-centric model for technology development in collaborative digitization projects. *OCLC Systems & Services: International Perspectives on Digital Libraries 25*(4), 249–262. Retrieved from http://dloc.com/IR00000041/

Wooldridge, B., Taylor, L. N., & Sullivan, M. V. (2009). Managing an open access, multi-institutional, international digital library: The digital library of the Caribbean. *Resource

Sharing & Information Networks 20(1–2), 35–44. Retrieved from http://dloc.com/
AA00004150

Wooldridge, B., Taylor, L. N., Vargas-Betancourt, M., Rogers, J., Mendoza, A., Silvera, V.,
Williams, G., Rickmann, J., Barradas, E., & Widmer, L. (2011). Digital library of the
Caribbean (dLOC) comprehensive sustainability plan. *Digital Library of the Caribbean
(dLOC).* Retrieved from http://www.dloc.com/AA00015400/00001/pdf

Appendix: dLOC – Links to Collections, Exhibits, and Publications Mentioned

Digital Library of the Caribbean (dLOC), www.dloc.com

dLOC, Scholar Curated Digital Collections:

Caribbean Newspaper Digital Library in dLOC, http://www.dloc.com/cndl

Efrain Barradas Mexican & Cuban Film Posters Collection in dLOC, http://dloc.com/
filmposters

Efrain Barradas Mexican & Cuban Film Posters Exhibit in dLOC, http://dloc.com/
exhibits/carteles

Teaching Guides & Resources Collection in dLOC, http://dloc.com/teach

Vodou Archive in dLOC, http://www.dloc.com/vodou

dLOC Online Exhibits:

About Face: Revisiting Jamaica's First Exhibition in Europe, http://exhibits.uflib.ufl.edu/
aboutface/

Haiti: An Island Luminous, http://dloc.com/exhibits/islandluminous

Journals Digitally Published and as Digital Acquisitions in dLOC:

Jamaica Journal, http://dloc.com/UF00090030

MaComère, http://www.dloc.com/AA00000079

Planters' Punch, http://dloc.com/AA00004645

Sargasso, http://www.dloc.com/UF00096005

The Public Knowledge Project: Open Source e-Publishing Services for Your Library

James MacGregor, Karen Meijer-Kline, Brian Owen, Kevin Stranack, & John Willinsky

Simon Fraser University & Stanford University

2 IN THIS CHAPTER

Theme

The embedded workflow in Open Journal Systems

Highlighted Service

Journal hosting & management

Software/Platforms Utilized

Open Journal Systems & Open Monograph Press

Resources

Examples of workflows for authors, reviewers, and production managers

The Public Knowledge Project,[1] a collective of academics, librarians, and software developers, has since 1998 been building free, open source software publishing platforms that create an alternative path to commercial and subscription-based routes for scholarly communication. The project's goal from the outset has been to find ways of increasing public and global access to research and scholarship, as well as to develop tools to enable scholars around the world to participate in the knowledge creation and sharing process. As such, it was an early participant in the open access movement, as it sought to develop ways of creating peer-reviewed journals that did not need to charge readers for access to their content and gave voice to researchers, particularly from the global South, that were often unheard by the traditional publishing system. By expanding both the consumers

Consortia & Inter-Organizational Cooperation

and producers of research, the project believes that the opportunities for learning, connecting, understanding, and innovation are significantly increased. The Public Knowledge Project continues to be a major contributor to the scholarly publishing world, with over 5,000 active and regularly published journals using its software, and in turn has developed a long-term sustainability plan to ensure continued funding for ongoing work.

> ## This [collective] wisdom has found its expression in...the active development of the international PKP community; and the feedback of users in guiding software and workflow design decisions...

Its various website platforms, including Open Journal Systems (OJS)[2] and Open Monograph Press (OMP),[3] provide a guided path through the editorial workflow of submission, review, editing, publishing, and indexing. Thousands of faculty members around the world are now using the software to publish independent journals on a peer-reviewed and open access basis, greatly increasing the public and global contribution of research and scholarship. What success the project has achieved over the years in developing software that is used by journals in many different parts of the world can be attributed to the collective wisdom, as well as trial and error, of the team involved in this project. This wisdom has found its expression in, for example, the early adoption of open source and community development models; the active development of the international PKP community; and the feedback of users in guiding software and workflow design decisions that reflected principles of simplicity, interoperability, accessibility, and openness, without sacrificing capability.

Today, PKP continues to look forward and adapt to the reality of an evolving scholarly world, where increased automation, online presence, and a shift towards a more sustainable funding model are called for.

Development of Editorial Workflow

Electronic/online publishing provides many benefits to publishing teams and readers alike over the more traditional print publishing methods, but transitioning from print—or even starting from scratch online—is not necessarily an easy or painless process. A primary goal of PKP has been to make electronic publishing as easy as possible while also adhering to the standards and requirements of the print world. Themes of simplicity and interoperability underlie our approach to supporting the managers, editors, authors, reviewers, copyeditors, layout designers, and proofreaders involved in the scholarly publishing workflow. Our systems aim to provide an easily understood checklist for all members involved in publishing, enabling those who have not been previously part of the traditional scholarly publishing community to participate and contribute, as they are guided through the process by the software design.

We have, in this process, pursued a number of important objectives, including the design of intuitive systems and the production of more automated pre- and post-publication workflows. We continue down this path, having realized that scholarly publishing is not an inherently intuitive process, nor one that can be readily automated. We have significantly reduced the clerical tasks and greatly increased the portability of the editorial office, with an organized, exclusively online workflow; if necessary the whole editorial team can be geographically distributed.

Visible Workflow

Submission

Each application's submission process has been refined to be as simple as possible for new and experienced authors alike. Each application uses a step-by-step submission process. Each step serves a specific purpose, from informing the author of any copyright or other requirements, to providing submission indexing metadata, to requesting submission and/or supplementary files, to confirming the submission. Authors are aware at all times of which step is the current one, and what is needed of them. This process ensures that all information relevant to the submission is gathered at the very beginning, saving editors valuable time during later stages.

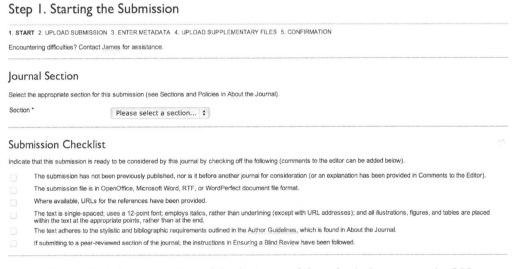

Figure 1. A demonstration of the first step of the submission process in OJS.

Review

While implementations differ as required by the publishing format, all three applications approach review and editing workflows in a philosophically similar way. Peer review is the key quality control for scholarly communication, as well as a source of improvement for this work. The review process, in particular for reviewers, must be kept as simple and quick as possible, as reviewers often have the least incentive to use the system and may balk at any impediment between themselves and the review proper. Typically, in the review process, the reviewer must

361

Consortia & Inter-Organizational Cooperation

agree to complete the review, download the submission files, and upload review comments and/or review files to the system. Reviewers may log in directly to the system to complete the review process, or editors may act on their behalf. To assist editors in selecting reviewers, the system tracks a reviewer's previous record on areas of interest, time taken, number of reviews, and editor rating.

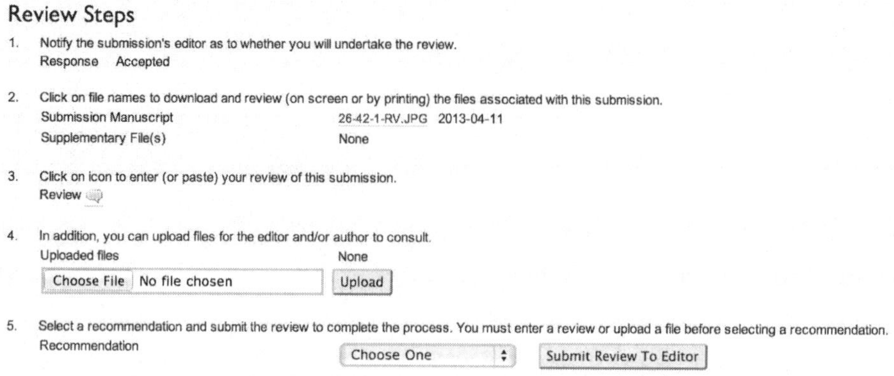

Review Steps

1. Notify the submission's editor as to whether you will undertake the review.
   Response   Accepted

2. Click on file names to download and review (on screen or by printing) the files associated with this submission.
   Submission Manuscript   26-42-1-RV.JPG 2013-04-11
   Supplementary File(s)   None

3. Click on icon to enter (or paste) your review of this submission.
   Review

4. In addition, you can upload files for the editor and/or author to consult.
   Uploaded files   None
   [Choose File No file chosen]   [Upload]

5. Select a recommendation and submit the review to complete the process. You must enter a review or upload a file before selecting a recommendation.
   Recommendation   [Choose One ‡]   [Submit Review To Editor]

Figure 2. The reviewer's review workflow in OJS.

> # The review process, in particular for reviewers, must be kept as simple and quick as possible, as reviewers often have the least incentive to use the system and may balk at any impediment between themselves and the review proper

Editing and Production

OJS and OMP have full-scale editing workflows that can include input from copyeditors, proofreaders, layout editors, and others. OJS groups copyediting, layout editing, and proofreading under the same general post-review "editing" workflow: Submissions accepted after review are sent to copyediting, then to layout editing, and finally, to proofreading. Authors are actively involved in the copyediting and proofreading process; separate copyeditors, proofreaders, and layout editors may be used by the system, or the editor in charge of the submission may choose to act in those roles. Once all stages are complete, a final galley file (typically HTML or PDF) is uploaded, the article assigned to an issue, and the issue eventually published.

In the case of OMP, editing and production workflows are handled separately: Copyediting of final draft files are handled in an editing stage, in collaboration with the manuscripts' editors, authors, and assigned copyeditors, while the creation of production-ready files (e-books, PDFs, etc.) and the completion of all catalog information for that particular manuscript are managed in a final production stage. This separation is due to the increased amount of work related to the production of final publication formats (paperback, e-book, etc.) and the manuscript's public catalogue; and also because of the increased number of people (translators, editors, illustrators/ designers, etc., along with the authors, editors, copyeditors, and so on) potentially involved. OMP effectively includes sub-workflows within the production workflow: one for the catalogue itself, and one for each publication format. The catalogue and each publication format must be vetted and approved before the final product is publicly available online.

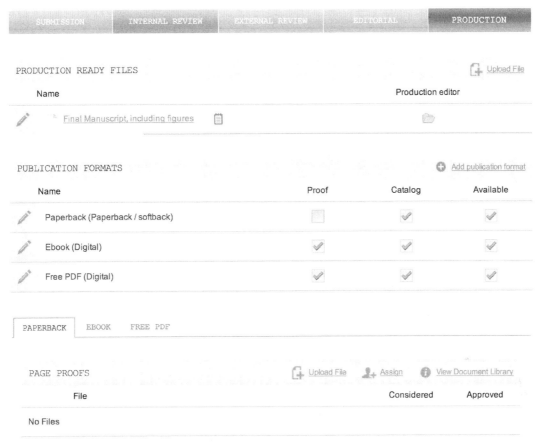

Figure 3. The production workflow in OMP.

"Invisible" Workflows

While the visible workflow is aimed to be as simple as possible, a great deal of behind-the-scenes automation and task/service management is included in OJS and OMP, offering far more capability than may be assumed from their relatively straightforward configuration processes. Most of these services involve promoting accessibility and visibility of the journal's published content on the Web. For example, Google Scholar requires article information to be available to its Web crawlers in very specific ways; OJS does this automatically, with no further configuration needed.

This "invisible" aspect of the editorial workflow is becoming as important as the actual review and editing processes. Modern online workflow is no longer just between humans, but also between the publishing platform and systems like CrossRef,[4] PubMed's MEDLINE indexing service,[5] Zotero,[6] or institutional repositories, without any intervention at all. These services are usually implemented as plug-ins, and allow different levels of access to data and metadata for different online services and platforms, typically with very little needed in terms of additional setup. Most importantly, however, the service standards and protocols are open, understood, and widely accepted throughout the scholarly and academic library communities, ensuring a broad level of support and interoperability for PKP applications. In this fashion, journals may have their content harvested by OAI-capable metadata harvesters, can provide article DOI information to CrossRef, and can deposit it into PubMed's MEDLINE indexing service.

Web 2.0

As with other open source software initiatives, community collaboration is at the forefront of the PKP development model, and the PKP user community continues to grow and influence application development. Both OJS and OMP have been developed to include options for widespread sharing of articles, chapters, and books through tools such as Twitter, Facebook, and Delicious, thus facilitating open online communities around the publications and increasing the visibility of the articles and chapters beyond anything previously possible.

Sustainability

PKP software applications have always been released as open source software, under the General Public License.[7] The software is free in two ways: It is free to download and use; and the source code is freely available to download, view, and modify.

Originally, a range of different government and foundation grants sponsored the project.[8] Grant funding continues to play a significant role in supporting PKP, especially for new software development initiatives and PKP's related research activities. In 2012, however, PKP introduced two new funding models to ensure its financial sustainability, which involved growing responsibilities around the expanding number of journals, books, and conferences dependent on its software. The first model involved strengthening PKP's hosting and software customization services for libraries, universities, and other publishers using its free software; the second involved creation of an institutional sponsorship program for research libraries, many of which are now providing PKP software as a new publishing service model to their institutions.

On the hosting and customization side, what was once a fledgling, ad-hoc initiative at Simon Fraser University Library[9] (PKP's home institution) to mount journals was established as a distinct venture, dubbed PKP Publishing Services (PKP|PS).[10] The growth and professionalization of PKP|PS has required a deeper level of commitment to infrastructure: hardware, network uptime, and software management across hundreds of installed instances of OJS, OCS, and

OMP. PKP|PS currently hosts over 450 journals and conferences (with the first OMP instances on the way), and now acts as a significant funding resource for PKP, not to mention a critical vector for feedback from day-to-day users of the software.

Perhaps more significant in providing a stronger institutional base for PKP is its sponsorship program, which has now over 30 participating institutions.[11] Interested research libraries can sponsor the project directly on an annual basis, or can become more involved as Development Partners. Development Partners are just that: they have access to the core PKP development team and are deeply involved in long-term technical and administrative planning. All sponsors are eligible to join the newly created Members and Technical Committees, and all Development Partners participate on the Advisory Committee.

This represents a new model for PKP, which has traditionally been a very small and tight-knit group of librarians and developers. Opening the team to a larger community is not without its challenges in coordinating the work among different teams and locations. It is important to stress here, however, that this isn't simply a way for PKP to become financially sustainable. The sponsorship program provides a venue for PKP to interact with the larger scholarly community in a way that previously did not exist. It is an open invitation to participate as a patron and a peer in this project, and the investment of participation is equally if not more important to the fundamental goals of the project as any financial contribution.

Conclusion

The Public Knowledge Project has worked closely with many organizations and institutions, editors and publishers, and librarians and software developers over the last decade-and-a-half to increase the options and alternatives available to the global community of scholars and researchers. In the face of a rapidly evolving publishing landscape that has transformed so many aspects of communication, and with even more changes clearly in the offing, it is too early to know or even predict what models and methods are going to prevail as the digital era of scholarly communication continues to unfold. Our project has always been to demonstrate ways in which these new directions and opportunities might uphold long-standing historical principles of openness, community, cooperation, experimentation, and questioning that are at the very core of librarianship and continue to underwrite the work of research and learning. The continuing success of this work relies not only on the open nature of the project, but on the passion and interests of this larger community in their desire to contribute ideas and knowledge, as well as the always appreciated instances of well-formed code.

Endnotes

[1] Public Knowledge Project, http://pkp.sfu.ca

[2] Open Journal Systems, http://pkp.sfu.ca/ojs

[3] Open Monograph Press, http://pkp.sfu.ca/omp

[4] Crossref, http://www.crossref.org/

[5] MEDLINE, http://www.nlm.nih.gov/bsd/pmresources.html

[6] Zotero, http://www.zotero.org/

[7] General Public Licence, http://www.gnu.org/licenses/gpl-2.0.html

[8] Current and Prior Research Grants, http://pkp.sfu.ca/research_proposals

[9] Simon Fraser University Library, http://www.lib.sfu.ca

[10] PKP Publishing Services, https://pkpservices.sfu.ca/

[11] PKP Sponsorships, http://pkp.sfu.ca/sponsorships

Building a Community-Driven Organization to Advance Library Publishing

Sarah Lippincott & Katherine Skinner

Educopia Institute

3 IN THIS CHAPTER

Theme
Establishment of a membership based cooperative to strategically plan and develop shared resources & infrastructure

Highlighted Project
Planning & development of a consortium

Resources
Discussion of the organizational structure & strategy of the LPC

Over the past two decades, academic libraries have partnered with faculty, graduate students, and undergraduates to produce e-journals, conference proceedings, technical reports, monographs, scholarly editions, and database-driven websites. What began as a set of one-off experiments undertaken by libraries, usually in response to individual faculty/student requests, began to solidify as a set of services in the mid-2000s under the label "library publishing." A 2007 Ithaka S&R report noted that "library publishing" efforts tended to be directed inwardly (toward campus-based scholarship), in contrast to the externally focused work of university presses, and it drew clear conclusions regarding the need for presses and libraries to collaborate in order to propel the scholarly communication field forward (Brown et al., 2007). A 2008 ARL report provided a snapshot of "library publishing" practices, defining this work as "the organized production and dissemination of scholarly works in any format as a service provided by the library" (Hahn, 2008).

Other studies quickly reinforced both this definition and the growing significance of these emerging library-based publishing endeavors. In particular, the seminal, IMLS-funded *Library Publishing Services: Strategies for Success* project and report (Mullins et al., 2012) documented the active development and implementation of publishing services in a range of academic libraries, from small liberal arts colleges to premier research institutions, as well as the enthusiastic support these were receiving from faculty, staff, and students. The report also showed that most of these programs were built in ad hoc ways and operated in relative isolation from one another. Such "siloization" limits the impact these initiatives can have upon the broader academic library community. To help library publishing services mature into a consistent field of practice, the report advocated raising the visibility and understanding of these practices profession-wide to establish library publishing as a strong sub-field with viable models that may fit a variety of campus needs and resource levels.

Organizing the Community

The well-documented need to establish a strong community of practice(s) served as the primary motivation for the Library Publishing Coalition project initiated by Purdue University, University of North Texas, Virginia Tech, and the Educopia Institute in May 2012. A proposal written and circulated by this group in August 2012 described a project to develop a network/community of libraries and to promote the emergence of this important publishing sub-field. More than 50 academic libraries responded to the proposal, contributing seed funding and staff time to found the Library Publishing Coalition (LPC), a new collaborative network of libraries.

Over a two-year period, these participating institutions (including additional institutions that joined the open initiative during the project period) are designing and implementing the LPC from the ground up. The design of this initiative thus differs greatly from other start-up endeavors: this project seeks to mobilize the community to create an organization that meets the broad needs of the emerging library publishing community. The governance, services, and business model for the organization are being built in the community by the libraries that comprise the core of its future membership. The process of building the LPC models the values we hope to see practiced in the broader community of library publishing: inter-institutional collaboration, knowledge- and resource-sharing, and networking.

> ...this project seeks to mobilize the community to create an organization that meets the broad needs of the emerging library publishing community.

To this end, Educopia serves as the facilitator, not the leader, of the initiative. It incubates the community, providing an apparatus of support and a catalytic environment for producing a new organizational structure and set of services, and ensures that the project engages each of the participating libraries in the process of designing and implementing this organization.

To address the challenge of balancing over 50 institutional voices, LPC delegates the project work to several complementary groups.

At the broadest level, libraries self-selected into two categories of involvement. **Founding Institutions** commit greater financial and staff resources to the initiative, and provide primary oversight by designing the governance, organizational structure, and services of the LPC. At the project's launch, the Founding Institution category closed in order to ensure a level of stability in this core team. **Contributing Institutions** serve in an advisory capacity and ensure that the initiative addresses the broad needs of the community.

Two small groups are responsible for high-level leadership and management of the project. An **Executive Group**, comprising seven representatives from Founding Institutions, works to implement the vision laid out by the project team. This group provides guidance on critical decisions, formalizes documentation, and ensures that the project makes progress towards its goals. An **Initiators Group**, which includes representatives from Purdue University, University of North Texas, Virginia Tech, and the Educopia Institute, provides ongoing vision for the project.

Two **working groups** have been convened to produce the main deliverables for the first year of the project: a directory of library publishing services and an annual forum for library publishing. Additional working groups will be formed as needed over the course of the project.

Finally, a **program manager** moderates communication between all of these groups and facilitates their work.

Building the Library Publishing Coalition

The project is designed to accomplish two core goals: 1) building the LPC community and organization, and 2) establishing a core set of LPC services to support this field.

Project Goal 1: Building Community and Raising Visibility

The primary focus of the LPC project is to establish and mobilize the community—building a shared sense of ownership of the emergent effort among all players, including those from large programs (e.g., Michigan, Columbia, and CDL) as well as those from smaller programs with large impacts (e.g., Illinois Wesleyan and Pacific University). These programs vary not only in their institutional contexts, but also in their scopes, objectives, and ambitions.

While acknowledging the diverse perspectives of its constituents, the project promotes the development of a shared identity to help libraries establish themselves in relation to other players in the scholarly communication ecosystem.

From the outset, LPC recognized the importance of coalescing the field around a set of shared values and common practices. The project focuses on finding common ground, building consensus around critical decisions, and providing frequent opportunities for formal and informal interaction.

Participants collectively wrote the following definition of library publishing, which aims to encompass the variety of publishing activities in libraries and articulate the unique values that distinguish libraries from other publishers. LPC therefore defines library publishing as:

> ... the set of activities led by college and university libraries to support the creation, dissemination, and curation of scholarly, creative, and/or educational works. Generally, library publishing requires a production process, presents original work not previously made available, and applies a level of certification to the content published, whether through peer review or extension of the institutional brand. Based on core library values and building on the traditional skills of librarians, it is distinguished from other publishing fields by a preference for open access dissemination and a willingness to embrace informal and experimental forms of scholarly communication and to challenge the status quo.

The project team also developed and formally approved a statement of values that will guide the organization and elaborated a set of services that LPC will provide. Composing these documents prompted important conversations about the library publishing community's priorities, aspirations, and practices and helped the participants begin the process of solidifying a group identity. These documents have laid the groundwork for producing the organization's mission and goals—the cornerstone of the LPC's governance documentation.

The project team recognizes that libraries are but one player in the scholarly communications landscape. A major goal of the initiative is to foster conversation between the library publishing field and other stakeholder communities, including consortia of presses, research centers, and libraries; advocacy groups; technical platforms/providers; digital scholarship collaboratives; and others. Engaging directly with these "strategic affiliates" during the formative stages of the LPC helps us to assess gaps in the current landscape, avoid duplicating existing work, and share information broadly regarding the project's mission and activities. Reaching out to other organizations as a coalition of over 50 libraries lends weight to library publishing and establishes libraries as active and significant contributors to the publishing field.

> # A major goal of the initiative is to foster conversation between the library publishing field and other stakeholder communities

Goal 2: Service Development and Sharing Knowledge

The value of the LPC will be defined in large part by the services it provides to its membership. The following services, representing the highest priorities for the first year of the project, will be shaped and implemented with effort and input from the community. Additional services will be added as requested and approved by the project participants and eventual membership.

Targeted research and annual directory

The LPC will conduct and support targeted research on significant, practical topics that lead to concrete advancements in publishing services. Working with institutional representatives, the LPC will produce a set of research reports that document replicable models.

The LPC will also compile and publish a directory of library publishing (missing in the current landscape). The directory will describe library publishing activities at a wide range of institutions, and will contribute to defining the field and raising the visibility of library publishing, identifying trends, and facilitating collaboration and knowledge exchange among practitioners and newcomers.

Models of practice

As this field matures, libraries will continue to experiment with organizational and business models, services, technologies, and partnerships. The LPC can support their work through hosting a shared set of documentation and models—particularly those deemed high-priority in *Strategies for Success*: "guides to business issues, information on publishing platforms, and examples of policy and process documents" (Mullins et al., 2012, p. 4).

The LPC will collect and distribute exemplar resources produced in the field. This resource gateway will include a range of documentation and model agreements on topics, including legal, economic, policy, workflow, standards, assessment, marketing, discovery, and technical platforms. The LPC will also help its constituent libraries develop shared lists of consultants, freelancers, and volunteers that they are using to fill a variety of roles in their publishing production cycles. Aggregating documentation will help libraries reduce duplication of effort and speed the pace of program development.

Community hub and annual forum

As discussed above, the LPC's primary focus, particularly during the project period, is to build community. To this end, the LPC is creating a virtual community hub for collaboration on

371

Consortia & Inter-Organizational Cooperation

organizational documents, surveys, and other key components of the project. The project team also assembles for regular conversation—both to discuss major topics and to build consensus around significant decisions. The LPC is also now hosting in-person "meet up" gatherings at key events in the field (e.g., conferences/meetings by CNI, ACRL, AAUP, Charleston, etc.) to bring its members face to face.

The LPC will also host an annual forum that deliberately fosters engagement from all attendees through panel discussions, action-oriented breakouts, and focused meetings for groups that share important strengths/interests that would benefit from alignment activities. The first forum will be held in March 2014 and will focus on alignment of library publishing practices.

Professional development

LPC participants note that there is no graduate-level digital publishing training that adequately prepares information managers for the full range of theoretical, practical, and organizational issues involved in publishing. The project is exploring the creation of a range of training opportunities, from webinars and tutorials to the design and launch of graduate badge/certificate programs. Throughout the project period, the LPC will coordinate webinars that take advantage of the knowledge and expertise already present within the community. Hosted by institutional representatives, these webinars will allow practitioners to learn and benefit from the experiences of their colleagues.

Conclusion

The LPC project brings organized leadership to the field to enable collaborative exploration of pressing issues, facilitate information sharing, and encourage the creation and advancement of library publishing services. The project will result in a strong collaborative network that intentionally addresses and supports an evolving, distributed, and diverse range of library production and publishing practices. The process of building the LPC serves as a model of collaboration around an emerging and increasingly important service area for libraries.

References

Brown, L., Griffiths, R. J., Rascoff, M., & Guthrie, K. (2007). *University publishing in a digital age*. New York, NY: Ithaka, S&R. Retrieved from http://www.sr.ithaka.org/research-publications/university-publishing-digital-age

Hahn, K. L. (2008). *Research library publishing services: New options for university publishing*. Washington, DC: Association of Research Libraries. Retrieved from http://www.arl.org/storage/documents/publications/research-library-publishing-services-mar08.pdf

Mullins, J. L., Murray-Rust, C., Ogburn, J. L., Crow, R., Ivins, O., Mower, A., Nesdill, D., Newton, M. P., Speer, J., & Watkinson, C. (2012). *Library publishing services: Strategies for success: Final research report*. Washington, DC: SPARC. Retrieved from http://docs.lib. purdue.edu/cgi/viewcontent.cgi?article=1023&context=purduepress_ebooks

Conclusion

Katherine Pitcher

Milne Library, SUNY Geneseo

The case studies and interviews included in the *Library Publishing Toolkit* are library strategies for dealing with an important question, "How do we sustain our role in providing content to our users?"

As libraries and librarians of all types ponder that question, we are looking for models, advice, and a set of best practices to help us answer the question and move forward. We want to share our stories and gain practical strategies for developing services that sustain our role as content providers and developers, whether that role is as curator, host, or publisher. One way we can accomplish these goals is to collaborate and create community-based resources for sharing solutions and developing applications to provide new services to our users, as well as providing the opportunities for the formalization of skills and training in publishing. Many libraries are searching for best practices to improve services, but few document and record their successes in a systematic manner. Thus, the *Library Publishing Toolkit* itself becomes one example of a community-based resource, designed to share and disseminate best practices to the larger library and publishing community.

Many of the academic library case studies in the *Library Publishing Toolkit* were initiated through librarian recognition of the need for publishing strategies that align libraries with the institutional mission. We should be "*...aligning the value in our new publishing services with the strategic goals of the academic library and its home institution by diving head-first into open access business models and fee-based service provision...*"[1] In this respect, new business models are taking shape at all types of academic libraries, as the need for transforming scholarly communications becomes a priority.

At public libraries, too, the mission and role of the library as content procurer is morphing from simple content provider to new roles as community publisher and content developer, along with strong publishing and writing services to support this growing need. Thus, librarians recognize publishing as another strategy in developing stronger ties and collaborations with our communities, whether academic or public. Author and scholar services are developing at all

---

[1]   Mullins, J. L., Murray-Rust, C., Ogburn, J. L., Crow, R., Ivins, O., Mower, A., Nesdill, D., Newton, M. P., Speer, J., & Watkinson, C. (2012). *Library publishing services: Strategies for success: Final research report.* Washington, DC: SPARC. Retrieved from http://docs.lib.purdue.edu/purduepress_ebooks/24/

types of institutions, where librarians are *"...assuming responsibility for acquiring a comprehensive understanding of editor and author needs, along with the suite of value propositions..."*[2]

As libraries develop and share library publishing best practices, what are the next steps and future priorities? How do we sustain these new roles?

What we see in the future are bright opportunities for libraries to learn, to share, and to grow as libraries, authors, and readers. Specific to our next steps, we are looking to develop the next edition of the *Library Publishing Toolkit* within the following key areas:

Marketing: How will libraries promote their content to other libraries, to new readers, to their current audiences? How do public libraries promote their community's works? How do we get new readers? Some of the options worth exploring include documenting processes for ISBNs and MARC record creation and their distribution via WorldCat, Amazon, or other utilities, in conjunction with publicity and marketing support for these methods. There are opportunities, too, for libraries to share best practices on the myriad efforts to disseminate metadata for free e-book collections—what results from these efforts?

Distribution: How will libraries get their content to readers? What new distribution models are created in light of new library publishing operations? Future best practices may include library development and work with EPUB standards and other e-book platforms.

Author Services: In particular, in academic libraries, what are the scholarly communication models and services that libraries are providing to their authors (i.e., their faculty and scholars)? Are print-on-demand, open access, and hybrid publications driving a new service model for libraries? What are our communities demanding? With the dramatic growth of social media sites for videos and blogs, and self-publishing services for text, photos, and even audio, a place to be creative in social environments seems to be the answer. Services ranging from writing groups to digital media equipment checkout, and from referral services to support programs are adapting to these needs.

Curation: What level of curation do we add to the content being published? What kinds of service models can we create? What curation roles do we encourage in both authors and readers? Libraries have an opportunity to use their unique position as curation and preservation specialists to enrich future publications and resources, whether through organization and advice or by active participation in the creation and publishing of these products.

Transforming library roles and activities to leverage new publishing and service opportunities can enrich our communities and scholarly communications. Because libraries provide a resourceful, inspiring, and sustaining place for both authors and readers, libraries developing publishing serves communities in a holistic manner. Tradition and innovation in libraries provide a dynamic learning environment for everyone.

For the next edition of the toolkit, what tools and practices still need to be documented? How can we give our libraries the support they need to effect important change in their communities? Please join us at http://www.publishingtoolkit.org to share your library's stories, thoughts, documentation, and experiences for effecting that important change.

[2]   Ibid.

Index

Errata

Library Publishing Toolkit. IDS Project Press, 2013

Corrections for the first printing & ebook download prior to Aug 26, 2013

Page Number	Correction
vii, line 6	Suzanne Guiod, & Suzanne E. Preate should read: **Suzanne E. Guiod, & Suzanne Preate**
195, line 15	Suzanne Guiod, & Suzanne E. Preate should read: **Suzanne E. Guiod, & Suzanne Preate**
215, line 7	Suzanne Guiod, & Suzanne E. Preate should read: **Suzanne E. Guiod, & Suzanne Preate**
378, column 2, line 37	Guiod, Suzanne should read: **Guiod, Suzanne E.**
379, column 2, line 11	Preate, Suzanne E. should read: **Preate, Suzanne**

These corrections are reflected in this printing of the *Library Publishing Toolkit*